LIGHT
REVEALING
ARCHITECTURE

MARIETTA S. MILLET

Illustrations by
CATHERINE JEAN BARRETT

 VAN NOSTRAND REINHOLD
I(T)P™ A Division of International Thomson Publishing Inc.

New York · Albany · Bonn · Boston · Detroit · London · Madrid · Melbourne
Mexico City · Paris · San Francisco · Singapore · Tokyo · Toronto

Front cover photo: Light patterns cast by the west-facing glass block wall in the stairwell in the Carpenter Center for the Visual Arts (Atelier Le Corbusier, 1961-64) at Harvard University in Cambridge, Massachusetts. Photograph by Marietta S. Millet.

Back cover photo: A changing cabana (Jersey Devil, 1992) glows at Seaside, Florida, the lighting fixture carefully designed to make all the surfaces luminous, yet dim enough so the baby sea turtles that gather on the beach at night are not disturbed. Photograph by Bill Sanders Photography, ©1994.

Interior photographs by Marietta Millet, unless otherwise credited.

Cover design: Paul Costello

Van Nostrand Reinhold Staff
Production Editor: Carla M. Nessler
Production Manager: Mary McCartney
Designer: Paul Costello

Copyright © 1996 by Van Nostrand Reinhold

I(T)P™   A division of International Thomson Publishing, Inc.
The ITP logo is a trademark under license

Printed in the United States of America

For more information, contact:

Van Nostrand Reinhold
115 Fifth Avenue
New York, NY 10003

Chapman & Hall GmbH
Pappelallee 3
69469 Weinheim
Germany

Chapman & Hall
2-6 Boundary Row
London
SE1 8HN
United Kingdom

International Thomson Publishing Asia
221 Henderson Road #05-10
Henderson Building
Singapore 0315

Thomas Nelson Australia
102 Dodds Street
South Melbourne, 3205
Victoria, Australia

International Thomson Publishing Japan
Hirakawacho Kyowa Building, 3F
2-2-1 Hirakawacho
Chiyoda-ku, 102 Tokyo
Japan

Nelson Canada
1120 Birchmount Road
Scarborough, Ontario
Canada M1K 5G4

International Thomson Editores
Campos Eliseos 385, Piso 7
Col. Polanco
11560 Mexico D.F. Mexico

  2   3   4   5   6   7   8   9   10   CP   01   00   99   98   97

Library of Congress Cataloging-in-Publication Data
Millet, Marietta S.
    Light revealing architecture / Marietta S. Millet ; illustrations,
  Catherine Jean Barrett.
       p.   cd.
    Includes bibliographical references.
    ISBN 0-442-01887–8
    1. Light in Architecture.   2. Lighting, Architectural and
  decorative.   I. Barrett, Catherine Jean.   II. Title.
  NA2794.M55   1996
  729'.28–dc20   95–20192
                                                        CIP

CONTENTS

ACKNOWLEDGMENTS

Advice, information, and material from many people have contributed to making this book. Many of the observations, ideas, and attitudes expressed here were germinated and grew throughout years of schooling, practice, research, and teaching. William Lam first introduced me to the mysteries of light in buildings. Joel Loveland, teaching colleague and consulting partner, has shared teaching and lighting design work. During the process of shaping the book, many colleagues have helped with critical information or review at crucial points: Ed Allen, Donald Canty, Virginia Cartwright, Frank Ching, Peter Cohan, Jennifer Dee, Barbara Erwine, Mary Guzowski, Grant Hildebrand, Lance Lavine, Peter McCleary, Rick Mohler, John Reynolds, Martin Schwartz, and Susan Ubbelohde.

Funding from the Graham Foundation helped defray the costs of the illustrations. The financial support of the Graham Foundation has indeed made this book possible, as the images and illustrations form the core of the book. Working with Catherine Barrett on the illustrations has been a real pleasure; her contributions range far beyond pen and ink. Many friends and colleagues have contributed their slides as illustrations; both their expertise and their generosity are gratefully acknowledged. Museums, archives, and professional photographers have also been most helpful.

In the publishing world, I want to thank Wendy Lochner for having faith in the potential of this book; Carla M. Nessler for seeing it through production; and Paul Costello for his fine graphic design.

The help of Amanda Knowles, who organized everything, and Carl Dominguez, who was both research assistant and permissions coordinator, was essential and is greatly appreciated. Finally, the support of my family has been more than generous, particularly that of my mother, Lillian Sprague Pollock, and my husband, Charles Radican.

Light Revealing Architecture is an engaging book which inspires creative thinking about light and lighting in architecture. Author Marietta Millet, who teaches at the University of Washington, relates her extensive experiences with meticulous examinations of the way buildings reveal themselves in light, physically and experientially.

The four chapters of this book focus the reader on the author's primary method of examining how light is utilized in the design of buildings. In each of the chapters the author has chosen examples which exemplify the issues and provide a vehicle for investigating the role of light in the built world. "Light Revealing Experience" is a method of investigation which focuses on the experiential use of light, both personal and universal. "Light Revealing Form" is a discussion on the formal uses of light and how parts of buildings reveal themselves in light. "Light Revealing Space" shows how the spatial ambiguities of light are related with an emphasis on the relationship of the inside to the outside environment. "Light Revealing Meaning" is a search for the symbolic meaning of sacred light as related to the mind and spirit.

Anyone who has written about light and lighting realizes the enormous challenge in trying to describe such an elusive and intangible commodity. Edith Wharton's many books reflecting her interest in architecture and the landscape and John Summerson's masterpiece *Heavenly Mansions* thrill us with elegant prose and descriptive narrative describing places in light. Most recently architects and lighting designers have written numerous articles and books on light. Marietta Millet's contribution continues in the tradition of such noted publications as Leslie Larson's *Lighting and Its Design*, Henry Plummer's *The Poetics of Light*, Junichiro Tanizaki's *In Praise of Shadows*, and John Lobell's *Between Silence and Light*, to name but a few.

Light Revealing Architecture shows the importance of the role of light and lighting in architecture and captures the interaction between the individual and the environment. For practicing architects, architectural educators, and students of architecture, they will find this book an invaluable resource.

Richard C. Peters, FAIA
Professor Emeritus of Architecture
University of California, Berkeley

I N T R O D U C T I O N

Beauty must be seen; this requires light.[1]

—KARSTEN HARRIES

Our lives are intimately bound up with light. We literally cannot live without it. It is one of the basic immutable forces of nature. Light is a primary element, animating life here on earth. The sun animates the weather patterns and is a determining factor in climate. It sustains plant life, thereby providing food for animal life. It allows us to see, both by the light of day and also by "delayed light": candlelight, or gas light, or electric light, all of which are dependent on material that once was sustained by the light of the sun. Even hydroelectric power is produced by means of dams that depend on the water cycle, that process of evaporation and deposition of water which is sustained by the sun. Buckminster Fuller reminded us of this dependence simply and eloquently: "Pointing to the logs burning in the fireplace, one child asked me, 'What is fire?' I answered, 'Fire is the sun unwinding from the tree's log.'"[2]

We see by contrast, we live by contrast, and we are aware of qualities only through their opposites. There is always light to counter darkness and vice versa. Variety in our environment stimulates us and keeps us aware. As René Dubos warns, "We must shun uniformity of surroundings as much as absolute conformity in behavior and tastes. We must strive instead to create as many diversified environments as possible."[3] Part of this diversity is accomplished through lighting: the flames of a fire, a candlelight dinner, the suffused glow of colored light in a cathedral, sunlight filtering through leaves or reflected from a smooth surface of water, neon signs, and searchlights crossing the night sky at a grand opening. Light is an indelible part of our experience of life.

We take light that enables us to see for granted, but we are dependent upon it in more ways than we perhaps know, psychologically as well as physiologically. The pineal gland, located at the top of the head, is sensitive to light received through the skull as well as through the eyes. Controlling the hormones, it determines our reactions in response to patterns of daylight occurrence. The short days of winter make us want to hibernate and the long days of summer make us want to play. Emotional well-being is caught up in this cycle, as evidenced by the recognition during the past decade of the SAD (Seasonal Affective Disorder) syndrome. How many other effects of light on our emotions, our behavior, and our spiritual lives remain to be "discovered"?

Before the advent of electricity, human beings were probably much more aware of our place in the universe than we are now. Starlight and moonlight were the definers of the night—parts of a larger whole of which humans are but a minuscule part. The mysteries of the universe were open to wonderment, and myths carried their message. After dark, light was scarce, and the night was bathed in mystery:

> *At that time the light one carried defined the 'room' around the body, the body participated in the light and was inseparable from its source. ... The enemy of night is artificial light. When man conquered darkness the latent generosity of night ceased to exist. In the totality of light the fairy tale disappeared. The night was deprived of imagination.* [4]

Now our night-world is often defined by street lamps and advertising with few opportunities to look beyond to the wonders and the mystery of the night.

Light that is visible to the human eye occupies an extremely small area of the electromagnetic spectrum. This confluence of the visible part of the spectrum and the structure of the human eye and entire perceptual system seems more miraculous the more you think about it. Each one of us sees in a unique way, although average sensitivity ranges to light and color have been established through experimentation. The availability of this data may lead us to view the interaction between light and an individual as defined by these limits, while in fact much of our response to light is associative and emotional.

The properties of light are dual: it is both a particle form (packets of photons) and a wave form (electromagnetic radiation). It is a vibration, and the many different kinds of light operate on different levels of vibration, with the result that they affect us differently. Some striking examples from the field of medicine are the use of ultraviolet light to treat jaundice in newborns, and the use of lasers for accurate surgical cuts, such as in removing cataracts from the cornea of the eye. Light clearly has the capacity to change matter. If it can change coarse physical matter of our bodies, then why not the more subtle areas such as our thoughts and our feelings?

Although light is variable, the laws of physics controlling it are immutable. Unexpected effects often occur with light, but upon investigation, they can be seen to have occurred according to the rules. Intensity falls off with the square of the distance. Reflection is reciprocal: the angle of reflection equals the angle of incidence for specular surfaces, such as mirrors and polished surfaces. Surfaces with a matte finish spread reflected light diffusely and evenly in all directions. As a surface is turned away from a light source, it receives light at an angle, and the illumination on the surface is reduced by the cosine of the angle of incidence—it drops off.

For all light sources, the luminous effect depends upon four factors: the source (its intensity, its directional characteristics, its color); the geometry (its relationship between the source and the receiver or receiving surface); the surfaces that receive and modify light, becoming secondary light sources in themselves by reflecting, redirecting, and coloring light; and the person who views the source and illuminated surfaces as he or she moves around. By observing how light behaves, we can work with it to reveal architecture.

Architecture depends on light. As light reveals the forms of architecture and the places made by it, it simultaneously reveals the meaning and the intentions that are released through the process of conceiving, designing and building. These meanings are both particular and universal.

Lighting is often considered at one of the ends of the spectrum of its capabilities: either solely for aesthetic purposes, or solely for providing visibility for tasks. In fact, it always renders both. Where there is very little light quantitatively (as in restaurants or churches) in order to establish a mood or aura, most of us can still see well enough to read if we will wait for our eyes to adjust and tolerate reading slowly.

Where there is enough light to perform intricate surgery, there is still a mood, a character of the room. These moods can be designed intentionally and not left to chance.

Light acquires meaning in architecture relationally, that is, as part of a sequence of luminous relationships. These relationships in turn set up a series of associations in the inhabitants that transfer meaning from the intentional realm of the designer into the personal realm of the inhabitant. Personal experience is the vehicle for interpretation for both designers and inhabitants. When we can understand the intentions inherent in the way a building is revealed in light, along with the techniques for doing so, then we have the basis for forming both our own intentions and the techniques that can realize them.

The author's intention is to explore light as an architectural medium, and to present light in a cohesive way as it relates to buildings. Ways of characterizing the use of light in architecture are presented in order to open up possibilities of dealing with light more directly and more meaningfully. Light is approached in an integrated way, both conceptually and practically. Included are the poetic and the practical, daylight and electric light, urban streets and building details, and intention and realization. The examples are presented in the spirit of a lighting sketchbook to which one can add his or her own examples.

Light is only one of the many aspects of architecture. But light reveals the building, its intentions, its place, its form, its space, and its meaning. Light reveals architecture and, in the best instances, architecture reveals light.

I believe in an emotional architecture. It is very important for humankind that architecture should move by its beauty: if there are many equally valid technical solutions to a problem, the one which offers the user a message of beauty and emotion, that one is architecture.[5]
—LUIS BARRAGAN

ENDNOTES

1. Harries, Karsten. 1989. *The Broken Frame.* (Washington, D.C.: The Catholic University of America Press), p. 4.

2. Fuller, R. Buckminster. 1981. *Critical Path.* (New York: St. Martin's Press), p. 62.

3. Dubos, René. 1968. *So Human An Animal.* (New York: Charles Scribner's Sons), p. 175.

4. Fjeld, Per Olaf. 1983. *Sverre Fehn: The Thought of Construction.* (New York: Rizzoli), p. 50.

5. Ambasz, Emilio. 1976. *The Architecture of Luis Barragan.* (Boston: New York Graphic Society) p. 8.

LIGHT
REVEALING
EXPERIENCE

. . . architecture, beyond providing

physical frames for human activities,

also interprets to human beings

their place in nature and society.[1]

—*KARSTEN HARRIES*

We can only know what we experience. Our experience of light begins in the personal and proceeds to the universal. We learn, in the environment of our childhood, how forms are revealed in light. We learn what forms mean, from the small forms of our toys to the large forms that shelter us. We do this in the light of the particular place or places where we grow up. A desert dweller cannot imagine the sunlight filtering through leaves, nor a forest dweller the sparkling expanse of the sea. Our experience of light is grounded in the place or places with which we are familiar. Many people live in environments that provide multiple settings and experiences. People travel, read, and watch television, so one's personal realm of virtual experience can encompass many environments. Environments in industrialized countries are dominated by electric lighting, so that the dynamics of the natural cycles of day and night and the change of seasons are muffled by the constancy of electric lighting, both inside and outside.

The patterns of light with which we grow up, and which attract our attention in later times, have meaning for us. Some of these meanings are universal, archetypal images that humanity shares. Some of these meanings are cultural, absorbed through rituals and their settings or simply reflecting an attitude to life. Some of these meanings are personal, associated with particular events or persons. Just as we may pick a certain dress to wear or not wear, because of certain associations, so may particular patterns of light remind us of a place and its associations. Our cumulative experience of light in places is complex, multilayered, and rich.

Although today, at least in Western industrialized countries, there is no common sacred belief system that begets a set of symbols of clear and universally accepted meaning, there is in the human subconscious a primal set of connections that relate us to light and darkness. These connections are of course tempered by cultural, social, and personal experience. But almost all human beings have experienced daylight, moonlight, starlight, and firelight. It was not abstract reasoning, I would guess, but a deep intuition drawing on experience that caused Richard Kelly to designate three types of light for design purposes: focal glow, ambient luminescence, and the play of brilliants.

> Focal glow is 'the campfire of all time, ... the sunburst through the clouds, and the shaft of sunshine that warms the far end of the valley. Focal glow commands attention and attracts interest. It fixes the gaze, concentrates the mind, and tells people what to look at. [It] separates the important from the unimportant.' ... Ambient luminescence is 'a snowy morning in open country. It is underwater in the sunshine, or inside a white tent at high noon. Ambient luminescence minimizes the importance of all things and all people. It fills people with a sense of freedom, of space and can suggest infinity.' ... Play of brilliants is 'the aurora borealis, ... the Versailles Hall of Mirrors with its thousands of candle flames. Play of brilliants is Times Square at night, ... the magic of the Christmas tree, Fourth of July skyrockets. It quickens the appetite and heightens all sensation. It can be distracting or it can be entertaining."[2]

It is exactly this kind of metaphorical thinking about light that can make buildings be places that have special meaning for us, extending their value beyond mere functional use.

If we as designers intend to create a certain lighting effect, it is usually because we have experienced that effect and know it to be right for a certain setting. Creating a setting in a particular place, either outside or inside, usually starts with fitting it gracefully to its locale and providing comfort for the people who will inhabit it. These intentions all fit under the general umbrella of experience: our experience of the world, and our cultural and sensory associations. Our experience of light is connected to specific places where light contributes to the identification of a *genius loci*, the peculiar character of a place as it is impressed upon our minds. Climate is also a defining element of genius loci. The use of light in a building affects our feelings of comfort in relation to the thermal variables in each climate zone. Light is indelibly connected to time in our experience, and can express or stifle the expression of changing time in buildings. Our reliance on light to be able to read and write and see people and places is so pervasive as to seem mundane, but the relationship between light and the task can range from the uncomfortable to the poetic. Ideally light not only fulfills its function of providing illumination for visual activities but does so in a way that enriches our experience.

LIGHT AND PLACE

Each particular place has its light. Light expressing place encompasses two distinct aspects: the place itself, its physical features and characteristics that determine how it differs at any given moment from any other place; and the particular set of changes that take place within it over time, creating distinctive patterns of diurnal and seasonal changes.

Especially when we have lived in a place, we know its rhythms of light and dark, clear and cloudy, and bright and dull. We know that a winter day in Boston can feel much brighter and more "cheery" than a much warmer winter day in Seattle due to the welcome winter sunlight reflected from the snow-covered ground. And we know that the "lazy, hazy, crazy days of summer" are much hazier in the Southeastern parts of the United States and semitropical areas everywhere, due to the high levels of water vapor in the air that affect the visual scene as well as human comfort.

FIGURE 1–1 *The continental United States, covering a large land mass and 24 degrees of latitude (25° North to the 49th parallel), encompasses a broad range of places characterized by their own particular light.*

A *The double rainbow near Taos, New Mexico (37° North, elevation: 7,098 feet) is not an unusual occurrence in autumn, when afternoon thunder showers typically break the heat of the day. The Sangre de Christo mountains in the distance to the east change color during the course of the day, first being silhouetted by the morning sunlight, then warming up in the color of the afternoon light.*

B *In the Palouse region of southeastern Washington and northern Idaho (latitude: 47° North, elevation: 2,500 feet), the rolling hills of stubble present a continuous surface that is voluptuously modeled in light. The gentle curves of the surfaces are distinctive of this region. The color of the ground surface and the light are characteristic of autumn.*

C *A little farther west and slightly farther north, the view of Mt. Index (latitude: 48° North; elevation: 6,100 feet) from the Skykomish River is blurred by autumn fog. The cold gray light of winter is already evident, the water surface reflecting the steel gray of the sky and the foliage of the evergreens absorbing the light that enters the trees, rendering them almost colorless.*

D *On the coast of Washington at Copalis Beach on the western edge of the Olympic Peninsula (latitude: 48° North; elevation: sea level), the sea reflects the color of the sky on a calm summer evening.*

E *On the other side of the country, the coastal waterways of Maine (latitude: 44° North; elevation: sea level) reflect the deep blue of the sky on a midsummer day.*

FIGURE 1–2A *A summer pond in Old Chatham in upstate New York.*

FIGURE 1–2B *Autumn.*

FIGURE 1–2C *Winter.*

FIGURE 1–2D *Spring.*

Particular sky conditions are repeated around the world, but at different times of the day and year. For example, a clear blue summer sky in northern Canada may have the same appearance as one seen in Washington, D.C., in the wintertime. The procession of particular sky conditions composes the typical patterns of light from the sun and sky that we expect in each place. In addition to regional patterns of typical sky conditions, specific places each retain their own identity within the general region. For example, people living on the east side of a mountain range experience sunrises and an early disappearance of the sun in the evening, while those living on the west side experience late mornings and sunsets. People living in the valley experience a shorter period of direct sunlight than do those people living on the mountain tops. People living on the eastern edge of any land mass view the sunrise across the water, while those people on the western edge view the sunset. These differences and many more can lead to habits and rituals having to do with the daily rhythms of light, such as gathering to watch the sunrise on east-coast beaches or the sunset in the west.

Water, by reflecting the sky and the surroundings, intensifies the light effects of a particular place. A pond in Old Chatham, near Albany, New York, photographed through the course of the seasons of one year, reveals the light of the place. On a summer evening the green of the leaves is darker, absorbing the sunlight. The grass has also taken on a deep hue, and the dark areas of the trees and lawn in shade frame the trees at the end of the pond catching the low rays of the sun. The sky is somewhat hazy, laden with moisture at the end of the day. The surface of the water reflects the greens, ranging from the tender new shoots of the cattails to the deep purple-green of the tree shadows. The darkest parts of the pond are the darkest surfaces in view.

In the fall, the sky is darker, the air crisp, and the colors of the leaves extend from green through yellow and orange to red. In late afternoon light, the pond is partially shaded, almost black. The colors of the trees are reflected in the water, forming a pattern of bright color against dark background that is similar to that of the lawn dotted with fallen leaves. The multiple colors and textures are emphasized in the crisp light. The pond surface reflects the plants at its edge, sharing the brightness of the reflected light with them.

The winter sky is deep blue, the bottom of the woods lost in darkness as the noon sun casts long shadows over the snow-covered pond. The contrasts are intense. The pond surface is now brighter than the sky where it is in full sunlight. The palette is condensed, and contrasts arise from shifts in value rather than hue.

These harsh contrasts soften in early spring when the snow has receded to uncover the muted tans and greens of cattails and lawn. A morning mist blurs the edges of the trees and the pond. The sky is light blue. The surface of the pond, ruffled, reflects the lower woods, mediating between the tangled darkness of the woods and the civilized darkness of the lawn.

Each place, and each prospect from a place, is defined uniquely due to the myriad combinations that reveal it in light. This light shapes both the prospect from the building and also the light that enters the building.

Genius loci

The spirit of a place, its *genius loci*, can be conveyed by responding sensitively to its light. The importance of light to spirit of place is evident in the words and images in Christian Norberg-Schulz's book *Genius Loci: Towards a Phenomenology of Architecture*. There are certain places that are memorable for their quality of light, and certain architects who are skilled in their evocation of place in light.

The particular light quality of the Pacific Northwest has been described by the Canadian architect Arthur Erickson: "The West Coast is a particularly difficult area with its watery lights, which are capable of soft and subtle moods." It is northern light, which "is remote and hidden above the clouds." Erickson's architectural response to this light is "transparency in buildings, or skylights bathing walls with a gentle introspective light, or water reflection to bring the sky's brightness onto the earth's dark surfaces."[3] Water reflections add a luminous quality to the otherwise dark and light-absorbing ground. Reflections in water put the sky at our feet. Erickson has placed expanses of water outside the windows of buildings in order to lighten the ground and reflect the sky to the occupants. At the British Columbia Government Services Complex (1973–79) in Vancouver, pools are part of the park setting for the building, with water cascading over waterfalls and skylights and lending its animating, light-reflecting substance to the experience of the place.

Forests provide an ever-changing palette of colors and textures in light, and each one is particular to its own part of the world. The tall evergreen trees of the northwestern United States bathe that area with a far different light than do the quaking aspens in the high Rocky Mountains. The tall spare pines of Finland thinly filter the light. In certain buildings, the image of the forest light is present.

Connected with the link between light and spirit of place is the link between light and culture. Junichiro Tanizaki explores this connection between light and culture in his book *In Praise of Shadows*, in which he explains the traditional preference of Japanese people for shadows and darkness:

> And so it has come to be that the beauty of a Japanese room depends on a variation of shadows, heavy shadows against light shadows—it has nothing else. Westerners are amazed at the simplicity of Japanese rooms, perceiving in them no more than ashen walls bereft of ornament. Their reaction is understandable, but it betrays a failure to comprehend the mystery of shadows. Out beyond the sitting room, which the rays of the sun can at best but barely reach, we extend the eaves or build on a verandah,

FIGURE 1–3 *Water reflects the sky. British Columbia Government Services Complex in Vancouver.*

FIGURE 1–4A *The pines outside the Villa Mairea (Alvar Aalto Architect, 1937–39) in Noormarkku, Finland.*

FIGURE 1–4B *Interior of Villa Mairea. The screen of poles that encloses the stairwell echoes the form of the tall straight trunks of the trees outside. They break up and filter the daylight and evoke the light quality of the Finnish woods inside the house. Photographs by Elaine Day LaTourelle.*

putting the sunlight at still greater a remove. The light from the garden steals in but dimly through paper-paneled doors, and it is precisely this indirect light that makes for us the charm of a room.[4]

The paper-paneled doors, or *shoji*, are only one piece in a complex set of parts of the traditional Japanese house, which was designed to provide comfort in the most difficult season—the hot humid summer. A broad roof overhangs the house, sheltering the interior from exposure to light, heat, and rain. Sets of shoji, lattice panels, rain shutters, and recently, glass panels slide in parallel tracks around the perimeter. By alternately opening and closing these panels, the house can be opened to the cross-ventilation of summer breezes or closed against the biting cold winds of winter, with many variations in between. The cedar-framed panels with rice paper, the shoji , transmit a soft and muted light that creates the shadowed interior described by Tanizaki. Interior sliding panels called *fusuma*, covered with several layers of denser paper, transmit less light and are used for partitions where light transmission is not so important.

The shoji do not ameliorate all environmental conditions, however. Shoji do not block sound. Due to a need for privacy, there is a psychological distinction between areas separated by these partitions that serves as a rule for daily living. This psychological barrier is expressed in the word *kekkai*, which was originally a lattice partition similar to a fence that separated the area for worshippers from the inner sanctuary in temples. It is a physical object that represents a psychological barrier. The shoji are a psychological barrier to sound transmission. If you are not supposed to listen to something, you do not hear it.

In the winter, the exterior panels provide only minimal protection from the cold. At least two rituals combat the cold that pervades the house: the inhabitants gather around a fire pit from which a robe extends to cover their laps; and they soak in public hot tubs. These two methods of warming the body help the inhabitants to withstand the cold temperatures in the house.[5]

Due to the fragility of the rice paper shoji, they are customarily repapered twice a year, traditionally in the spring and autumn. With all these associated rituals, shoji are linked to cultural and thermal conditions as well as to light quality. The shoji cannot be understood as a single element that controls the quality of light, but must be comprehended in the totality of patterns of dwelling in a traditional Japanese house.

The windows of the Netherlands are as distinctive as the shoji. They are unusually large. Dutch architect Herman Hertzberger has noted: "That you can look straight into Dutch livingrooms and can almost take part in what goes on inside is a tradition that never fails to amaze visitors to this country."[6] He attributes this open-window policy to the openness of Dutch society. Certainly the Dutch people like to display themselves and their possessions. There are picture windows for prostitutes in the red-light districts, and large windows at the front and back of row houses that allow passersby to see through the rooms and into the back garden. Windows, as a means of seeing through things, are a part of the culture.

There are functional and historical roots as well. Much of the land mass of the Netherlands has been wrested from the sea through the arduous task of erecting dikes around water-covered areas and pumping the water out, originally by means of windmills and later steam- and diesel-driven pumps, into canals. The land won in this manner was precious, especially in the cities. In order to give as many houses as possible frontage on the canals, the house fronts were kept very narrow. The houses shared common walls on the sides and extended deeply into the narrow lots. Areas for windows were therefore restricted to the two ends—the canal front and the garden back. Since light is prized in this northern climate characterized by cloud-filled skies, the windows claimed as much area of these walls as possible.

FIGURE 1–5A *Shoji, glazed panels, and bamboo shades in a traditional house, Yoshijima Residence, in Takayama, Japan.*

FIGURE 1-5B *The enclosed garden filters the daylight before it reaches the shoji. In turn, the shoji frame the view of the garden. Photographs by J. William Curtis.*

FIGURE 1–6 *Typical Dutch windows in buildings fronting the canal in Groningen in the northern part of the Netherlands.*

FIGURE 1–7 *View through a front window and livingroom to the garden in a house in Amersfoort, the Netherlands.*

And yet the large areas of glazing are a liability, too, allowing heat loss. The local climate is largely determined by the sea. A northwest maritime climate, it is raw and cold in winter, mild but cool in summers. And yet Hertzberger claims that "The exceptionally large expanses of glass in our buildings ... are possible thanks to the mild climate ..."[7] This perception is one with which a southerner would violently disagree, and makes evident the fact that response to climate is relative. The climate of the Netherlands is mild when compared to that of the Scandinavian countries, but harsh in comparison to that of southern France or Spain. That it seems mild to a Dutchman is appropriate. He had better be used to it.

The paintings by Jan Vermeer, done in his studio which fronted on the market square in Delft, reveal the variations in lighting conditions possible with the combination of large windows, wooden shutters, sheer curtains, and heavy draperies, all of which were used to control the flow of light. The resulting light quality could be varied at will, from large swaths of precious sunlight to tiny glimmers of light sneaking through wooden shutters. In *The Geographer* (1669), direct light coming through the window falls on the geographer and his charts on the table, and also highlights additional rolls of charts on the floor and a globe of the world behind him. Light is reflected from the side wall and cabinet behind the geographer as well. Curtains block light from the foreground of the scene. The light was manipulated to provide the appropriate luminous setting for the expression of the painting.

Italian windows respond to the benign climate and also to the social rituals of conversing with friends and family in the street below. The tall casement windows open fully for ventilation and allow one to go out on the balcony and participate in the life of the street below. The exterior shutters are louvered to reject sunlight and its accompanying heat while still allowing ventilation. The resulting dark interior also con-

FIGURE 1–8 The Geographer, *1669, by Jan Vermeer. Photograph by Artothek, reproduced courtesy of the Städelsches Kunstinstitut, Frankfurt.*

veys a psychological sense of coolness. Bottom sections of the shutters flip up to increase the ventilation area, at the same time allowing one to see the street. Solid wood shutters on the interior provide a third line of defense against light, heat, and sound. Positioning the casements and the two sets of shutters provides individual and subtle control of these three environmental elements.

Norberg-Schulz singles out the window as being especially important in defining the spirit of place: "It does not only express the spatial structure of the building, but also how it is related to light. And, through its proportions and detailing, it participates in the functions of standing and rising. In the window, thus, the *genius loci* is focused and 'explained'."[8] By considering the window as an interpretation of genius loci, we can find an expression of cultural attitudes to light that extend far beyond the practical needs for light and air. It stands to reason, then, that when designing a window, we have the opportunity to do much more than offer a view or let daylight into the building. The way windows are made reveals the character of the people, and also the character of the wall, hence building materials and methods. The numerous layers of Dutch and Italian windows require a thick wall in which to position them. The masonry walls in the Netherlands and Italy provided that along with weather protection. The series of sliding panels—rain shutters, glass, lattice, and shoji—in the traditional Japanese house are only part of the construction that protects the interior. The verandah with its broad eaves shelters these panels from the brunt of the weather. In each case, the window fits the wall and reveals it in addition to the light of the place.

If the windows of a building are to fit into a place, to be of that place, then they must respect the light quality of that place. Our perception of light-quality is intertwined both with our response to the local climate as well as with the task at hand. Two libraries built in the 1980s offer two different approaches to making windows for southern California light: the San Juan Capistrano Library (Michael Graves, 1982); and the Frances Howard Goldwyn Regional Branch Library (Frank Gehry, 1983–85) in North Hollywood.

The settings for the two libraries are different, although they are only 60 miles apart and both are near the coastline. The San Juan Capistrano Library is located on an open suburban site, while the Hollywood Library is set on a busy city street. The light quality of southern California that attracts people like a magnet—the golden sunlight that makes the landscape seem luminous—is evident in San Juan Capistrano. In Hollywood, however, the sunlight is often obscured by a haze of smog.

Michael Graves chose an interpretation of the Mission Style for the form of the San Juan Capistrano Library. The formal language of the library responds to the place symbolically by borrowing the forms of previous builders. These forms do not, however, celebrate or modify the light of the place for the current task, reading. For example, numerous cupolas and small windows suggest from the outside that the hot and bright light will be filtered to a cool interior. The daylight *is* mod-

FIGURE 1–11A *San Juan Capistrano Library entry.*

FIGURE 1–11B *Interior view of "light cupola" visible behind the trellised arch of the entry in the photograph of the entry. The determination of the light quality of the place by means of the electric lighting fixture is typical of the experience of the library.*

FIGURE 1–11C *View of the adults' lounge in mid–afternoon. An enclosed garden is adjacent to this room through the glass doors.*

FIGURE 1–11D *View from garden to children's reading room shows the separation of inside and outside rooms.*

FIGURE 1-11E *Layers of trellis separate an outside reading room from the children's fiction room.*

ified, but in the process it is often restricted to a point where it must be supplemented constantly with electric lighting, as in the entry and in the adults' lounge. Then it is the quality of the electric lighting that determines the light quality of the rooms in spite of the abundance of daylight outside, daylight that carries with it the nuances of that particular place, a place noted for its beautiful light. The windows reject the light of the place.

Neither do outdoor reading areas invite one to read outside in this most temperate of climates. Most outdoor reading areas are on the western side of the building where afternoon sunlight and heat build-up make reading uncomfortable in the afternoon during much of the year. Nor are the reading areas built to temper the southern California light in ways that would make reading comfortable. Trellises, for example, cast strong patterns of light and shadow that are disruptive to reading. Again the formal design strategy is autonomous and does not respond to the site and climate conditions to temper the light for the task.

The orientation of the Hollywood Library is determined by its street front, its main façade facing east. This orientation proves sensitive in balancing light and heat. Morning sunlight can be welcome inside, but it is accompanied by heat that can hang around all day. So the fact that large areas of the east façade are glazed could pose overheating problems for the library patrons. The fact that morning sunlight is often lost in fog and smog helps. Additional glazing is all located in the north facing façades of the three reading rooms, facing away from direct sun. The north and south reading rooms are capped by light-grabbing boxes that reach out and capture additional daylight, delivering it from the top and boosting the light levels away from the windows. This additional top-light evens out the light gradients across the room.

The formal design strategy opens to the site and its lighting conditions. Views of trees, buildings, and sky surround the reading rooms. They are buffered from the street, however, by courtyards with light-colored walls that reflect light back into the room. The result is a light-filled room that is visually connected to its surroundings, yet private. The light at the edge invites one to read in a spot where light is tempered for the task by overhead panels, yet visually connected to outdoors by the large amount of glazing and light entering through it. The windows accept and celebrate the light of the place. The library is "open" to its neighborhood in a similar sense that Los Angeles culture is "open"—a mixture of races, classes, and creeds where almost anything goes.

As originally designed and built, the Hollywood Library also incorporated water as a cooling and light-reflecting element in the courtyards. Due to leakage problems, the courtyards have now been drained and paving blocks installed, so that the special quality of water reflecting light, so precious in a hot climate, has been lost. This situation does point up the extent to which lighting is connected with the details of a building, in this case even its waterproofing details.

The role of light is defining when it is revealed through the experience of a building. In order for this place-defining light to be revealed, the formal strategy used in designing buildings must be flexible enough to be able to respond to the local light conditions as tempered by the immediate surroundings.

Light as image of nature

Counter to revealing the spirit of the place where we are, light can suggest other places and other times. In the face of having lost our constant and natural relationship to the landscape and its light, light can still remind us of places that we know through recreating their particular patterns of light, such as shafts of light that penetrate into deep forests. And patterns of light can suggest places that we

FIGURE 1–12A *Frances Howard Goldwyn Regional Branch Library. View of entry (behind tall fence) with children's reading area above. The north reading room is to the right behind the glazing that wraps around the corner of the building, with the glazed box on top.*

FIGURE 1–12B *Interior view of the north reading room.*

FIGURE 1–13A *Les Halles (Victor Baltard, 1845–57, now demolished). Photograph taken in 1972. Light seen through the grille in the former market halls in Paris is reminiscent of the light in a forest. The shutters filter the daylight as do the leaves of the trees, and the vertical members of the grille recall the tree trunks. The daylight picks up a green cast as it passes through the green shutters.*

FIGURE 1–13B *Light in the forest in northern Vermont.*

might not have experienced, such as the Northwest Coast Indian villages that are intimated in the Museum of Anthropology at the University of British Columbia (see "Experiential Light" on page 37).

Images of light in nature can be used as powerful models for designing the luminous qualities of rooms. The poetic use of light adds new qualities to a given place. When light creates an image of nature inside a building, associations are evoked through the type of light (intense, filtered, weak), the patterns of light (speckled, dappled, smooth, wispy), the direction of the light, the color of the light, and the relation of the light to the surroundings. Light in this case creates a visual connotation, suggesting the presence of something perhaps far distant. The representation may be as abstract as an impressionist painting or more literal.

A major concern in the residential design work of Frank Lloyd Wright was providing connections, both real and metaphorical, between inside and outside. He used patterns abstracted from nature in windows of many of his early houses, including those in the Robie House (1908–10) in Chicago, Illinois. A window on the north side of the living room creates patterns of light that mingle with the patterns of light in the trees beyond the window. The abstracted image of nature introduced in the colors, textures, and shapes of the window glazing is set against the view of nature, so that the barrier between inside and outside seems to dissolve and the two images merge in a phenomenal transparency. The image of nature was also projected into the interior by means of the patterns cast by light entering through the colored glass in the windows. Mr. Robie, the original owner of the house, referring to the sunlight entering through these windows, stated that the interior "seemed *alive*, because of the movement of the sun ..."[9]

Numerous other examples are evident in Wright's work. Much later, in Taliesin West (1938–59) in Maricopa Mesa near Phoenix, Arizona, Wright recalled another image of nature by means of electrical light. The image of the starry sky is repre-

FIGURE 1–14 *View out a livingroom window in the Robie House. The transparency of the clear glazing overlays the ornamental pattern of the window onto the view outside. Used with permission of The Robie House, University of Illinois, Chicago; and The Frank Lloyd Wright Foundation.*

FIGURE 1–15 *The ceiling lighting in the cabaret at Taliesin West evokes the image of the starry sky. Used with permission of the Frank Lloyd Wright Foundation.*

FIGURE 1–16A *A mountain stream in Maine, late autumn.*

sented in the cabaret by stringing fairy lights across the ceiling. Evoking a sense of mystery and fantasy, the allusion to the night sky sets the stage for festivity. The power of these lighting effects that recall a natural lighting condition is connected with our associations with natural phenomena, as Richard Kelly's classification of lighting reminds us. The starry sky is "the play of brilliants."

The image of water can also be evoked with light. Water, a powerful symbol, may be suggested in the fluid way that light moves over objects, as in the patterns that moving water casts on the surfaces below it. This similarity is suggested in two images: one of a mountain stream, and the other of Hagia Sophia (Anthemios and Isidoros, 532–37) in Istanbul, Turkey. As in the likening of the image of Les Halles with the image of Vermont woods, this particular natural scene certainly did not influence the design of the building. But in seeing these similarities between natural and built images, we can use the images of natural lighting phenomena as models for luminous conditions in buildings. Knowing how an effect was created in a building can suggest similar built conditions where images of nature may be evoked.

The suggestion of water by light is clearer and intentionally symbolic in the baptistery of St. Matthew's Episcopal Church (Charles Moore, John Ruble, and Buzz Yudell; Richard Peters, lighting consultant; 1979–83) in Pacific Palisades, California. Water, by which the sins of the world are washed away, is the material with which the ritual of baptism is performed in the Episcopal church as in many others. The baptismal font holds water, and the entire alcove surrounding it recalls the image of water by means of daylight filtering through colored glass. The glazing pattern and coloration is designed to suggest the numerous colors encountered in water, the constant movement, and darkness increasing with depth.

FIGURE 1–16B *Interior view of Hagia Sophia. The light passing through the stone screen is reminiscent of the image of air bubbles and refracted light in a mountain stream. Light touching the side of the screen's perforations recalls light striking the air bubbles in the stream, as do the glass candleholders in the chandelier. The silhouetted shapes of the holes in the screen are similar to the patterns that the surface of the water overlays on the stones beneath the surface.*

FIGURE 1–17 *The image of light arriving through water is suggested by the glazing in the baptismal alcove in St. Matthew's Episcopal Church.*

LIGHT AND CLIMATE

The interaction between light and climate is multidimensional. It has to do with the spirit of place, with thermal comfort, and also with culture, since climate affects people, their habits, and their rituals.[10] The character of the light, its colors and rhythms, is one of the great contributors to genius loci.

Light plays a dual role in ameliorating the thermal conditions in a building. Firstly, it can provide a visual counterpoint to them, softening the harsh reality of difficult environmental circumstances such as pervasive heat or cold. Secondly, the manner in which light is introduced also produces a physiological reaction. Light is the package in which heat is wrapped, so that light and heat are connected with regard to thermal comfort. Light is often shunned in hot climates, while it is welcomed in cool climates. Where it becomes bitterly cold, a battle is waged between the dual necessities of excluding the cold and admitting the light. In temperate climates, there are few thermal restraints, and the interaction between inside and outside is often maximized. Interaction between inside and outside can be maximized in extreme climates as well, but usually only at great expense, which makes a statement of wealth and power. This struggle between the thermal aspects and the light-giving properties of windows was summarized by Le Corbusier in a discussion he called The Problems of Sunshine: "the history of the window is also that of architecture, ... at least one of the most characteristic slices of the history of architecture."[11]

There are several thermal aspects connected with the introduction of light. Glazing offers little resistance to heat or cold. Losing heat to the exterior is a liability in cold climates and in the wintertime. But glass also admits heat along with direct sunlight, and then traps it inside—the "greenhouse effect." Fire, gas, and electric lighting sources also introduce heat to the interior.[12] Admitting heat to the interior adds thermal stress and the need for additional cooling in hot climates and in the summertime. Cooling can be required even in the winter in buildings where high internal thermal loads result from a concentration of people, heat-generating equipment such as computers, and electric lighting fixtures. Providing balance, both visual and physiological, among these factors falls to the architect.

The visual effect

Light can convey a visual message that transforms the uncomfortable realities of a particular climate condition. For example, the admission of even a small beam of sunlight into a building in a northern climate on a cold winter day can add a sense of vitality and sparkle to the interior. This fact may seem obvious, but there are many buildings in northern climates that exclude sunlight or, conversely, admit it unrestrained so that it presents a visual burden due to its intensity and the glare conditions it creates as well as a thermal burden through the heat that accompanies it.

Similarly to presenting the sound of water to create "psychological cooling" in hot climates, light can be presented in ways that alleviate unpleasant visual conditions, whether too dull or too bright. The use of gold to add contrast to an otherwise dull setting of dark skies and dark surfaces is one response to lighting conditions in northern climates. By its warmth and

FIGURE 1–18 *Places such as Victorian greenhouses, follies, or wintergardens become the foci for sensual pleasures that relieve the exigencies of a difficult season. The Wintergarden, 311 South Wacker Drive, Chicago (Kohn Pederson Fox Associates, completed 1991).*

FIGURE 1–19 *In the Netherlands, a gold finish lends sparkle to the ornamental top of a fence at the Royal Palace in Het Loo.*

FIGURE 1–20 *Wood and brick bathed in sunlight create a visual sense of warmth in the Stock Exchange Building in Amsterdam.*

FIGURE 1–21 *Color from the electrical lighting fixtures in the entry lobby to the Centraal Beheer office building in Apeldoorn brighten the restrained palette of materials and the cool sky light.*

FIGURE 1–22 *A glass canopy and handrail add light and interest to the entry of the Montessori School in Amsterdam.*

sparkle, even under the diffuse light of overcast skies, gold provides psychological relief. This same detail in the desert would blind the eye and seem garish. But gold-tipped fences and domes stud northern European cityscapes, brightening the otherwise monochromatic winter scene. Inside, finishes that look warm as well as feel warm can help mitigate the chill. In the Stock Exchange building (Hendrik Berlage, 1898–1903) in Amsterdam, The Netherlands, the reddish tones of the wood lend their warmth to the light that spills past them onto the floor and the structure. The wood feels warm to the touch because, having a high thermal resistance, it does not wick heat away from the body. We have associations built up from the experience of wood that contribute to our perception of it as warm.

The balance of daylight and electric lighting is crucial in achieving the appropriate visual effect. In the Centraal Beheer (Herman Hertzberger, 1968–72), an office building for an insurance company in Apeldoorn, the electric lighting fixtures add a perceptible warmth to the interior. Daylight enters into the building through well-placed central skylights as well as at the perimeter, but since the skies in the Netherlands are predominantly overcast, that light is often dull and gray. The major building materials of concrete and concrete block are neutral in their reflection of the light, neither warming nor cooling it, so that differing light qualities are readily apparent. When the electric lighting fixtures are on, however, the yellow Plexiglas pieces that have been added at the corners of fluorescent fixtures provide bright spots that counter the cool daylight. The glow of strategically-placed incandescent fixtures, such as those on the reception desk, suffuse the surfaces with a warm light. These spots of colored focus provided by the electric lighting fixtures suggest a warmth that alleviates the coolness of the light and outside temperatures.

In northern climates where light is prized, the conflict between protecting an exterior area from rain or snow and yet admitting light is one that can be resolved through the use of glass. In the entry to the Montessori School (Herman Hertzberger, 1980–83) in Amsterdam, The Netherlands, the entry area is protected but not darkened by its frosted glass canopy. The outer section of the stairs is made of heavy glass treads and wire-mesh risers, allowing light to filter through to a play area below. The stair rail is made of frosted glass, allowing additional filtered light to reach the play space underneath through the light-diffusing treads and risers. The play space has been kept dry yet daylit by using glass and wire mesh rather than opaque materials. The glass and the coloring of its frame also enliven the monochromatic building.

In southern locales, on the other hand, intense light renders surfaces too bright to be viewed comfortably. The ornamental motif on the walls of the gate-

FIGURE 1–23 *The patterns on the wall of the Finca Güell in Las Corts de Sarriá, a suburb of Barcelona, relieve the brightness of the surface with their cast shadows.*

FIGURE 1–25
Arbors such as the one in the garden of General Vallejo's house in Sonoma, California, offer both visual and thermal respite from light and heat.

FIGURE 1–24 *In Turkey, the interiors of the sixteenth-century Topkapi Palace pavilion illustrate another method of introducing "cool daylight": limiting its entrance through screens; coloring it blue with colored glass; and reflecting it from blue and white glazed tiles. Photograph by Candis Allison Miles.*

house to the Finca Güell (Antonio Gaudí, 1884–87) in Las Corts de Sarriá, a suburb of Barcelona, creates a rich pattern of light and shadow. This type of ornamentation is typical in Barcelona and other parts of Spain, where the sunny climate provides the means for dramatic modeling of form. Indeed, a flat wall of this light stone would reflect so much sunlight that it would seem glaring to the eye. The deeply sculpted forms, on the other hand, produce a delightful pattern of shadows, that relieve the brightness. The forms create a series of changing compositions as the sunlight moves over them. The deep overhanging arches insure that shadows will be cast when the sun is overhead and also to the side. The indentations in the raised hemispheres are kept in shadow, even when sunlight barely grazes the outermost tips. The harsh sunlight of Spain emphasizes these forms, which in turn celebrate the light.

The provision of shade often signals a comfortable respite from the glaring sun with its too-bright light, radiating heat, and accompanying high temperatures. In Tempe, Arizona, a cool grotto reached through a sequence of descending stairs gives entry to the museum of the Performing Arts Center (Antoine Predock, 1987–89) on the campus of Arizona State University. This underground space provides welcome relief, both real and psychological, from the outside conditions, which can be hot even in winter. The concrete surfaces exude coolness, as does the interior of a cave. A small pool supplies both evaporative cooling effects and the psychologically cooling sound of water. The light is dim, so dim that electric lighting fixtures are turned on during the daytime. Daylight is admitted through small openings—square holes punched in the concrete shell and the wire-mesh covered risers of the stairs over-

FIGURE 1–26 *The entry to the Performing Arts Center in Tempe, Arizona, provides a contrast to the external light and heat.*

FIGURE 1–27 *Visual and thermal options are presented in the garden room of Taliesin West in Maricopa, near Phoenix, Arizona. The photograph was taken on a January morning looking southwest. Photograph by Carol A. Prafcke, used with permission of the Frank Lloyd Wright Foundation.*

head. In contrast to the glaring brightness beyond, the partial darkness lends a sense of coolness that is corroborated by the physical experience of it.

The images of the entries to Centraal Beheers (see Figure 1-21) and to the Performing Arts Center are similar in overall tone, coloration, and light distribution. Upon close examination, critical differences become apparent. The diffuse daylight washing the surfaces of the Centraal Beheers enters through a large sloped clerestory. That amount of clear glazing in Arizona would bring in a broad swatch of sunlight and obliterate the cave-like atmosphere. The daylight openings to the grotto of the Performing Arts Center are small and incremental, spreading the entering sunlight over the adjacent concrete surfaces. Each entry receives its sense of warmth or coolness relative to the conditions outside: in the Netherlands, a cool gray overcast; in Arizona, hot sunshine and blue skies.

At Taliesin West (1938–58), Frank Lloyd Wright's winter residence and community near Phoenix, Arizona, a number of strategies are used to provide a visually cool yet light-filled setting in the middle of the desert. The Garden Room is an interesting example because it functions as a retreat from the diurnal hot/cool cycle of winter even when sunlight is shining into it. On a winter morning, low sunlight strikes various surfaces in the room while leaving other areas in shade. The orientation and shape of the room allow morning sunlight to enter, responding to the desert climate where nights are cold and days are hot, so that the warmth of the sun is welcome in the morning and unwelcome in the afternoon. The rock pylons at the left form deep baffles against the direct sunlight and the skylight. A roof over this low outer section blocks light from the center of the room, while clerestory windows above admit light and sunlight to the opposite side of the room. The ensuing pockets of deep shadow in the protection of the rock pylons offer refuge from the desert light. The sense of protection from the heat and glare of the sunlight is intensified by this contrast. The choice is presented to sit either in the sunlight or in the shade, to be exposed or protected.

The physiological effect

There are thermal realities associated with the introduction of light into buildings that cannot be avoided: the introduction of heat along with direct sunlight, heat loss through glazing when the temperature outside is lower than inside, and the addition of heat to interiors when electric lighting fixtures are operating.[13] A building that provides both comfort and delight in its locale must respond to these realities.

The connection with light, especially sunlight, and heat is evident in small rooms with large windows that face south where the occupant cannot escape from the dazzling light nor the high temperatures produced by the trapped heat from sunlight. A famous example that illustrates this quandary, and its ultimate resolution, is the Cité de Refuge (Atelier Le Corbusier, 1929–33) in Paris.[14] In this dormitory for homeless people run by the Salvation Army, Corbusier had designed the south-facing glazed façade of the sleeping rooms as a double skin that, in concert with refrigerated cooling coils, was intended to control heating and ventilation. He called this system "respiration exact."[15] But single-glazing was installed instead, the cooling coils were not installed, and there was no provision for natural ventilation. In fact, the system as built practically cooked the occupants. Although originally defensive of his design, Le Corbusier faced the facts, especially after he himself became the victim of the heat produced by east-and-west-facing glazed façades in the apartment building he designed and occupied in 1933 near the Porte Molitor in Paris. He was also involved in the difficulties of mitigating the intense heat in Algiers and Barcelona, for which he was designing apartment blocks. He had observed and been impressed by shading and cooling techniques used in North Africa during his visits there. Due to these influences, his office eventually added a *brise-soleil* to the south façade of the Cité de Refuge. In 1946, Le Corbusier, with hindsight and poetic flourish, described his development of the brise-soleil.[16] After that time, the brise-soleil and other forms that controlled the admission of sunlight and heat to buildings became part of his formal vocabulary to be used for both climate-responsive and also expressive strategies.

The opposite quandary, that of not losing too much of the building's heat to the exterior when it is cold outside, is one faced in northern locales. Aalto designed buildings in light in a way that celebrates the climate conditions of Finland. In this region of long cold winters, daylight was not provided at the expense of comfort. In the library in the town complex of Seinajoki (Alvar Aalto, Architect, 1963–65), a large area of glazing that admits light to the main bookstack and reading area faces south. In midwinter, heat would be lost through this glazing almost all the time, the sun peaking over the horizon only three hours a day, and then weakly. The windows are placed at the top of a high wall, with a curved ceiling section rising to it. This location effectively shields people in the library from losing their body heat to the cold glazing through radiative heat loss since the cold surfaces are distant and therefore form a smaller part of each person's radiant field.

It may seem odd to find sunshades on a building in Finland, but the very short winter days are balanced by very long summer days when the result of the sun shining on the land for 20 or more hours a day heats it up considerably. As welcome as the sun is, as with anything persistent, one begs for relief. The sunshade

FIGURE 1–28A *The south–facing façade of the Cité de Refuge as originally constructed.*

FIGURE 1–28B *The same façade after the addition of the brise-soleil.*

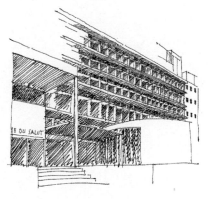

FIGURE 1–29A *The design of the windows in the Seinajoki Library in Finland responds to both the lighting and thermal conditions of the climate.*

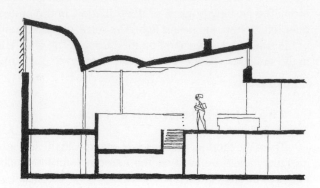

FIGURE 1–29B *Section.*

FIGURE 1–29C *Exterior view of south–facing louvers.*

baffles redirect sunlight when it comes from high in the sky in summer, so that the light that reaches the interior has been bounced from the outside of one slat to the inside of the one above, and thence through the glazing to the great curve of the ceiling and back to the bookstacks and exterior wall. In winter, sunlight from very low angles is admitted, in small pieces, into the building to play on the columns supporting the outer section of the ceiling and the reading counter. The entire curved perimeter section of the library works as one great daylighting fixture that controls the admission of light into the library without imposing too great a thermal load on the building either for winter heating or summer cooling. Light and heat are balanced, the seasons respected, and the light celebrated.

Parasol/parapluie

We can find a conceptual model for the combination of luminous and thermal comfort in *parasol* and *parapluie*—two French words meaning, respectively, a sunshade that protects one from the sun ("against the sun") and an umbrella that protects from the rain ("against the rain"). Images speak perhaps more eloquently than words. In John Singer Sargent's watercolor *Simplon Pass: Reading* (1911) a light-blue parasol casts luscious shadows on a white summer dress. The two women are protected from the sun by it. The features of the reclining woman are clearly visible in the light diffused by the parasol, while the face of the woman shaded by the bonnet as well is less clear. The parasol, adjustable at will to provide thermal and visual relief from the sunlight, has been used to create a micro-climate around these two women.

Parasols are usually lightly or brightly colored. Umbrellas, however, are usually black, at least in the West, although parapluies in China and Japan are made of oiled paper. The major purpose of the parapluie, to shed rain, is beautifully depict-

FIGURE 1–30 *John Singer Sargent, American, 1856-1925,* Simplon Pass: Reading, *1911, watercolor on paper, 20 x 14 in. Hayden Collection. Charles Henry Hayden Fund. Courtesy, Museum of Fine Arts, Boston.*

ed in Gustave Caillebotte's *Paris Street, Rainy Day* (1876–77), with the parapluies held in several typical positions by people who are strolling while those without parapluies move quickly, huddled against the rain. The light quality, the gray shadow cast by the black parapluie, is also portrayed.

The parasol/parapluie analogy emerges from a way of thinking that incorporates thermal and luminous comfort in the design of the building envelope. The history of the window continues, the struggle for admitting light without losing or admitting too much heat. And the struggle is not restricted to the physical form of the window. It is waged with the entire building form.

The parapluie represents the winter condition, providing protection from the elements—snow, rain, and stormy weather. Buildings and their occupants need even greater protection in winter. But at the same time they need to be exposed to

FIGURE 1–32 *A literal parasol has been erected at Seaside, Florida over the boardwalk to the beach (Jersey Devil, 1992). Photograph by Bill Sanders Photography, © 1994.*

light in order to carry out their activities, and for a sense of connection to the outside. The buildings need to shed water, but also to admit light. The parasol affords protection from the sun both thermally and luminously. It is an analogy for a building that needs light, but also needs protection against the heat that accompanies the light. Therefore the maxim is to provide shade while admitting light. That light can be admitted selectively, even playfully, as it is through colored parasols. The significant difference between lighting concepts that emulate parasols and those that emulate parapluies is whether the construction is primarily "against the rain" or "against the sun." That distinction depends upon climate and upon the major climatic conditions that cause the most severe environmental comfort problems inside buildings that need to be redressed.

Japan has a difficult climate in which to provide comfort in houses because of its cold snowy winters and hot humid summers and the resultant need for both heating and cooling. The development of lightweight shoji that open the house to cross ventilation has to do partly with insuring as much comfort as possible during the hot season when cooling is needed. Along with the deep verandahs around the house, they also determine the quality of the light inside. The deep verandahs play a significant role in shading the house:

> *In making for ourselves a place to live, we first spread a parasol to throw a shadow on the earth, and in the pale light of the shadow we put together a house. There are of course roofs on Western houses too, but they are less to keep off the sun than to keep off the wind and the dew; even from without it is apparent that they are built to create as few shadows as possible and to expose the interior to as much light as possible.*[17]

As Tanizaki points out, the Japanese attitude to light is quite different from the Western approach which invites light inside. He likens the function of the Western roof to a mere weather-protection, no more than a rain cap. The Japanese roof clearly furnishes protection from precipitation and wind as well. Functionally, the

FIGURE 1–33 *The verandah spreads over the traditional Japanese dwelling like a parasol and also acts as a parapluie, protecting the layers of sliding panels from the weather.*

FIGURE 1–34 *An example of the parasol is a fiberglass-skin building, such as the British Columbia pavilion (Zeidler and Roberts, 1983–86) at Expo '86 in Vancouver, a big parasol that has become a tent. The building is now the British Columbia Convention Center.*

roof is a parapluie; metaphorically, it is a parasol. The response to climate and the attitude to light are inextricably mingled in the traditional Japanese house.

The simplest built equivalent to the parasol is the tent. In Australia, it has been said that the tent is, in many respects, "the ideal prototype of such an endemic architecture in so far as it is light and strong and responds in a most direct fashion to the climatic pressures of strong sunlight and dryness."[18] In the buildings designed by Glenn Murcutt in Australia, the suggestion of a parasol is often there, as in the roof forms of the Kakadu Visitors Centre (completed 1994). The administrative office building sits lightly on the land, not interfering with it, sufficient unto itself. The essence of a parasol, light and variable protection against the sun, is presented in the durable medium of metal.

For buildings as for hats, open-work membranes work well in hot climates because their open spaces allow the heat to rise and escape so that the cooling effect of the shade is not counteracted by trapped heat. Such a parasol has been erected at the urban scale in Phoenix, Arizona, (Robert R. Frankeberger, 1980) to provide a shaded public space in the heart of downtown at the site of the city's first structures. The quality of light under this parasol is strikingly different from that of the surrounding urban area. The shaded and patterned surfaces afford visual as well as thermal relief from the brightness and heat of the adjacent city streets.

The parapluie affords protection against the rain. For buildings that mimic parapluie, the battle becomes one for light: how to admit light without compromising the sheltering role of the roof. Depending upon prevailing climatic conditions, either the parasol or the parapluie may be the conceptual model for introducing daylight into buildings in an appropriate way. In some locales, however, with hot summers and cold wet winters, both concepts are applicable and the "struggle" becomes one of accommodating both conditions.

A beautiful example of the resolution of this struggle is the Zimmermann House (William Turnbull, 1972–75) in Fairfax County, Virginia, outside of Washington, D.C., in a climate similar to that of Japan. The roof, made of translucent fiberglass placed on wood rafters,[19] resembles the Far Eastern oiled-paper umbrellas with numerous

FIGURE 1–35 *The roof of the administrative office at the Kakadu Visitors Centre in Australia resembles a parasol conceptually without mimicking its form. Photograph by J. Bradford Hubbell, © 1994.*

FIGURE 1–36 *The Lath House in Phoenix, Arizona, shades the outdoor area of the community activity center for large public gatherings as well as the lone stroller.*

FIGURE 1–37 *The roofs of Pacific Northwest Indian lodges, made of slabs from huge trees, are wood umbrellas that shed rain. During the winter, wooden planks are also extended over the spaces between the lodges, forming a continuous sheltered area for the community.*

FIGURE 1–38 *The steeply-sloped roofs of Timberline Lodge (Works Progress Administration, Gilbert Stanley Underwood, 1936–37) at Mt. Hood near Portland, Oregon, shed snow as well as rain for much of the year, the steep slope encouraging the snow to slide off it. Numerous dormers lift the roof to let in light.*

FIGURE 1–39 *The steel parasol of the Maison de l'Homme (Le Corbusier, 1963–67) in Zurich, Switzerland, also functions as a parapluie. Described as a brise–soleil, the raised roof was constructed first, allowing the construction of the lower portion to proceed undeterred by weather. The roof does not affect the quality of light that enters the house, however, but only affords protection to the roof deck.*

FIGURE 1–40 *The fiberglass roof of the Zimmermann House acts as both a parasol and also as a parapluie.*

small ribs that transmit a lovely, slightly warmed, diffuse light. The house unfolds under it, the walls of the house beneath weatherproof so that the roof can be likened to a parapluie carried by someone wearing foul-weather gear. The form of the house is the result of meeting two potentially conflicting design requirements: providing a large porch, and filling the house with light. The places between the house walls and the lattice of the outermost skin form a series of porches—living spaces perched between inside and outside. The house *is* a big porch. The roof protects the porches from the heat of summer and from the snow and rain of winter while introducing and celebrating light. Like the roof of the traditional Japanese house, the roof of the Zimmermann House plays a dual role as parasol and parapluie. Whereas the purpose of the traditional Japanese roof is to "throw a shadow on the earth," the purpose of the Zimmermann's fiberglass roof is to let light bathe the porches and the interior.

LIGHT AND TIME

Light marks our experience of time. Many cultures have constructed means of marking the time on this planet in relation to our galaxy, as at Jaipur in India, the pyramids in Egypt, and Stonehenge in England. Today we seem to be largely unaware of those larger units of time. We are still, however, biologically attuned to the change of light through the course of the seasons, wherever we may live. At the equator, day and night are equal every day. On the Arctic and Antarctic circles, the length of day varies from two hours at the winter solstice to 24 hours in midsummer.

Painters who are particularly responsive to light have recorded its subtle and not-so-subtle effects due to its daily and seasonal changes. A very well-known and sensitive example of this artistic research is Claude Monet's series of "grainstack" paintings. Although he painted series of other places and forms as well, such as the façade of Rouen Cathedral, rows of poplars in the countryside, and the water lilies in his gardens in Giverny, the haystacks are particularly compelling for the story they tell of the changing light of the seasons. The artist, who spoke little about his art, wrote in a letter about these paintings: ". . . the further I go, the more I understand that it is imperative to work a great deal to achieve what I seek: 'instantaneity,' above all . . . the same light present everywhere and more than ever easy things that come in a single stroke disgust me. In the end, I am excited by the need to render what I feel . . ."[20]

Monet portrayed the grainstacks as the colors and shadows and reflected

FIGURE 1–42A *View of the Gamble House from the entry drive. The front door is at the top of the steps.*

FIGURE 1–42B *Front door panels, designed by Charles Greene. Exterior view.*

FIGURE 1–42C *Interior view, afternoon. Photographs used with permission of The Gamble House.*

FIGURE 1–43 *In the south–facing studio in the Carpenter Center, summer sunlight penetration is restricted to the perimeter area of the brise-soleils.*

light shifted during the course of the days and the seasons. He portrayed light: the light of late summer that made the sky yellow and the shadows violet; the light of winter that turned the mountains a cool blue and revealed color in the snow; and the light of sunset that engulfed the haystack in every color in the rainbow.

Viewing these paintings together reveals to us the constant shifting of light and color that occurs. These changes are natural cues that we read in the landscape. They remind us that we have evolved in an environment of constant change, and that change is part of our experience of life. Change is revealed in the light of day. Louis Kahn stated: "I have no color applied on the walls in my home. I wouldn't want to disturb the wonder of natural light. The light really does make the room. The changing light according to the time of day and the seasons of the year gives color."[21]

The way light is let into a room can suggest a particular season forever. The light that filters through the large stained glass door at the Gamble House (Greene and Greene, 1907–09) in Pasadena, California, is reminiscent of a warm fall day with yellow leaves gleaming in the sunshine—the last warmth of Indian summer intensified by the bright color with the promise of colder days to come. Perhaps this artificial seasonal shift is necessary in southern California where the seasons blend into one another, where people go to escape the seasons. The glass panels represent the native Californian oak trees outside, thereby forging a connection between inside and outside. This connection is made with the quality of the light as well as the image of the tree.

A building can mark the course of the days and the seasons as does a sundial. In the Carpenter Center for the Visual Arts (Atelier Le Corbusier, 1961–64) at Harvard University in Cambridge, Massachusetts, the brise-soleil in the third-floor south-facing studio casts its moving shadows across the floor as the days and the seasons progress. In this building, as in his own studio, Le Corbusier did not follow the maxim that artists' studios should face north, an orientation to the part of the sky that maintains fairly constant color from day to day. Instead he viewed intense sunlight as a stimulant to work more precisely. He said of his studio:

> . . . the light, contradictory, coming from the east, from the west, not at all from the north as a result of the arrangement of the house, light unfavorable at each instant, at each hour of the day, all year long, permanent adversary (abominable from the classical point of view of a painting studio) but in fact a useful adversary, seeing that here again it plays a role, that of forcing one . . . to concentrate, to condense, to express.[22]

The active role that the light plays in the studio of the Carpenter Center marks time and keeps one continually aware of the natural conditions outside at the same time as making one more aware of one's work revealed in that changing light.

The biggest shift in light comes as day turns to night, and then reappears. We take this for granted—perhaps more so when we rely on electric light, thereby blurring the differences. Forms at night are rendered differently than in the broad brush stroke of daylight, for no amount of electric light can reproduce the qualities of daylight. Nor should they. Instead they can celebrate the difference. Night is celebrated in the Cannery (Joseph Esherick and Associates, Richard Peters, lighting consultant, 1968), a shopping complex recouped from a 1909 canning factory in San Francisco. Brick walls that reflect the

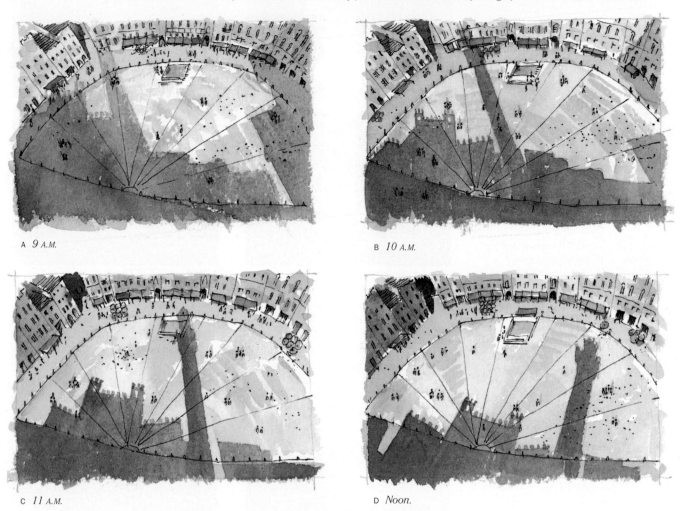

FIGURE 1–44 *The Torre del Mangia casts its shadow over the fourteenth–century Piazza del Campo in Siena, Italy. As the day progresses, the shadow moves like the hour hand of a clock, touching each of the façades in turn. Illustrations adapted from* Natural Light and the Italian Piazza, *Plate 3.5, published for Comune di Siena, 1992 and 1994, by Alsaba Grafiche, Siena; by permission of the author/photographer, Sandra Davis Lakeman.*

A *9 A.M.*

B *10 A.M.*

C *11 A.M.*

D *Noon.*

daylight are cut away to reveal warmly colored stucco walls illuminated at night. The clean exterior lines of the old warehouse buildings are the backdrop to the courtyard by day, but by night the shops and interior walkways are highlighted. The focus and the color change. At night the exterior walls are illuminated only at specific places, such as the incandescent lighting fixture backlighting the tree and providing illumination to the ground at the same time. But for the most part it is the inner surfaces that are emphasized. The emphasis has changed from the daytime bright spots of the sky, the sunlit exterior walls, and a patch of sunlight on the ground to a nighttime focus on the inside walls, the entry sign, the patterns of light on the wall, and the lighting standard at the foot of the stairs. At night, light is used to pick out specific parts of the composition and to guide one through the complex. The darkness demands a different design approach than does daylight.

In most industrialized countries of the world, we are used to mixing daylight and electric light, or even depending almost entirely on electric light. There might be windows for views, but we flip the switch when we need to "see." Where electricity is expensive, unreliable, and not so readily available, as in India, the norm for illumination is still daylight; electric lighting still has a special character of privi-

FIGURE 1–45A (RIGHT) *During the course of the day, the colors and patterns of light and shadow shift, so that a person familiar with this view knows the approximate time immediately. S. Andrea della Valle (Fra Fr. Grimaldi and Giacoma della Porta, 1591), Rome, in the morning light.*

FIGURE 1–45B (FAR RIGHT) *Afternoon light. Photographs by Catherine Jean Barrett.*

lege, of the ability to spread light in the darkness. At the opposite end of the spectrum is Las Vegas, where the illusion of the casinos is dependent upon total separation from the marking of time that daylight brings. In pushing back the frontiers of the night, we may lose the significance of the difference between night and day and their related rituals and symbolic meanings. Recognition of the daily and seasonal rhythms of light and dark is one of our primal connections to this world. It is rewarding to celebrate them.

FIGURE 1–46A *Entry courtyard in the Cannery during the daytime.*

FIGURE 1–46B *Night view.*

LIGHT AND THE TASK

Much of our experience of light comes from working in it. We are most acutely aware of light when there is either not enough of it, or too much, to be able to comfortably do what we want to do. Working conditions range from full daylight in open fields to the murky darkness of barns at night, from brightly lit factories with moving assembly lines to construction work on roads at night, and from uniformly illuminated office landscapes to candlelit restaurants. Some people have physical difficulties that affect their vision, and everyone has their own preferences as to the distribution and level of light. As we grow older, we all need more light and more time to perform visual tasks with the same accuracy and speed as we did when we were 20 years old.

Levels of illumination have most often been used as criteria for specifying lighting conditions for work environments, although in some countries considerations of the quality of the light have been used as well.[23] Although based on scientific evidence, recommended levels of illumination have historically risen with the technical and economic ability to provide them. For example, the Illuminating Engineering Society of North America has issued recommended levels of illumination for various tasks since 1913. During this time the illumination recommended for office work has moved from a range of 2 to 4 foot-candles[24] to a high of 100 foot-candles in 1960 and then, following the "energy crisis" of 1973, to its current level of a range of 50 to 100 foot-candles.[25] There are, however, additional ways of improving visibility other than adding light—presumably from an electric source—to the task. In the end, the responsibility falls on each of us as designers to draw from our clients the particularities of their personal conditions and visual tasks and try to accommodate them in the luminous environments that we design. We can also observe exemplary buildings as well as the luminous conditions that afford us comfort and bring these observations to bear in our designs.

We can find examples of innovative office lighting in the work of architects who went beyond traditional approaches in designing work environments, such as Frank Lloyd Wright. Two of his executed designs stand out in this regard: the Larkin Building (1903–06) in Buffalo, New York, and the Johnson Wax Administration Building (1936–39) in Racine, Wisconsin. The lighting concept for the Larkin Building was not innovative in and of itself—daylight entered from a large central skylight and perimeter windows—but it was an integral part of the design concept for the building, which placed workers at long desks perpendicular to the windows along the mezzanines and in the central court under the skylight. The desks on the mezzanines were illuminated by daylight from two sides: the windows in the exterior wall and the light from the central court. Globe lanterns were mounted four to a pole at the ends of the tables in the central court, bringing the electric lighting source into the vicinity of the working surfaces. Each person worked in diffuse light that would not cast shadows on their work: daylight diffused from above or from two sides, and light from electric lighting fixtures on two sides.

The lighting concept for the Johnson Wax Administration Building was, however, unique: "Work itself is correlated in one vast room . . . day-lit by the walls and

FIGURE 1–48 *Larkin Building central court.*

FIGURE 1–49 *The Great Workroom of the Johnson Wax Administration Building in Racine, Wisconsin. Photograph by Kenneth McKelvie, used with permission of The Johnson Wax Company.*

roof becoming crystal wherever light will be most useful."[26] The "crystal" effect was achieved by wiring Pyrex glass tubing to specially shaped aluminum racks to form two layers of glazing, one interior and one exterior. Incandescent lamps were mounted between the two layers so that light always entered the room from the same places. Wright wrote that "In the interior the boxlike structure vanished completely."[27] Added to the open workspace and unique organizational plan for the company was a new expression of structure and construction.[28] Employees held varying opinions concerning the lighting; some remembered good lighting conditions, but there were also some complaints of glare from direct sunlight coming through the glass tubing.[29] The lighting cannot be separated from the building— from its concept, its structure, its construction, or from the resultant work environment.

Reading is a preeminently visual task that has inspired special approaches to building with light. The Finnish architect Alvar Aalto is esteemed for the wonderful quality of light in buildings he designed, among them libraries. During the several years that he had to design the Viipuri Municipal Library (1927–35), he searched for an appropriate quality of light for reading. This search is documented in his preliminary study sketches for the library. On one page he investigated the distribution of daylight, on the other, electric light. On both pages his explorations range from sketches of one man with a book to sections across the main library room showing the reflection and distribution of light. He studied a man and a book from the front and from the side, showing that light reaching the book

FIGURE 1–50A *Aalto's 1927 sketch of proposed daylighting distribution in the Viipuri Municipal Library.*

FIGURE 1–50B *Sketch of expected distribution from electric lighting fixtures. Sketches courtesy of The Alvar Aalto Foundation.*

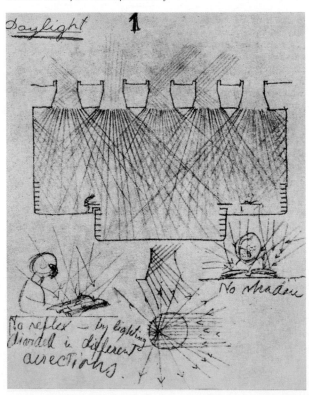

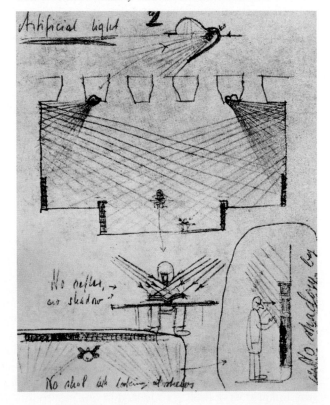

would arrive from all directions: a diffuse light free of shadows. The way in which round skylights provide this light coming from all directions is diagrammed here also, both in section and in plan in the lower center of the "daylight" page. In the section, the lines tracing the path of incoming skylight diverge from the splayed interior of the skylight well. In the circle below, showing a horizontal cut through the skylight well, the light entering from one direction is reflected in many directions from the curved sides. The skylight well acts as a daylighting fixture, redistributing the light from the sun and sky.

The electric lighting fixtures were designed to produce the same effect of diffuse light. On the page of sketches entitled "artificial light," a man looking at books on a bookshelf is shown, in a section sketch, with the direct light from above casting a shadow on the lower part of the bookshelf. In a plan view of the same situation, the reflected light coming from both sides is shown canceling out that shadow.

The result of this careful, formal, and qualitative study of light for reading was an understanding of light quality that became part of Aalto's formal vocabulary. The study was formal in that it investigated the relationship between light and form: how form shapes light and changes its directional qualities. The study was qualitative in that it used as criteria the distribution of light relative to the reading task rather than the quantity of light: "a shadow-free, diffuse light was obtained—ideal for the reader who could take his book to any point in the room without being bothered by shadows or stark sunlight."[30] Aalto manipulated his formal vocabulary in the several libraries that he designed in later years (see Chapter 3, "Spatial Light," for a discussion of some of them), but the basic characteristic of reflecting daylight and electric light from the surfaces of the building and the lighting fixtures to obtain "a shadow-free, diffuse light" remained intact.

FIGURE 1–51 *View of carrels in the Library at Phillips Exeter Academy in Exeter, New Hampshire. Photograph by Martin Schwartz.*

The light quality in the libraries designed by Louis I. Kahn is distinctly different but no less concerned with the conjunction of reader, book and light: "...the reader should be able to take the book and go to the light."[31] Just such a place is provided in the perimeter carrels of the Library of the Phillips Exeter Academy (1965–72) in Exeter, New Hampshire. The honey-colored wood of the carrels contrasts with the deep red brick and concrete floor, inviting one to sit and read by the window. Each carrel has its own window with sliding wooden shutter to control light, heat, and view. "Reading light" spills in through the tall windows above. This place for reading is located between the outer brick wall and the bookstacks in their concrete building, in an interstitial space that mediates between light outside and the dim light of the central hall. It is the space "between" that has been captured for reading, for taking a book to light. It is, in the beginning and the end, the relationship between a reader and a book in light that defines a library.

A museum is defined by the relationship between a viewer and a work of art in light. Kahn investigated this relationship in three museums: The Yale University Art Gallery (1951–53), the Kimbell Art Museum (1966–72; see Chapter 4, "Sacred Light"), and the Yale Center for British Art (1969–77, completed posthumously by Pelecchia and Meyers, Architects; Richard Kelly, lighting consultant). The relatively low levels of illumination in the Yale Center for British Art were carefully considered: "I allowed the amount of window that each space needed on the periphery to be dictated by the interior space."[32] The visitor is thus invited to view each painting from close up, encouraging an individual and intimate experience.

FIGURE 1–52 *A young reader turns her book to the light in the children's reading area at the Frances Howard Goldwyn Regional Branch Library (Frank Gehry, 1983–85) in North Hollywood, California.*

FIGURE 1–53 *A viewer with a painting in daylight in the Yale Center for British Art.*

FIGURE 1–54 *Modern painting display with traditional side–lighting in the Louisiana Museum (Jorgen R. Bo and Vilhelm Wohlert, 1959–82) in Humlebaek, Denmark, provides good conditions for viewing paintings. Incandescent lighting fixtures furnish additional light to the painting surfaces. The sculpture is silhouetted against the window.*

FIGURE 1–55A *The Viking Museum: Viking ships are clearly visible displayed against the backdrop of the sea due to daylight entering through skylights.*

FIGURE 1–55B *The wall display is shaped to deliver task lighting to each individual panel.*

FIGURE 1–56 *Frank Lloyd Wright's reading and writing table in his room at Taliesin East. Used with permission of The Frank Lloyd Wright Foundation.*

Objects other than paintings are displayed in many museums, and call for equally careful integration of the building concept and structure, the lighting design, and the display strategies. A stunning collection of Viking ships is displayed with the sea as their backdrop in the Viking Ship Museum (Erik Christian Sørensen, 1963–69) in Rothskilde, Denmark. The extreme contrast between the brightness of the sea and sky and the dark, almost black surface of the ships would prevent a clear view of the ships (they would appear only as black silhouetted shapes) if it were not for skylights that cast a wash of daylight over the front of the ships.[33] The dramatic setting of the sea could be presented and the major museum activity—viewing objects—be accommodated by balancing the light beyond the window with light on the inside.

Many comfortable luminous environments for visual work or play are the result of sensitive observation and common sense. Toward the end of his long life of designing and observing buildings, Frank Lloyd Wright once again renovated Taliesin East, adding a reading and writing area to his bedroom. It suited his needs. He would sit in the chair at the table under the ceiling raised over clerestories that provided light and a sense of this space as a room within a room. Daylight flooded in from the two sides and behind him while in front of him stretched the long hallway leading to the front door. Overseeing the entrance, in a space released from the low ceiling, he defined his working place with light.

ENDNOTES

1. Harries, Karsten. 1984,"On Truth and Lie in Architecture," *Via 7, The Building of Architecture*. (Cambridge, Mass.: The M.I.T. Press), p. 51.

2. Cialdella, Philip, and Clara D. Powell. 1993."The Great Illuminator," *LD+A*, 23 (5): pp. 59–60. Reprinted with permission of the publisher.

3. All three quotations from: Erickson, Arthur. 1975. *The Architecture of Arthur Erickson*. (Montreal, Quebec: Tundra Books), p. 33.

4. Tanizaki, Junichiro. 1977. *In Praise of Shadows*. (New Haven, Conn.: Leete's Island Books), p. 18. Reprinted with permission of the publisher.

5. Stinchecum, Amanda M. 1981. "Enduring Cold the Japanese Way," *Natural History*. 90(10): pp. 50–55.

6. Hertzberger, Herman. 1991. *Lessons for Students in Architecture*. (Rotterdam, The Netherlands: Uitgeverij 010 Publishers), p. 216.

7. Ibid.

8. Norberg–Schulz, Christian. 1980. *Genius Loci: Towards a Phenomenology of Architecture*. (New York: Rizzoli), p. 179.

9. Hoffmann, Donald. 1984. *Frank Lloyd Wright's Robie House*. (New York: Dover Publications, Inc.), p. 67.

10. See Heschong, Lisa. 1979. *Thermal Delight in Architecture*. (Cambridge, Mass.: The M.I.T. Press), pp. 50–72.

11. Boesiger, Willy, Editor. 1946. *Le Corbusier: Oeuvre Complète, 1938–1946*. (Zurich: Les Editions d'Architecture), p. 103. Author's translation.

12. Additional environmental issues include the pollutants introduced by fire and gas as well as combustion dangers.

13. Glazing products are available that change the thermal properties of glazing so that heat can be rejected to the exterior or retained in the interior. The most honest and responsive experiences of the naturally combined forces of light and heat, however, are still provided by a well-designed building envelope.

14. See Sobin, Harris J. 1980. "Le Corbusier in North Africa: The Birth of the 'Brise-soleil'" in *Desert Housing*. Clarke and Paylore, Editors. (Tempe, Ariz.: University of Arizona), pp. 168–69; and Taylor, Brian Bruce. 1987. *Le Corbusier: The City of Refuge, Paris, 1929/33*. (Chicago, Ill.: The University of Chicago Press), pp. 107–25.

15. Boesiger, Willy, Editor. 1935. *Le Corbusier et Pierre Jeanneret: Oeuvre Complète, 1929–1934*. (Zurich: Les Editions d'Architecture), p. 101.

16. Boesiger. op. cit., 1946. pp. 103–15.

17. Tanizaki. op. cit., p. 17.

18. Drew, Philip. 1985. *Leaves of Iron: Glenn Murcutt, Pioneer of an Australian Architectural Form*. (Auckland, New Zealand: Harper Collins Publishers Ltd.), p. 134.

19. William Turnbull has noted that, as originally designed, there were more rafters in the roof. They were intended to provide a baffling effect to the sunlight. The number of rafters was reduced for reasons of cost. Personal communication with the author.

20. Written in a letter to Monet's future biographer, Gustave Geffroy, on October 7, 1890. Quoted in Tucker, Paul Hayes. 1989. *Monet in the '90's*. (Boston, Mass.: Museum of Fine Arts), p. 3.

21. Wurman, Richard Saul, Editor. 1986. *What Will Be Has Always Been: The Words of Louis I. Kahn*. (New York: Rizzoli), p. 175. From a 1972 issue of House & Garden.

22. Boesiger, Willy, Editor. 1953. *Le Corbusier: Oeuvre Complète, 1946–1952*.

(Zurich: Les Editions d'Architecture), p. 57. Author's translation.

23. For example, the British building code has included standards for lighting based on a glare index.

24. The foot-candle is the unit of illumination on a surface in English units; in international units, illumination is measured in lux. If you hold a lit candle one foot from a book in a dark room, the amount of light falling on the book will be approximately one foot-candle or 10 lux.

25. Osterhaus, Werner K.E. 1993. *Office Lighting: A Review of 80 Years of Standards and Recommendations.* (Berkeley, Calif.: Lawrence Berkeley Laboratory), pp. 2–8.

26. Lipman, Jonathan. 1986. *Frank Lloyd Wright and the Johnson Wax Buildings.* (New York: Rizzoli), p. 183. Statement by Frank Lloyd Wright from 1936 document prepared for the Johnson Company.

27. Wright, Frank Lloyd. 1957. *A Testament.* (New York: Bramhall House), p. 171.

28. Wright developed the actual construction method for the glass tubing in consultation with Corning Glass after more than a year of experimentation, having originally envisioned using custom-shaped glass blocks. See Lipman, op. cit., pp. 62–83.

29. Lipman, op.cit., p. 93.

30. Fleig, Karl, Editor. 1963. *Alvar Aalto, Volume 1: 1922–1962.* (Zurich, Switzerland: Les Editions d'Architecture Artemis), p. 49.

31. Lobell, John. 1979. *Between Silence and Light.* (Boulder, Colo.: Shambhala Publications), p. 100. From an unpublished transcript of a talk by Kahn.

32. Wurman. op. cit., p. 240. From a conversation with William Jordy.

33. The contrast in the photograph is greater than that experienced by the human visual system since photographic film does not have the ability to accommodate differences in brightness as well as do the human eye and brain.

Experiential Light: Museum of Anthropology, University of British Columbia

Vancouver, British Columbia, Canada
1972–76

Arthur Erickson Architects
Project Architects:
Ron Bain, Rodger Morris, and Alex Kee

Qualities of light have profound responses within us; they are the wellsprings of feeling … With light as the palette, architecture can be supreme in the arts. It is a source of expression that we tend to ignore and the one aspect of architecture that we cannot divorce from meaning in our determined nihilism as long as night and day and sun and moon work their pattern upon us. It is with light that we can bring soul and spirit back into architecture and perhaps find our own souls in the process.[1]

—ARTHUR ERICKSON

"With light as the palette," Arthur Erickson has created a setting for the artifacts of the Northwest Coast Indians that expresses to the visitor the essence of their original natural setting. From the entry through the sequence of galleries and outside to the replicas of native villages, the modulation of the light suggests the forest passage to the village where forest and beach meet and the vista opens to the water. The architects have expressed the light of the place in a way that can deepen the visitor's appreciation of the meaning of natural forces and forms in the life and rituals of the Northwest Coast Indians.

The climate of the Northwest coast of the North American continent is temperate and mild, with relatively warm, rainy winters and cool rainy summers interspersed with warm spells. Until massive logging occurred in the early twentieth century, the area was heavily forested with huge evergreen trees, mostly fir, hemlock, and cedar. The sky,

often overcast, offers a gray light that dwindles as it passes through the deep forest canopy. When the sky is clear, spots of sunlight create bright pools of green in the forest. In this setting, traditional coastal villages were usually located at the juncture between forest edge and shale beach on an inlet.

The design concept for the Museum of Anthropology was to create conditions similar to the settings of the native Indian villages which were the origin of the museum's collection.[2] The architects visited the native village sites and photographed artifacts in their natural settings. The transition from dark towering woods to bright exposed sea provided a dramatic setting that Erickson tried to recreate on the museum site. The design concept relies on the power of the physical setting. Located on the Point Gray Cliffs overlooking the Georgia Strait, the museum has been surrounded by trees but has yet to be graced with a mock coastal inlet due to predictions that water would seep from it and erode the cliff on which it rests.

The experience of the building begins with the site. The visitor descends from the parking lot and approaches the entrance through free-standing post-and-beam frames. As one proceeds from the brightness of the parking clearing into the museum, the openness to the sky is gradually cut off, first by trees that form a channel to the entrance, then by the post-and-beam frames, then by the ceiling of the lobby. The materials are concrete, roughly poured so that textures are presented that suggest the bark of trees. The floor is covered with a neutral carpet, providing a quiet background visually and acoustically. The building finishes are neutral; the artifacts and the light are on display.

There are views opening out into the woods from the lobby through floor-to-ceiling glass—the experience of the site is not terminated as one enters the building, just interrupted. Skylight slots also bring daylight down to wash over totems, revealing them as they would be revealed in the forest by the filtered light from above. The experience of the light in the lobby is similar to that in the deep woods where you can see through clearings and light filters through the tree canopy overhead. The visitor has been prepared to enter the deep forest.

Beyond the entry door, one enters the exhibits through the Ramped Gallery. It is suggestive of a route through the dark woods, with totems and other carvings lining the skewed path (you can't go straight in the woods). The gallery ramps down, as does the shore as one approaches the beach. There are large structural posts that act as metaphorical tree trunks and, at the same time, divide the gallery into bays for the display of carvings. Daylight enters from above, from the top of these side bays, with the result that there is never daylight directly above you, only filtering down from the sides. The illumination levels are low. Ahead the light and the view through the glass wall of the Massive Carvings Gallery draws you on down toward the "inlet," which as planned would have presented an even brighter scene with water reflecting the sky or the sparkle of sunshine. The passageway suggests the typical approach to a village site one would experience passing through the columnar forest of tall trees that opens onto the beach. Light is seen beyond, but before reaching it, one arrives at a crossing with a long, wide corridor that exposes the surrounding woods in the distance through glass walls at both ends. It is as if one has reached a clearing in the forest where some limited views are presented and light is more abundant. Ahead opens the Massive Carvings Gallery, with totems sitting before the tall glass wall as if in front of the Haida Indian longhouse itself, which can be glimpsed through the glazing. The glazing is supported with glass mullions so as not to interfere with the connection between inside and outside.

The Massive Carvings Gallery appears to open out into the landscape. Central to that impression are three glazed walls and a series of long skylights overhead. The columns at the ends of the spaces are heavy, in the proportions of tall tree trunks, offering the impression that the woods are thinning out around this enclosure of carvings.[3] The skylights above are carried by deep inverted-U-shaped channels that rise progressively higher as they proceed toward the glass wall, thereby blocking the view of the skylights. These skylights balance the light coming through the glazed walls so that all surfaces of the carvings are illuminated. The skylights are glazed with two layers of quarter-circular sections of bronze plastic. The bronze plastic colors the daylight as it enters and absorbs some of it, lessening the amount of illumination coming from above so that the glazed north wall is the focus of attention. The skillful balancing of the daylight from three sides and the top affords comfortable viewing conditions in this gallery without sacrificing the drama of the connection to outside through the north wall.

A certain tension between the inside and outside is established by the sequence of light-to-dark-to-light. It continues at the far right end of the Massive Carvings Gallery as a curved concrete wall[4] gently gathers the visitor into the low, dimly lit Koerner Masterpiece Gallery, as if beckoning one back into the forest. The relative darkness and compressed spatial experience of the Koerner Masterpiece Gallery causes one to pause to adjust to the cooler, quieter room. Beyond the glazing stands a row of evergreen trees lending their shade and their color to the room. The exhibits of small precious objects seen against this backdrop take one back once more to the forest primeval. The objects take on a sense of sacredness in the hushed setting. In contrast to the noisy exuberant openness of the large gallery, sounds are muted as one stops to gaze at each small object. Large spaces for large carvings, grand gestures, and movement toward light determine the mood of the large gallery; compressed space for small objects, quietness, and subdued light define the Koerner Gallery. The relative darkness con-tributes to the stillness, as does the simple geometry of the room.

Several different kinds of display cases have been installed in this gallery through the years, the most successful being those that showed a glimmer of incandescent reflector-lamps through bronze acrylic shields at the top while casting a flood of warm light through glass shelves onto the objects below. The display cases have also been moved around the room over time. The best viewing conditions are presented when the cases are set against the glass wall and the objects are seen as though nestled in the branches of the trees outside. When the cases are in the center of the room, reflected glare is easily picked up when the glass of the display case reflects the pattern of light seen through the exterior glazing.

Exiting the dark gallery space, one turns to the right around a curved concrete wall that holds the auditorium into the long, wide corridor that leads to the woods on the opposite side of the building. A bright focal spot before you is *The Birth of Man* wood sculpture by Bill Holm, flooded with light from a domed skylight above and silhouetted against a dark concave wall (the inside curve of one of the bunkers). The skylight has been covered with sailcloth to temper and soften the light, and to block heat that could crack the wood that was carved *in situ*. In such a dark setting, the burst of full daylight, especially sunlight, was too intense. Dark curtains cover a glazed wall that leads to an unused outdoor courtyard. The ovals of incandescent light thrown onto the walls by perimeter lighting fixtures are weak, almost unnoticeable, in comparison to the daylight, subdued as it is.

Farther down the hallway a few steps lead invitingly down to the "storage gallery," a large room with the remainder of the collection that would normally be housed "in storage" but here is on display. The idea behind the display extends to the architectural concept for the room itself: everything is exposed—structure, electric lighting, and mechanical ducts. Lighting fixtures are track-mounted so that they can be moved and focused on displays. Filters and baffles are attached as necessary to prevent exposure of the artifacts to certain wavelengths of radiation or to prevent glare in viewers' field of vision. Many displays are in drawers so that they are exposed to light only when being viewed. The room is located in the center of the building, an obvious planning strategy since the environment in this room is maintained totally by mechanical means and therefore requires no direct connection to the exterior.

The electric lighting fixtures are integrated into the structure of the building in such a way that they are hardly noticeable. In the Massive Carvings Gallery, ambient light is provided by fluorescent strips mounted on top of the channels just inside where the curved plastic skylight sections rest on them. Incandescent exhibit lighting fixtures are tucked up into the channels.

The experience of visiting the Museum of Anthropology can be likened to a metaphor for the journey through life in addition to the journey to a Northwest coastal village. Having approached the village through the contracted sequence of the entry lobby and the Ramped Gallery, one experiences a release to the light filled Massive Carvings Gallery that suggests a village site. One leaves the life and light of the village and enters the contracting space of the Koerner Gallery, the setting for symbolic and sacred objects used in spiritual ceremonies. On the journey back to the beginning, one is attracted to the focus of the sculpture *The Birth of Man,* which is central to the native world view. Surrounded by darkness, the sculpture representing birth also suggests death and the endless continuation of the cycle.

The practical and the experiential go hand in hand. The major exhibition spaces recall the original native settings of the artifacts through an interplay of light and form. They tell their story through the sequential experiences of the rooms as well as through the objects with their labels. The museum experience suggests the setting of the actual coast villages. This is largely due to the lighting and its relationship to form. The rhythm of the lighting and the rhythm of the forms are one. There is an overall rhythm of light and dark at the building scale, and a particular rhythm of light and dark for each room. There is light from above (Entry Lobby, Ramped Gallery, Massive Carvings Gallery) and light from the side (Entry Lobby, Great Carvings Gallery, Koerner Masterpiece Gallery). There is light delineating structure (Massive Carvings Gallery) and light dematerializing structure (dappled light in the Koerner Masterpiece Gallery). There is light washing surfaces and light silhouetting forms (Ramped Gallery). There are many different ways of admitting light, many different patterns of light, many different levels of illumination—all employed with the intention of suggesting the experience of a typical Northwest Indian village while at the same time allowing for the display of artifacts. On a conscious or even a subconscious level, the innate human reactions to changing patterns of light and darkness enrich one's experience of the exhibits and establish a connection to these special objects in a way that is deeper than seeing them totally removed from any semblance of their origins. It is a unique collection in a unique setting and the two are woven together with light.

I have been anxious to find, wherever I build, the right response to light.[5]
—ARTHUR ERICKSON

ENDNOTES

1. Erickson, Arthur. 1964. "The Weight of Heaven," *The Canadian Architect* 9(3):50. Reprinted with permission of the publisher.

2. Millet, Marietta. 1980. "University of British Columbia Museum of Anthropology" in *Daylighting Window Design Re-source Package: Vol. 3, Case Studies.* (Berkeley, Calif.: Lawrence Berkeley Laboratory, University of California), pp. 5-6.

3. The columns were the subject of careful study. A model was prepared to observe the effects of having the split columns run parallel or perpendicular to the end walls, so that they would appear solid (parallel) or open (perpendicular). A parallel orientation was chosen as the more solid side had the appearance of large tree trunks.

4. The curving wall surrounds one of three World War II bunkers, part of the site that could not be removed and has been skillfully incorporated into the building.

5. Erickson, Arthur. 1975. *The Architecture of Arthur Erickson.* (Montreal, Quebec: Tundra Books), p. 33.

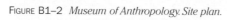

FIGURE B1–1A AND B *Northwest coast forest in sunshine and in fog.*

FIGURE B1–2 *Museum of Anthropology. Site plan.*

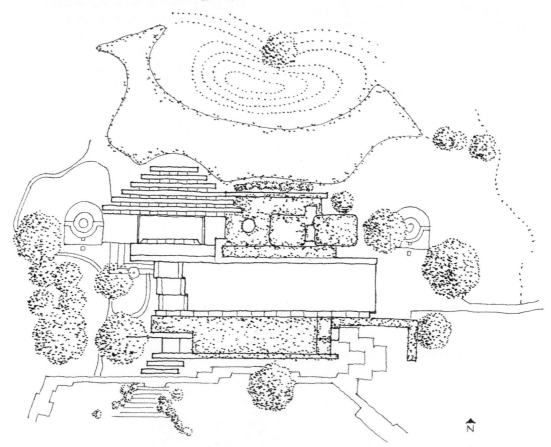

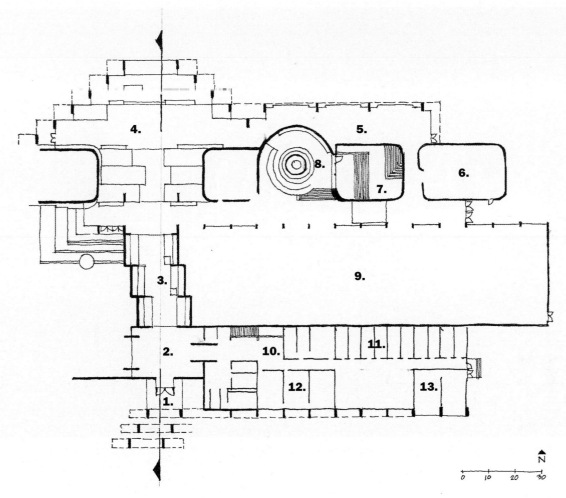

FIGURE B1–3 *Building plan.*

1. Entry
2. Lobby
3. Ramped Gallery
4. Massive Carving Gallery
5. Koerner Masterpiece Gallery
6. Theater
7. Outdoor Court
8. Lounge with Birth of Man
sculpture
9. Systematic display gallery
10. Reception
11. Offices
12. Seminar rooms
13. Mechanical

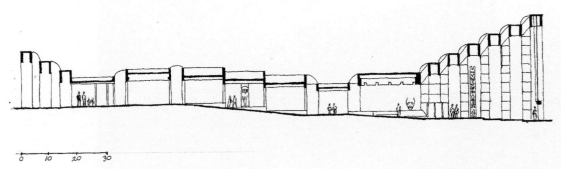

FIGURE B1–4 *Building section.*

FIGURE B1–5 *Model of the museum with the pond that was proposed to suggest an inlet in front of the Massive Carvings and Koerner Masterpiece galleries. Photograph courtesy of Arthur Erickson.*

FIGURE B1–6 *Entry from parking lot.*

FIGURE B1–7 *Lobby; view to the left upon entering.*

FIGURE B1–8 *The Ramped Gallery.*

FIGURE B1–9 *Emerging from the Ramped Gallery into the Massive Carvings Gallery.*

FIGURE B1–10 *The Massive Carvings Gallery, looking toward the entry to the Koerner Masterpiece Gallery.*

FIGURE B1–11 *The Massive Carvings Gallery at night.*

FIGURE B1–12 *Exterior view of the Massive Carvings Gallery.*

FIGURE B1–13 *The Koerner Masterpiece Gallery.*

FIGURE B1–14 *View of the exterior wall of the Koerner Masterpiece Gallery.*

FIGURE B1–15 *View along the corridor with the lounge to the right, the systematic display gallery to the left.*

FIGURE B1–16 *Entry to the systematic display gallery.*

FIGURE B1–17 *The Birth of Man, sculpture by Bill Holm in the lounge.*

LIGHT REVEALING FORM

Our eyes are constructed to enable us to see forms in light.[1]

—LE CORBUSIER

Light is not perceptible without form—even the diaphanous form of swirling smoke—to reflect it. Conversely, form is not perceptible without light to reveal it, at least not to our vision, on which we rely to provide the majority of our information about our surroundings. Light *is* an architectural material, but an intangible one. Like sound and heat, it is dispersed by means of materials and their forms. Many architectural forms that are much admired have been shaped *for* light, such as Le Corbusier's *brise-soleils* at the Carpenter Center (1960–63) and Kahn's cutouts in the National Assembly Building (1962–83; successor architects: D. Wisdom and Associates) in Dhaka, the capital of Bangladesh.

The light that renders form visible is always changing. The nature of daylight *is* change, both qualitative and quantitative change. The nature of electric light is constant, but electric lighting sources are turned on and off with regularity, and can be dimmed. Form remains constant; light changes. We perceive the form as stable, however, due to our perceptual processes.[2] The presentation of a wall to our eyes can change drastically as the light moves over it, and yet we perceive the form as stable.

LIGHT AND FORM

All building forms express an attitude to light. Christian Norberg-Schulz has noted that: "The additive spatial structures of the Renaissance demand a uniform illumination, while Baroque structures based upon dominance and contrast admit a more 'dramatic' illumination."[3] The forms to which he alludes respond to the light, and the light, in turn, is shaped by the form. The forms that we see in a building, and

FIGURE 2–1 *Brise-soleils on the west façade of the Carpenter Center, Cambridge, Massachusetts.*

FIGURE 2–2 *Screen walls of the National Assembly Building, Dhaka.*

the way that we see them, are due to the way in which light is admitted by the form as well as the way in which the form then models the light that has been admitted.

The clerestory windows of S. Lorenzo (Filippo Brunelleschi, 1421–60) in Florence, Italy, admit an even illumination to the nave by means of their even spacing and their high placement. The pattern of light and dark that we see results from the spatial modeling and from the different materials employed in the composition. The side aisles are naturally dimmer than the central area of the nave, since they are set back behind the arcade with a lower ceiling, receiving light reflected from the high walls above the arcade. Small circular windows set in deep niches above the side chapels balance the light received from the nave. The surfaces of the side chapels receive only reflected light, so that they are darker and recede in the overall composition. The columns and capitals use the light to provide depth and modeling. The transition from column to capital and to the arches and upper walls is particularly rich. Deep shadows cast by the Acanthus leaves of the Corinthian capital and the square plate from which the arch springs darken these stone parts which are already naturally darker than the plaster wall surfaces. Within the arch banding, shallow modeling creates gentle gradations of gray on gray. The use of light in these gradations from nave to side aisle to chapel, and from column to capital to arch to wall, reinforce the spatial organization and the role of each part in the overall composition.

The material, the form, and the light are all introduced as discontinuous elements that are related in a strict hierarchy. The light has its own separate and discernible forms—the rectangular windows in the clerestory wall and the round windows under the semicircular vault in each side chapel. Each structural and ornamental part is clearly articulated in form and light. Each element is then related to the whole by means of a hierarchy which provides a transition between parts. The form's hierarchy, from the overall spatial organization to the details, is reinforced by the light. S. Lorenzo is clearly made up of separate but related parts which are rendered through material, form, and light.

A more "dramatic" illumination that affords a different sense of organization is evident in the Baroque church of S. Carlo alle Quattro Fontane (Francesco Borromini, 1638–41) in Rome. Obviously the individual parts are still evident, but

FIGURE 2–3 *Articulation of form shifts with changes in light: Weisman Museum of Art (Frank O. Gehry and Associates, PHA Lighting Design, 1990–93) on the campus of the University of Minnesota in Minneapolis.*

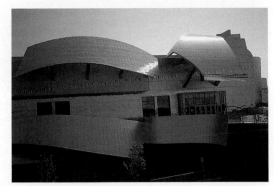

FIGURE 2–3A *The specular turned-up edge of the entrance canopy catches reflected sunlight on a clear day and seems to advance. The darker doorway recedes relative to the canopy.*

FIGURE 2–3B *Under overcast skies this reflective band "sees" the dark ground and, in reflecting it, becomes darker itself and seems to recede. The doorway advances relative to the canopy.*

FIGURE 2–3C *Inside in the corridor leading to the galleries, diffuse light from the overcast sky emphasizes the floor surface, leaving the ceiling in relative darkness.*

FIGURE 2–3D *The bright patch of sunlight on the floor bounces light to the ceiling but makes most other surfaces appear dark in comparison to it.*

FIGURE 2–3E *Plan of the Weisman Art Museum.*

1. Entry
2. Lobby
3. Museum store
4. Gallery
5. Seminar rooms
6. Auditorium
7. West lobby/exhibit

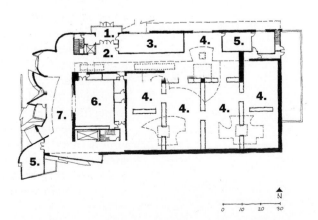

FIGURE 2–4A *Drawing of the nave of S. Lorenzo in Florence, Italy.*

FIGURE 2–4B *Drawing of a side chapel as seen from the nave.*

in this case the central space and the gesture of its dome in light are dominant. The plan shows that the four chapels, which before this time had been located in apses, are now incorporated into the central volume of the church. The side chapels and the central space of the church are illuminated equally by the central dome. The entablature follows the line of the exterior walls quite closely. Above the entablature, pendentives carry the oval dome. Apsidal half-domes beyond the pendentive arches are in shadow, contrasting with the light in the dome. The same pale stone is used for all these forms, so that the transition from wall to entablature to pendentive to dome is made up of gradations caused by light alone. The forms of the entablature, the pendentive arches, the dome ring, and the surface of the dome itself are all modeled. Each one presents its own distinctive pattern of tones of light and at the same time creates a continuous play of light over all the forms. The material, the form, and the light are all introduced as connected elements that provide a sense of a single unified volume.

Light and shadow animate the surfaces. Glazing fills four of the lowest coffers in the dome, allowing shafts of sunlight to move over the stone forms. The ridges of the coffers capture the grazing light from the windows and seem to detach themselves from the recessed portions that remain in shadow. Tree-like cut-outs spring from the dome ring, providing a physical screen over which light plays to heighten the drama of the layering of light and shadow. Sometimes a "tree" is seen in front of a dome window, seemingly dissolved in a ray of sunlight. Sometimes sunlight plays over a "tree," brightening it in front of the shaded coffers of the dome and seemingly increasing the distance between the two.

The lantern admits daylight from glazing on all eight of its sides, a continuous

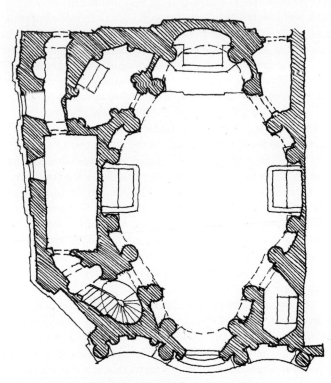

FIGURE 2–5A *Plan of S. Carlo alle Quattro Fontane, Rome.*

FIGURE 2–5B *View of dome. Photograph by Dennis Tate.*

light that bathes all parts of the dome equally. The gold ceiling of the lantern with the dove of the Holy Spirit appears to be in a burst of light—the light of the Holy Spirit—its representational rays merging with the light of day. Paolo Portoghesi has characterized Borromini's light as "above all a 'guided' light, an instrument that can bring out the characteristics of a structure by augmenting their perceptibility, a factor of *claritas* that, more than anything else, is logically coherent and has the capacity to identify the synthetic connections."[4] In S. Carlo, the dominance of the central unity is revealed through the subtle yet dramatic interplay between continuous light and continuous form.

Light emphasizing form

It seems an obvious statement that light emphasizes form. The truth is that sometimes it does and sometimes it does not. A form in light may be there in our visual field, but that does not necessarily mean that we see it clearly, or in the way intended, if there *is* an architectural intention attached. For example, forms that stand out clearly in sunlight may fade in the light filtered through clouds of the overcast sky. Many forms disappear in the darkness of night.

Relief letters on a building fragment at Pompeii (destroyed by an eruption of Mt. Vesuvius in A.D. 79) are clearly visible because of the shadows that they cast. We see the raised sections as slightly lighter than the background, but the cast shadows are more noticeable since they provide a greater contrast with it. Raised letters and their opposites, incised letters, work well in sunny climates, but lose their

FIGURE 2–6 *Relief letters on a building fragment at Pompeii. Photograph by Catherine Jean Barrett.*

FIGURE 2–7 *The gold letters of an entrance sign at Tivoli in Copenhagen, Denmark, glow in the dusk.*

FIGURE 2–8 *Column at the Baths of Caracalla in Rome modeled in sunlight. Photograph by Catherine Jean Barrett.*

impact in mostly cloudy climates where the diffuse daylight illuminates all the surfaces more evenly. Therefore the shapes of carved or incised letters are often indistinct and vague in locales with predominantly overcast skies, where value contrast or reflecting materials or luminescence (as in neon) are better used to make letters distinguishable. One of the entrance signs for Tivoli, an amusement park in Copenhagen, Denmark, demonstrates the effectiveness of gold surfaces to reflect even small amounts of available light. Light from street lamps reflects from the gold surfaces of the letters, which are especially noticeable in contrast to the background darkness. Direct and diffuse light articulate form in different ways.

Subtleties in the modeling of a column at the Baths of Caracalla (A.D. 212–16) in Rome suggest that part of the reason for its shape is the way it receives light. It is a fluted column, with flutes alternating between projected half-cylinders. The protruding ridges cast shadows onto the surfaces of the flutes, the shadows varying in length with the angle of the sun. The narrow half-cylinders that top these ridges also cast shadows of varying lengths onto the ridges, so that sometimes there is a thin line of light between the narrow shadow from the half-cylinder and the wide shadow cast into the groove by the ridge. As sunlight moves around the column, the pattern of light and shadow varies as a result of both the overall form of the column and also its articulation. Sunlight reveals the subtleties of the form while appearing to dance upon it.

Distinguishing form through patterns of light also tells us how to use parts of a building, such as a stairway, where the surfaces of the treads are usually distinguished from the risers by the way they are modeled in light. In some cases, stairways become sculpture revealed in light, as at the estate Vizcaya (F. Burrall Hoffman, Jr. and Paul Chalfin, 1914–16) in Miami, Florida. At any given moment the sun is at a constant angle in relationship to all the steps, so the pattern of light and shade on each one is the same. The relationship of these patterns shifts only with the eye of the beholder. The curve at the top of the polished masonry nosing reflects the sunlight in a horizontal line along its length. As the surface curves down to the riser, it falls into shadow. The horizontal strip just below the nosing also casts a shadow onto the riser. Together these pieces of light and shadow form a rich pattern of *chiaroscuro* against the mellow stone, which is enhanced by the cast shadows of two lighting fixtures as well as the deep shade at the top of the staircase. The form of the steps responds to the light, and in turn the patterns of light are shaped by the form.

In building interiors, the relationship between the light source and the form is shaped by geometry and the building envelope. Some situations call for a reciprocal relationship between the light source and the form, as when a special object or feature of a building is highlighted.

The cross above the altar is the focal point in Christ Church Lutheran (Eliel Saarinen, 1949) in Minneapolis, Minnesota. Its bold form is shaped to be highlighted by the light washing it and the brick wall behind it from the side. This sidelight emanates from floor-to-ceiling glazing and incandescent reflector lamps mounted in front of it along its height. The glazing is translucent, as it is elsewhere in the church, admitting light inside but no views out. The square bars of the cross are set on the diagonal so that they will reflect light to the congregation. The half of the vertical bar of the cross that is set at 45° to both the window and the congregation is the brightest surface as seen from the congregation. The cross stands out in contrast to the darker brick behind it that receives grazing light. The form inflects to the light in order to make the cross the focal point in the church.

Form is also emphasized by light when it is silhouetted, as is *The Shattered Cane* sculpture in the Kaleva Church (Reima and Raili Pietilä, 1959–66) in Tampere, Finland. The church is composed of tall curved concrete forms interspersed with glass, arranged so that parishioners sitting in the congregation do not look directly out of any of the glass segments except for the one directly ahead

FIGURE 2–9A *Stairway at Vizcaya in Miami, Florida.*

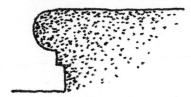

FIGURE 2–9B *Section of stair showing the form of the nosing.*

FIGURE 2–10A *View of the cross in Christ Church Lutheran in Minneapolis, Minnesota.*

behind the altar. In front of this tall glazed opening is the wood sculpture, its outline distinctly clear against the sky seen through the glass. The subtleties of the form of the sculpture, its bulges and wood textures, are also clear because of the daylight that falls on it from the other glazed openings which furnish complementary light. If there were no other sources of light illuminating the planes of the sculpture, then only its silhouette, its outline, would be clear, while the details would be lost in the perceptual darkness of the front of the sculpture due to the high contrast between it and the view of the bright sky beyond.

In all these cases the daylight openings and the objects they illuminate—the cross, the stairway, the sculpture—complement each other. In each case, the daylight opening was located to reveal the object within. The objects, in turn, have been located and shaped in response to the direction of the light.

A similar relationship exists between forms and electric lighting sources. Light sources can be placed more freely than windows, since they are not restricted to locations in the enclosing building form. The geometric relationship between the source and the object, however, and the distribution of light to emphasize the form, follow the same principles. Columns in the lobby of the Opera House (Wilhelm Holzbauer, 1979–88) in Amsterdam, The Netherlands, are articulated in electric light while still being washed with light from the setting sun on a late summer evening. The column lighting fixture provides an ornamental aspect to the column form by its vertical slit of light. From the top it washes the upper part of the column and the adjacent ceiling with light that emphasizes the circular form of the column in contrast to the flat plane of the ceiling. The ceiling is pulled back and stepped up where it surrounds the column, differentiating these two forms. The forms are expressed through a combination of focus (the light slit and the glow on the column) and ambient illumination (the light reflected from the column and ceiling surfaces). The column lighting fixture—holder of the light source—is also an object in the composition. The ceiling joint was shaped to express the difference between column and ceiling in both conditions of daylight from the side and electric light from the column fixture. The electric light source was located and shaped to articulate the column in light.

Larger groups of building forms are also revealed through the modulations of

FIGURE 2–10B *Relationship of the cross and light sources.*

FIGURE 2–12 *The column in the lobby of the Amsterdam Opera House is articulated in light.*

light and shade. In Sta. Maria in Cosmedin (eighth century) in Rome the form of the semi-circular side apse is articulated by daylight. Set behind the brightness of the flat plane of the end wall, the apse is softly modeled in graded shadow. The glass of the side window joins right into the end wall, emphasizing the planar quality of the wall. In the middle, two carved stone screens filter the glow of daylight. The insubstantiality of these broken forms emphasizes the solidity of the walls. Light defines the concavity of the apse in relation to the flat wall from which it departs.

In the church of Germigny des Pres (810) in the Loire Valley in France the entire geometric composition of the interior is articulated in graded shades of daylight. The openings are placed so that the upper regions of the crossing have the brightest surfaces and are more clearly defined than the lower planes. The undersides of the arches, receiving no direct light, are dark. Framing the views of the upper surfaces, they make the latter seem brighter in comparison. The Roman Catholic Church "Pastoor van Ars" (Aldo van Eyck, 1964–69) in The Hague, The Netherlands, produces the opposite effect with graded light, the floor and lower walls of The Sacred Way receiving the most daylight from the circular skylights

FIGURE 2–13 *The side apse in Sta. Maria in Cosmedin in Rome is articulated in light. Photograph by Catherine Jean Barrett.*

FIGURE 2–14 *The crossing in the church of Germigny des Pres is defined in graded light.*

FIGURE 2–15 *The Sacred Way in the Roman Catholic Church "Pastoor van Ars" is defined in graded light.*

above. The brightest surfaces—the inner surfaces of the skylight wells and the Japanese lanterns—are at the top. The spherical surfaces of the Japanese lanterns serve to reflect the daylight to the upper wall surfaces as well as to shield and diffuse the electric light emanating from them. Together the light-washed surfaces of the building and the bright reflecting surfaces of the skylight wells and Japanese lanterns surround the worshipper with light.

Light emphasizes the form of a room by defining its bounding surfaces with light. When these surfaces emphasize the shape of the room and organize its features, then the light becomes organizing light.[5] In the Mt. Angel Abbey Library (Alvar Aalto Architect, 1963–70) in Mt. Angel, Oregon, the curved clerestory, revealed in light, organizes the library in both plan and section (see Chapter 3, "Spatial Light"). Its daylight-washed surfaces define the reading areas below it and the circulation paths around it.

In the interior of the Amsterdam Opera House, patterns of electric light organize the room during intermissions. These patterns define an apparent ceiling plane and the edges of the balcony. Clear incandescent lamps mounted on a grid

FIGURE 2–16 *The form and volume of the Mt. Angel Abbey Library are defined by the light from the curved clerestory.*

structure imply a plane at the same level as the perimeter ceiling. These lighting fixtures perceptually hide the structure and stage lights that are above them. The grid disappears into the darkness of the upper reaches of the hall. The implied ceiling plane continues the real one that is at the perimeter and seems to enclose the space. In addition, clear lamps edge the curved balconies, whose front is a highly polished material that reflects the lamps and multiplies them in a sparkling effect. This design approach of defining an implied ceiling plane and outlining the balconies organizes the room by offering clear perceptible boundaries that provide both orientation and delight.

In these building examples, light articulates the form and organizes the room. The relationship of each part to the whole is important, as it is these relationships that inform our perceptions of a room, a building, and a place. Light emphasizing form in an organizing way creates visual order in the built environment.

Light dematerializing form

Light seemingly dematerializes form when form and light are juxtaposed in certain ways. The result makes it seem as if the form were created by and for light rather than by and for the heartier forces of gravity. The surfaces of the West façade of the Weisman Museum of Art seem immaterial in the dynamic light of Minnesota. The shapes, clad in shining steel, scintillate in the sunlight and reflect light patterns of the sky that obscure a clear view of the form. The material, reflecting sunlight and skylight, becomes a secondary light source for its immediate environment.

The coalescence of form and light is one of the essential ingredients of the Bavarian Rococo church: "... the white walls and pillars of the interior absorb this light, become immaterial and radiant. Light and matter fuse as stone and stucco are transformed into an ethereal substance."[6] In the Pilgrimage Church (Johann Michael Fischer, sculpture by Christian, stuccos by Feuchtmayr, 1744–65) in Zwiefalten, Germany, the intermediary space between the central space and the exterior layer of walls and windows becomes a lighting fixture, a modifier of light that is itself "a visually indeterminate, light-filled mantle."[7] This light-modifier allows large quantities of diffuse reflected light to reach the surface of the frescoes and render them visible. The forms of the lighting fixture itself, the interstitial space, seem to dissolve in the bright patches of sunlight. This brightness sets the interior surfaces into relief. The transition is a gradual one, with the surface modeling of the columns and the capitals gradually fading into a blur of white as it reaches the sunlit area. Form is made to seem immaterial to support the illusion of the heavenly realms that the interior represents.

A contemporary example of light dematerializing form occurs on sunny days in the Chapel of the Holy Cross (Pekka Pitkänen, 1967) in the Turku Cemetery in Finland. In the plain interior volume enclosed by bare concrete surfaces, the white-draped altar seems to dissolve in the burst of direct sunlight from the angled skylights. This effect is reproducible only at certain times, however, relying as it does on the extreme contrast between the concrete surfaces washed with daylight from a glazed wall to the side and the brilliance of the surfaces in the direct beam of sunlight.

Conversely, darkness also dissolves form and obscures the firmness of material. The mysterious atmosphere of Notre Dame de Chartres (1194–1260) is achieved partly by its darkness. Huge areas of glazing are interspersed with the delicate structural members so that the interior is bathed in light entering through the deep blue and red stained glass windows. These windows at Chartres have been described by Henry Adams: "No words and no wine could revive their emotions so vividly as they glow in the purity of the colours; the limpidity of the blues; the depth of the red; the intensity of the green; the complicated harmonies; the

FIGURE 2–18 *The forms of the west façade of the Weisman Museum of Art seem to dissolve in the changing patterns of light.*

FIGURE 2–19 *Form seems immaterial in the space between the inner and outer shells of the Pilgrimage Church in Zwiefalten, Germany. Photograph by Claus Seligmann.*

FIGURE 2–20 *The altar seems to dissolve in a shaft of sunlight in the Chapel of the Holy Cross in the Turku Cemetery in Finland.*

FIGURE 2–21 *Although the limits of the space are clearly defined by the luminous stained glass windows of Nôtre Dame de Chartres, the forms are indistinct in the darkness. Photograph by Grant Hildebrand.*

FIGURE 2–22 *The contrast of light and dark creates* sfumato *effects around the wall openings in Nôtre Dame du Haut at Ronchamp, France.*

sparkle and splendour of the light; and the quiet and certain strength of the mass."[8] The deep-colored glazing in these windows filters and colors the daylight that enters through it, so that the interior is dark and the heights of the vaults are almost lost to view in a vague luminosity.

Layers of forms are revealed successively as one moves through the great cathedral, with partial prospects leaving areas in deeper layers of shadow. The forms become shrouded in the darkness of the vast volume of the church. The gleaming stained glass windows define the perimeter of this vast obscure space. The patterns of colored light that they admit move over the columns and walls and floor inside, denying its material form and ornamenting it as with jewels.

A similar effect of light is given in a much smaller space in the chapel of Notre Dame du Haut (Atelier Le Corbusier, 1950–55) at Ronchamp, France. The interior of the chapel is also very dim. In contrast to Chartres, where large areas of deeply colored glass absorb the daylight, here there are small areas of daylight openings into the church. These openings are either deeply baffled (as in the three light towers) or the daylight is filtered through colored glass and passed through the deep south wall (see Figure 2–34b). The contrast between the daylight and the dim interior is great enough that the edges of the splayed openings are veiled in *sfumato*, the tones from light to dark blurring so as to conceal the exact form. The light decomposes the edges. The light that fills the chapel, as at Chartres, seems palpable, at first concealing, and then revealing, the forms of the interior. The visual process of adaptation plays a large role here, for on first entering the church it appears dark, with dark surfaces broken by bits of colored light. After spending some time inside, however, the interior surfaces of varying shades of gray are clearly disclosed as being white stucco. The perceived varying shades of gray are due to the way light falls on the surfaces. Some surfaces, such as the deep red surfaces of the light shaft that opens toward the pulpit, are barely discernible. The chiaroscuro effects are played mostly at the low end of the scale, with a few bright counterpoints, such as the window behind the altar that admits daylight unabated, maintaining the high end of the scale so that perceptions of form in light are made relative to that bright light. The materiality of the forms is denied by the way that light and shadow play over them.

Strong patterns of light and shadow can also decompose our perception of form by overlaying strong figures on the ground of a building form. For example, broken patterns of daylight coming through the grilled windows of Hagia Sophia (Anthemios and Isidoros, 532–37) in Istanbul, Turkey, are cast onto the carved stone walls. The walls seem to dissolve into limpid pools of light, the hardness of the stone succumbing to the soft edges of the patches of light. The grilled window at the end of the room beyond brings us back to hard-edged reality, but a veil of illusion has been cast before us.

In Juha Leiviskä's church at Myyrmäki, Finland (1984), a strong diagonal pattern of light and shade overlays another pattern of planes in space, so that the two together form a symphony of forms in light, a multilayered composition of light and shadow. Beams under the skylight and the mullions in the skylight split the sunbeams into patterns of light and shadow. Planes of parallel partitions channel daylight from the side, revealing successive layers of surfaces in light. The woven tapestries hanging in the space form additional layers of light, the looser and denser weaves alternately filtering and blocking light. The way the form and light interact gives primacy to the light, fulfilling Leiviskä's aim of producing a "shimmering, constantly changing veil of light."[9] The form is dematerialized in favor of the light.

FIGURE 2–23 *Patterns of light dematerialize the form of the walls in Hagia Sophia in Istanbul, Turkey.*

FIGURE 2–24 *Light patterns dematerialize the form in the Myyrmäki church in Finland. Photograph by Virginia Cartwright.*

LIGHT AND STRUCTURE

Light and structure are intertwined. Louis I. Kahn said that

…structure is the maker of light. When you decide on the structure, you're deciding on light. In the old buildings, the columns were an expression of light. Light, no light, light, no light, light, you see. The module is also light, no light. The vault stems from it. The dome stems from it. And the same realization that you are releasing light.[10]

FIGURE 2–25 *The Crystal Palace, London.*

FIGURE 2–26 *Bibliothèque Nationale, Paris.*

In some of the "old buildings," such as the Parthenon and the Pantheon, this expression is clear. "In the old buildings" covers a lot of territory, however, and history also holds examples of buildings where the intent clearly is not to reveal the structure in light.

In S. Lorenzo, discussed earlier, the relationship between the structure and the light is clear. The openings for light in both the exterior envelope and between nave and side aisles follow a clear order. In S. Carlo, however, the sources of light are concealed. Although still dependent on structure—the glazing is inserted at the bottom of the dome where stresses are least, and on the sides of the lantern—light is not ostensibly related to the form of the support.

Changes in the relationship between light and structure were associated with the advent of new technologies as well. Use of iron and glass in building systems revolutionized the building industry and the attitudes toward light in buildings. The Crystal Palace (Joseph Paxton, 1851), part of the Great Exhibition of 1851 in London, was made entirely of cast and wrought iron holding panels of glass set in wood frames. It was, essentially, an extraordinarily large see-through umbrella. Later, in Paris, Henri Labrouste conceived a taut balance of iron structure and glass, marrying structure and light, in the Bibliothèque Nationale (1854–75). Thin iron columns and arches carry lightweight terra-cotta domes, each with an oculus that spreads light widely over the reading tables below.

Light revealing structure

A simple correlation between structure and light is shown in the horse stables of the Finca Güell (Antonio Gaudí, 1883–87) outside Barcelona, now serving as a library for the Gaudí Foundation. The parabolic arches were used by Gaudí in an effort to "approximate the catenary of the line of pressures or of the 'true' arch, viz., an arch without moment or thrust."[11] Windows are set between the arches at the ends of parabolic-shaped vaults. The structure defines the place where light enters. The structural module provides the rhythm of light, no light. Where the structure is, there is no light. Between the structural elements, there is light.

Roof glazing usually reveals structure because the structure ends up being silhouetted against the light. In the renovated market building of Covent Garden (Charles Fowler, 1828–30; renovated 1974–80 by the Greater London Council Historic Buildings Division) in London, two variations on this theme occur that reflect the developments in materials and construction techniques that occurred during the nineteenth century. Above Central Avenue in the central market hall as designed by Fowler, simple trusses carry both roofing and glazing panels, the glazing area restricted to the inner half of the roof span. The structure is dark and seems heavy, so that it is very noticeable against the glazing. The truss supports the roof, and part of the roof is glazed to allow daylight to enter. It is a simple accommodation to provide light to Central Avenue.

The courtyards between the central hall and the north and south wings of the market were originally open to the air, but were roofed over in 1874–75. The iron roof of the south courtyard is carried on cast iron columns that are set against the brick walls of the building. Arches springing from these columns span the courtyard and support a glazed clerestory that runs down the center. Originally painted "two shades of light blue"[12] and covered entirely by glass, the roof structure is less dominant than the earlier one. The structure is more integral with the light as it supports only glazing. Compared to the earlier roof over Central Avenue, the effect is more one of structure supporting light, rather than light being allowed to enter between structural members.

The ten-story light well of the Rookery (John Root and Daniel Burnham,

FIGURE 2–27A *In the former horse stables in the Finca Güell near Barcelona, the structural system defines the places for daylight to enter.*

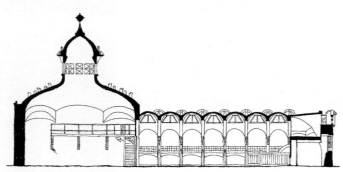

FIGURE 2–27B *Longitudinal section showing the relationship of structure and windows. Redrawn from Collins, George R. and Juan Bassegoda Nonell. 1983.* The Designs and Drawings of Antonio Gaudí. *(Princeton, N.J.: Princeton University Press), Plate 31B, drawn for the architect Juan Bassegoda, 1967.*

FIGURE 2–27C *Sketch of a window with solid wooden shutters that open inward from the center post to deflect direct sunlight.*

1885–88) in Chicago, Illinois, solved the problem of admitting daylight into offices on the interior of a large building before the availability of electric lighting. The walls of the light well were constructed as a skeleton frame, an advanced technology at that time that allowed the wall to have large windows so that offices opening onto the light well were as attractive (and could command a good rent) as those on the exterior walls, which were constructed with load-bearing masonry with windows opening onto the street. Structure was used in an innovative way to provide equal access to light and air. The surfaces of the light well were clad in white terra-cotta with gold decorative bands that reflect the daylight and sunlight, turning the light well into a building-sized lighting fixture.

Frank Lloyd Wright, who investigated the integration of structure with light throughout the course of his lengthy practice, renovated the light court at the bottom of the light well in the Rookery in 1905. A recent restoration (McClier, Donald Bliss, lighting consultant, 1988–92) has preserved Wright's work and added a skylight at the top of the light well to improve thermal performance and protect the terra cotta and the original skylight to the light court below. The light court celebrates the ability of iron to support glass and admit large amounts of daylight, the light revealing the structure and being the reason for it. Electric lighting adds to the effect. Twelve large chandeliers incorporating Wright's square and circle motif are suspended from structural crossings, thereby placing large glowing globes of electric light at key points along the mezzanine. Smaller globes hang from the corners, providing a pattern of light that is broken down into smaller components related to the human size. Rows of incandescent lamps march along the underside of the beams, providing a warm counterpoint to the daylight, reflecting their golden glow into the interstices of the openwork structural members. The black railing, stairwell, and lighting fixtures contrast with the white structure, giving each its clear role. This light is made possible by structure, by the spans allowable with this cast iron system. The structure that admits the daylight and the structures that provide electric light both celebrate light revealing structure.

Frank Lloyd Wright's passion with connecting structure and light is displayed in many of his buildings. A clear example is the Johnson Wax Administration Building (1936–39) in Racine, Wisconsin (see Figure 1–49). In Wright's words, "Glass tubing laid up like bricks in a wall compose all the lighting surfaces. Light

FIGURE 2–28A *The early roof (1828–30) over Central Avenue in Covent Garden, London.*

FIGURE 2–28B *The iron roof over the court-yard in the south wing of the market, built 1874–75.*

enters the building where the cornice used to be."[13] In the end the glass tubing was not laid up like bricks, but each length was tied to aluminum racks that span the five-foot-wide opening between the exterior brick walls and the ceiling pads supported by dendriform columns. The construction method required intense development and collaboration among Corning Glass, Wright's office, and the contractor Ben Wiltscheck. The racks were scalloped so that the Pyrex glass tubing would fit onto them snugly, and mastic was used to caulk the joints between tubes.

The fact that this five-foot-wide area "where the cornice used to be" could be opened up for daylight was due to the use of the specially designed columns. No

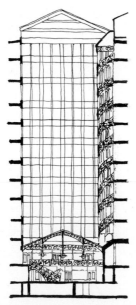

FIGURE 2–29A *Section of the ten-story light well of the Rookery in Chicago, Illinois.*

FIGURE 2–29B *View of the light court in the Rookery.*

FIGURE 2–30 *Structure and light at a small scale in the display niches/hollow columns in the model Usonian House.*

FIGURE 2–31 *A graceful structure determines the patterns of daylight in a passage built in the 1980s to link downtown to the train station in Jönköping, Sweden. Photograph by Peter Cohan.*

physical connection to the exterior wall is necessary for their support, thereby the gap between the exterior wall and the ceiling/roof construction is left free for glazing. The box is broken. The columns flare out at the top to support pads that form the solid part of the ceiling and Pyrex glass tubes are fitted between them—again the structure allows light to enter. Bare lamps were mounted between the inner and outer skins of tubing in both the cornice and also the ceiling of the Great Workroom. The innovative structural concept allowed light to penetrate to every part of the building so that "whoever will work there will feel as though he were among the pine trees breathing fresh air and sunlight."[14] Light was both part of the inspiration for the structural innovations and the end result as well.

At a much smaller scale, a detail of the Usonian House[15] that was part of the exhibition *Frank Lloyd Wright: In the Realm of Ideas* (1988–91 national tour) displays this conceptual approach to light and structure. Specially-shaped concrete blocks form U-shaped hollow columns on the outside wall of the loggia of the house. The concrete blocks are L-shaped with a hole in the middle, the hole wrapping around the corner. The holes are filled in with glass for weatherproofing, and sheets of glass are inserted into the grooves between the blocks to make display shelves. It is clear that the concrete blocks were not designed solely for structural support, but rather were designed to provide both structure *and* light. Structure could be accommodated in a way that allowed the free passage of daylight and connection between inside and outside.

The principle of structure defining the place for light is also evident in the Newton Library (Patkau Architects, 1990–92) in Surrey, near Vancouver, British Columbia. The glazing is part of an independent outer skin beyond the column line. On the south side of the main library room, the wall configuration is thickened to modulate the daylight and sunlight. Reading tables are sheltered under lowered roof sections. At the inner edge

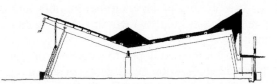

FIGURE 2–32A *Section of the Newton Library in Surrey showing the configuration of the south wall on the right.*

FIGURE 2–32B *View along the south wall to the west, with canted columns serving as large baffles.*

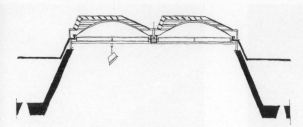

FIGURE 2–33A *View through the fourth-floor galleries in the Yale Center for British Art.*

of this low roof, clerestory windows bring daylight high into the library, spreading it through the bookstack area. At the outer edge of this low roof, exterior concrete wall sections serve as partial sunshades for the clerestory windows. The columns are canted, carrying the outward thrusts of the roof load. As one looks down the aisle between book stacks and reading tables at the windows, the slanted columns and concrete partitions serve to baffle views of this lower glazing and also the clerestory glazing above, so that the reading tables in their alcoves are revealed only as one proceeds down the aisle. The penetrating daylight, however, is apparent from the light-play on the columns and the illuminated surfaces around the clerestory window openings.

Structure orders and releases light eloquently only when it has been designed to do so. In Kahn's buildings, structure is the maker of light, and the two are indelibly intertwined. In the Yale Center for British Art (1969–77, completed posthumously by Pellecchia and Meyers, Architects; Richard Kelly, lighting consultant), the upstairs galleries are formed by the module of the structure which is consonant with the twenty-foot-square module of the "room." The deep concrete skylight wells baffle and interreflect the light, softening it and further diffusing it following its filtration through the skylight system.

It is important to note that the skylight system was long studied, and not resolved before Kahn's death, so it is impossible to know whether it might have ended up differently. This skylight system required careful design and three full-scale mock-ups to finally produce an arrangement that would reject ultraviolet light and direct sunlight while delivering diffuse daylight to the wall surfaces in quantities adequate for viewing the paintings without harming them.

As the skylight system ended up, a metal frame supporting fixed plates and louvers tops each skylight.[16] A sloped solid plate blocks all direct light from the north.[17] The louvers are arranged to allow some sunlight to reach the top of the skylight dome when the sun is low in the sky, early and late in the day and in the winter. Each skylight is a double-layered acrylic dome, the inner layer absorbing ultraviolet radiation. Below the skylight rest Plexiglas "cassettes," described by Anthony Pellecchia as "the boxes we collected the light in."[18] The top and bottom layers in each cassette are prismatic plastic lenses that diffuse and scatter the light to the side. Sandwiched between them is a parabolic louver that redirects the light from the top panel downward. The clear Plexiglas box that holds these layers was sandblasted on the sides, but the corners were left clear to allow the sparkle of sunlight to be observed at certain times. The goal of illuminating the walls so there was no discernible difference among them was achieved through the use of these multiple layers of baffles and diffusers. That the structure and light *could* work together was due to the technical realization of the skylight system.

What Kahn had hoped to achieve in the Kimbell Art Museum (see Chapter 4 "Sacred Light") —the coincidence of structure, light, and room[19]—was achieved in the Yale Center for British Art. The room is defined by the coincident module of structure and light. It required both the concept and also extensive and careful detailing of the skylight to achieve this goal.

FIGURE 2–34A *View toward the rear of the chapel of Nôtre Dame du Haut, Ronchamp, France, with the south wall on the left.*

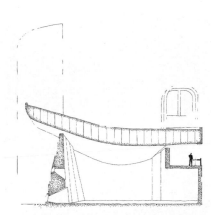

FIGURE 2–34B *Section through the chapel; south wall to the left.*

Light concealing structure

It seems unlikely that light could conceal structure, since light reveals what is there, and structure is always present in a building. However, sometimes structure is hidden purposefully or thoughtlessly. Sometimes the pattern and rhythm of the light contradicts the pattern and rhythm of the structure. Sometimes the way the structure looks and the way it really acts are not coincident, or are unfamiliar to us, leaving unexpected places open where light can enter counter to our expectations.

Such is the case in the chapel of Nôtre Dame du Haut (Atelier Le Corbusier, 1950–55) at Ronchamp, France. The shape of the ceiling/roof construction, sagging in the middle, suggests weight. And yet, along the top of the thick masonry walls that we assume are built so heavily in order to support the roof, a slit clearly allows daylight to enter. The structure remains a mystery. In fact, the roof rests on columns of reinforced concrete located inside the thick rubble walls. The roof itself is constructed in a manner similar to the wing of an airplane.[20] A thin external shell (six centimeters, approximately two inches, thick) is stretched over a framework of beams that defines the surfaces.[21] Although the roof looks heavy, and its surface is visibly concrete, it is in fact a relatively light-weight shell. Le Corbusier in fact intended the passage of light between wall and ceiling to cause consternation: "a horizontal beam of light ten centimeters wide will cause surprise ..."[22]

Light seems to substitute for structure in interior walls in the lobbies of the Arizona Biltmore Hotel (Albert Chase MacArthur, architect of record; Frank Lloyd Wright;[23] 1927–29). In a wall that backs a fountain, lighting fixtures with opal glass panels are interspersed with the "textile" concrete blocks of the wall.[24] The metal lighting fixtures support the glass panels that are patterned to complement the concrete blocks. The lighting fixtures are the same size as the concrete blocks. They are located at the corners of the configuration, seemingly defying any continuous support function of these otherwise solid piers. The openwork concrete blocks in the wall visually defy any load-bearing capacity as well, thereby proclaiming this construction to be purely ornamental. We do not know for sure, however. The lighting fixtures defy the structural role of these walls.

FIGURE 2–35 *Block wall around the fountain in the Arizona Biltmore Hotel.*

FIGURE 2–36 *Columns in the Pilgrimage Church at Zwiefalten Germany. Photograph by Claus Seligmann.*

In Bavarian rococo churches, light is manipulated by means of form and color to conceal structure—sometimes even to overwhelm it. This intention contributes to one of the five criteria for distinguishing a Bavarian rococo church: "Traditional architectural forms are transformed, isolated, and displaced."[25] These traditional forms include the structural forms, such as wall and columns. At Zwiefalten Abbey Church (Johann Michael Fischer, 1744–65), columns and pilasters are richly colored and textured in a technique called *scagliola*,[26] and thus visually separated from the white pedestals below and entablatures above: "they begin to float, exchanging their tectonic for a more purely ornamental function."[27] The reality of the structure is not sacrificed for an illusion; rather structure is manipulated by means of light and color to contribute to a complete art form, the Bavarian rococo church, in which painting, sculpture, and architecture were fused pictorially into "illusions of heaven descending right into its churches."[28]

In a contemporary church, St. Matthew's Episcopal Church (Charles Moore, John Ruble, and Buzz Yudell; Richard Peters, lighting consultant; 1979–83) in Pacific Palisades, California, several strategies recall the Baroque play of light, particularly the light of Borromini. The structure is at once revealed by the light, as the truss is silhouetted against the skylight glazing, but it also seems to be broken up by the light. Light makes the edges of the form seem to blur, a *sfumato* effect. The members of the fan-truss become luminous lines. Structure creates luminous effects at the same time as it serves its function of supporting the weight of the building form. Wall surfaces are broken up into stripes by vertical strips of wood applied to the walls, denying the continuity of their surfaces. The wall behind the altar, washed with grazing light from above and to the side, is seen through the layers of the suspended cross, the arched frame, and the altar sculpture. The organization of the church is also expressed in light. Daylight emphasizes the axes of the cross of the plan, while the electric lighting fixtures emphasize the semicircular curve of the seating. When daylight and electric light are both active, the two orders are interwoven.

When light conceals structure, it cannot escape the laws of physics that determine the rules for structural support. Rather light contradicts our expectation of structure and finds expression in an unexpected way.

FIGURE 2–37A *View toward altar in daylight, St. Matthew's Episcopal Church, Pacific Palisades, California.*

FIGURE 2–37B *The same view with the addition of the electric lighting.*

FIGURE 2–38 *The sculpture installation (1961–64) that Carlo Scarpa designed in the Castelvecchio Museum in Verona, Italy uses contrasting light to delineate form. The black cross absorbs the light around the sculpture so that the sculpture stands out. The form of the cross is carefully delineated in relationship to all three sculptures, forming a visual niche for the two figures at the sides. Their smooth surfaces are subtly distinguished from the rough stucco of the same color behind them by differences in texture. The light source is a window to the left. Photograph by Lucy Carter Sloman, © 1996.*

LIGHT AND MATERIALS

Light and materials are mutually dependent on each other. Materials are key to understanding light in architecture because they directly affect the quantity and the quality of the light. Two qualities of materials—their finish and their color—are most important in this regard. Specular materials, such as glossy finishes, reflect light as a mirror does, which can result in reflected images of the light source being visible "on" the surface. Matte surfaces, such as natural stone, wood, and plaster, reflect light diffusely, equally in all directions. Of the three aspects of color—hue, value, and intensity—value is the one that determines how much light is absorbed and how much is reflected. A white wall reflects approximately 82 percent of incident light, a light yellow wall 78 percent, and a dark green or blue wall 7 percent.[29] Colored surfaces lend some of their hue to light that is reflected.

FIGURE 2–39 *An application of red* stucco alla veneziana *in the Banco Popolare (Carlo Scarpa, 1973–78, completed following his death by Arrigo Rudi) in Verona, Italy. Photograph by Jose F. Talavera.*

A change in materials can alter the feeling of a room and the level of illumination as well. The cheapest way to increase the amount of light in a dark room is to paint the room surfaces white. A dark room, on the other hand, can be created either by using little light in a white room or through dark surfaces. With dark surfaces, a room will look dark during both daytime and at night. With light or white surfaces, however, the effect changes depending upon the light sources used. This effect can be exploited. For example, the interior surfaces of the chapel of Notre Dame du Haut at Ronchamp are white, but due to the small quantity of daylight admitted, perceptually the surfaces grade from light gray to dark gray (Figure 2-34A).

Materials are important emotionally in relation to light. The sparkle of glass, the glitter of gold mosaics, the depths of dark polished wood, and the shadows on white walls all hold emotional messages, some of them connected with cultural settings, some of them connected to individual recollection. Some regions have building traditions and materials that respond to particular local conditions, such as the *stucco alla veneziana* favored by Carlo Scarpa. Requiring a labor-intensive process of application with very particular materials, the stucco "over time takes on a softer, more moist look, a quality of fantasy and beauty."[30]

Light emphasizing materials

Emphasis on materials is grounded in the interaction between light and material. Highlights arise from glossy materials reflecting discrete points of light. Definition of surface texture comes from grazing light. Revelation of the inner qualities of materials results from light passing through them. Dark shadows result from light being deflected from the surface, and from material absorbing light.

Light emphasizes the materials in the Newton Library, discussed earlier, at the same time as the materials emphasize light and foster its distribution. As the archi-

FIGURE 2–40B *Detail of the rock wall.*

FIGURE 2–40A *In the Temppeliaukio Church (Timo and Tuomo Suomalainen, 1968–69) in Helsinki, Finland, light from above brings out the textures of the rock, both the rock that has been hewn out and the rock pieces that have been built up. The grazing light brings out the contrast between the rock and the copper surfaces, emphasizing both the roughness of the rock and the smoothness of the copper.*

FIGURE 2–40C *Detail of the copper surface of the ceiling.*

FIGURE 2–41 *At the monastery of La Tourette (Atelier Le Corbusier, 1952–59), the different textures of the walls reflect the apportionment of the narrow private cells for the monks. When sitting at the desk, one faces a smooth white plaster wall. The light from the windows is reflected uninterrupted from the smooth white wall to the desk area. The other wall surfaces are rough white stucco that interrupt the light, cast tiny shadows with it, break it up, and tone it down as the light from the side grazes over them. Photograph by Virginia Cartwright.*

FIGURE 2–42 *White-painted sheetrock defines the light-reflecting part of the ceiling at the Newton Library in Surrey, British Columbia.*

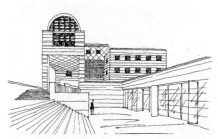

FIGURE 2–43A *Exterior view of the Museum of Contemporary Art, Los Angeles, California.*

FIGURE 2–43B *Interior view of the onyx glazing.*

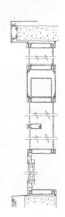

FIGURE 2–43C *The glazing detail was carefully developed so that the thin sheets of onyx would be sufficiently supported by the mullions and protected from the weather by an exterior layer of glazing. Redrawn from* ARCHITECTURAL RECORD, *p. 106. (January 1988), ©1988 by McGraw-Hill, Inc. All rights reserved. Reproduced with the permission of the publisher.*

tects have stated, "because the light of the Vancouver area can be very soft, even weak, under the frequently overcast skies of winter, the robust light-absorbing character of heavy timber and concrete, in themselves, are not appropriate to distribute natural light into a relatively deep floor plate."[31] The ceiling surfaces of the library have therefore been treated where needed with material that distributes light to the interior. Near the tall sloped north glazing, where the large area of glass provides abundant light for reading, the ceiling surface is the exposed underside of the wood decking. In such a situation, care must be taken so that the contrast between materials at the perimeter glazing and the sky is not too great, causing discomfort. Here the wash of daylight over the wood beams and onto the underside of the ceiling helps to mitigate the contrast at the edge as well as even out the brightness of the ceiling from the window wall to the center of the room. About midway between the glazing and the low center beam, sheet rock surfaces painted white were applied as the ceiling surface, better reflecting the daylight down to the area below. Each material is used honestly to do what is needed and no more, forming an economical building shell. The layering of materials discloses the role that each plays in the total realized construction.

Usually the glazing material is not the object of attention in a room. Special glazing materials, however, such as thin slabs of stone, can be emphasized by the way they transmit light. Under the barrel vault of the trustee's board room, overlooking the library at the Museum of Contemporary Art (Arata Isozaki, 1981–86) in Los Angeles, California, onyx has been used to glaze a semicircular opening and four windows below it. The onyx fits tight to the ceiling, so that the glow of the entering daylight is carried along the black concrete ceiling surface. Attention is called to the onyx as it is the brightest surface in the room. The thickness of the material saves the window from being a source of glare. Light reveals and celebrates the onyx, making it the identifying feature of the room.

In the central six-story light well in the Casa Batlló (Antonio Gaudí, 1904–06) in Barcelona, Spain, Gaudí designed the ceramic tiles that cover its surfaces to manipulate light. By modulating the hue, value, and texture of the tiles, he modi-

FIGURE 2–44A *Section through the light well of the Casa Batlló in Barcelona, Spain, showing the disposition of the windows. Redrawn from Collins, George R. and Juan Bassegoda Nonell. 1983.* The Designs and Drawings of Antonio Gaudí. *(Princeton, N.J.: Princeton University Press), Plate 49A, drawn by Roberto Carulla, Sixto Rosell, and Ramón Berenguer for the architect Luis Bonet Garí, 1960.*

FIGURE 2–44B (TOP LEFT) *View of tiled surface and a window at the top of the light well.*

FIGURE 2–44C (MIDDLE LEFT) *View of tiled surfaces and windows at the ground floor of the light well. Photograph by Gregory J. Bader.*

FIGURE 2–44D (BOTTOM LEFT) *View from the entry hall to the light well. Photograph by Gregory J. Bader.*

fied the qualities and quantities of light experienced in the light well itself as well as in the adjacent apartments. The tiles range in color from a deep blue through lighter shades of blue to an off-white. The deep blue tiles are placed in their largest concentration at the top of the light well, on the surfaces directly under the skylight glazing, interspersed with lighter tiles. The effect here is cooling, almost as if one were seeing the light underwater. At the bottom of the light well are placed the lightest tiles, interspersed with a few darker ones. In between, the colors gradually shift from dark to light. This distribution of the colored tiles evens out the perceived light gradient in the light well, establishing a balanced light. Thicker patterned tiles, which reflect the light from their corners, are scattered among the smooth ones along the entire height, adding a glint of sparkle. In addition to the use of materials to manipulate the light, the shape of the light well—wider at the top—and the sizing of the windows—larger at the bottom—serve to balance access to light for all residents. An additional geometric manipulation of the section of the light well is the insertion of balconies, with glass panels serving as flooring for the balcony and as a skylight for the room below. The light that enters the apartments through the windows in the light well is therefore more equal than in the usual situation where the rooms at the top garner all the light and the rooms at the bottom are in shadow. Ventilation apertures are separate from the glazed windows, thereby adding more light to the interior when they are open.

In the Casa Batlló, light was used in a thoughtful way with consideration for the well-being of the inhabitants, their need for light and air, and artful ways to provide them. Light was apparently considered at each step in the design process: concept, development of plan and section, window size and placement, surface shape and composition, and details. The tile work is not only beautiful, but also serves the purpose of modifying the daylight as it enters the building and is distributed to the apartments. Control and delight are both provided.

The materials of electric lighting fixtures are as important as those of building surfaces which are acting as daylighting fixtures. In the Resurrection Chapel (Erik Bryggmann, 1939–41, renovated 1984) in the Turku Cemetery in Finland, the brass lighting fixtures reflect daylight with a cool yellow that warms to an amber glow when the incandescent lamps are turned on. The material and details of the fixture respond to the incandescent light. The vertical blades that baffle views of the lamp glow with the light reflected between them. The "crown" of brass loops circling the top catch the light, as do similar "crowns" higher up. The pools of gold light in the cool interior lend a warmth and points of attraction similar to the glow

FIGURE 2–45A *View of lighting fixtures in summer daylight in the Resurrection Chapel in Turku, Finland.*

FIGURE 2–45B *Close-up view of the lighting fixtures.*

FIGURE 2–46A *View of wall-mounted lighting fixture in daylight, Henry's Church, Turku, Finland.*

FIGURE 2–46B *Fixture illuminated by incandescent light source.*

of a fire. The light furnished by electric lighting fixtures is contrasted with the daylight in both color and distribution. While the daylight washes the surfaces of the interior with fairly even light, the electric lighting fixtures act as points of focus.

In Henry's Church (Pitkänen, Laiho and Raunio, 1980) in Turku, Finland, the material of the lighting fixtures appears entirely different under daylight and under electric light. With daylight streaming in from large windows, the white screen material is almost transparent, and the brick wall shows clearly through it. When illuminated from below, the white material becomes a reflector, casting the light back down to the congregation. As it does so, it obscures the view of the wall directly behind it and casts a warm glow over the nearby wall surface. The material switches between revealing what is behind it and reflecting what is in front of it, as does a scrim curtain in theater productions. Through it, one becomes more aware of the difference between the nature of daylight and electric light.

Light muting materials

Materials can also be chosen to mute the effects of light, to make dissimilar materials appear similar, or to make the light seem unchanging. The shoji screens in traditional Japanese houses diffuse all the daylight that enters, whether the skies outside are sunny or overcast. The light is first shaded by the large overhanging roofs, acting as a parasol, so that the interior muted effect is constant (see Chapter 1). The interior surfaces, such as the ones pictured in the teahouse in the Zen Center at Green Gulch, California, are carefully surfaced to interact with the light:

> We do our walls in neutral colors so that the sad, fragile, dying rays can sink into absolute repose. The storehouse, kitchen, hallways, and such may have a glossy finish, but the walls of the sitting room will almost always be of clay textured with fine sand. A luster here would destroy the soft fragile beauty of the feeble light. We delight in the mere sight of the delicate glow of fading rays clinging to the surface of a dusky wall, there to live out what little life remains to them.[32]

FIGURE 2–47 *Tokonoma in Zen Center teahouse in Green Gulch, California.*

FIGURE 2–48 *Courtyard façade in the Isabella Stewart Gardner Museum, in Boston, Massachusetts.*

The *lume materiale* of Venice seems to glow in Boston, Massachusetts, at the Isabella Stewart Gardner Museum (Willard T. Sears, 1899–1901). The wall was prepared in a similar way to the traditional Venetian stucco, and consists of plaster impregnated with color introduced by using a wash of pink paint. The light of Boston is not the light of Venice, but the appearance can fool the eye on certain days. The surfaces seem to glow in and of themselves so that the light is more real than the material. Likewise, in the exhibition of glass balls, *Niijima Floats*, by Dale Chihuly (1992 at the Seattle Art Museum), the light that is cast by the glass seems to be the point of the piece. It is not the balls themselves that are so important, but the patterns of light that they cast on the surface below. The material (of the balls) transforms the light which then transforms material (the resting surface).

Kahn was very aware of the nature of a material's response to light. Kahn's selection of concrete and travertine as materials for the Kimbell Art Museum (1966–72) in Fort Worth, Texas, was related to how their surface characteristics shaped that response:

> *'Travertine and concrete belong beautifully together because concrete must be taken for whatever irregularities in the pouring' are revealed....Time, he believed, would unify all materials eventually, but the architect could achieve unity by carefully choosing certain materials—wood, travertine, concrete—'which are so subtle that each material never ruins the other ... And that's why the choice.'*[33]

The travertine, unfilled and unpolished, has certain characteristic ways of reacting with light that complements the reaction of concrete to light. As the light changes—outside and inside—the surfaces of the two materials shift subtly in relationship to each other. First one seems warmer, then the other does. First one appears to be lighter, then the other. One seems to have a glossy surface, and the other a matte finish, and then they switch.[34] One looks more mottled, then the other one does. The surfaces respond to the changing light. Light is the real material here.

I think light is as material as anything else.[35]
—JAMES TURRELL

FIGURE 2–49 Niijima Floats, *Dale Chihuly, 1992.*

FIGURE 2–50A (BELOW LEFT) *Exterior view of the Kimbell Art Museum, Fort Worth, Texas, showing the textures of travertine and concrete as revealed in direct sunlight. Photograph by Peter McCleary.*

FIGURE 2–50B (BELOW RIGHT) *Interior view with daylight lightening the concrete ceiling and bringing out its texture in relationship to the travertine. Photograph by M. Susan Ubbelohde.*

1. Le Corbusier. 1974. *Towards A New Architecture*. (New York: Praeger Publishers), p. 8.

2. Gibson, James J. 1986. *The Ecological Approach to Visual Perception*. (Hillsdale, N. J.: Lawrence Erlbaum Associates, Publishers), pp. 65–92.

3. Norberg-Schulz, Christian. 1965. *Intentions in Architecture*. (Cambridge, Mass.: The M.I.T. Press), p. 154.

4. Portoghesi, Paolo. 1968. *The Rome of Borromini*. (New York: George Braziller), p. 381.

5. For a more extended discussion of this concept, see: Schwartz, Martin. 1992. "Light Organizing/Organizing Light," *Places* 8(2):14–25.

6. Harries, Karsten. 1983. *The Bavarian Rococo Church*. (New Haven, Conn., and London: Yale University Press), p. 73.

7. Ibid.

8. Adams, Henry. 1985. *Mont-Saint-Michel and Chartres*. (New York: Gallery Books), pp. 88–89.

9. Poole, Scott. 1992. *The New Finnish Architecture*. (New York: Rizzoli), p. 102.

10. Wurman, Richard Saul. 1986. *What Will Be Has Always Been: The Words of Louis I. Kahn*. (New York: Rizzoli), p. 63. From "Silence and Light," address to students at the School of Architecture, ETH, Zurich, Switzerland, February 12, 1969.

11. Collins, George R. 1963. "Antonio Gaudí: Structure and Form," *Perspecta 8*:74.

12. Thorne, Robert. 1980. *Covent Garden Market*. (London: The Architectural Press), p. 32.

13. Wright, Frank Lloyd. 1957. *A Testament*. (New York: Bramhall House), p. 171.

14. Wright's words as recalled by his wife Olgivanna in: Lipman, Jonathan. 1986. *Frank Lloyd Wright and the Johnson Wax Building*. (New York: Rizzoli), p. 41.

15. Full-scale building of the Usonian Automatic House, designed in 1955 but constructed for the first time for this exhibition.

16. The description of the skylight construction is from Anthony Pellecchia, conversation with author, June 1995.

17. According to Anthony Pellecchia, the north light, rather than the south light, was blocked due to a misunderstanding about the significance of the relative quantities of ultraviolet radiation in north skylight versus direct sunlight. Although north skylight delivers more radiation per foot-candle in the ultraviolet range than does direct sunlight, the much higher intensities of sunlight still render it more damaging. Ibid.

18. Anthony Pellecchia, Ibid.

19. McCleary, Peter. 1987. "The Kimbell Art Museum: Between Building & Architecture," *Design Book Review 11*:50.

20. Pauly, Canièle. Translated by Stephen Sartarelli. "The Chapel of Ronchamp as an Example of Le Corbusier's Creative Process," in Brooks, H. Allen, Editor. 1987. *Le Corbusier*. (Princeton, N. J.: Princeton University Press), pp. 127–40.

21. Le Corbusier. 1989. *Le Corbusier: texts and sketches for Ronchamp*. (Switzerland: Association Oeuvre de Nôtre Dame du Haut, Ronchamp), Second English edition.

22. Ibid.

23. Morton, David. November 1981. "Wrighting wrongs?" *Progressive Architecture* 52(11): 110–14. According to information in this article, Wright's original sketches for the building were discovered in the vaults at Taliesin West in Scottsdale, Arizona, Wright's western office and residence, in 1975.

24. The patterns for the concrete blocks were all designed by McArthur and Wright and molded on site. "Arizona Biltmore, Phoenix, Arizona." *Architectural Record* 168(1):116–21.

25. Rupprecht, Bernhard. 1959. "Die bayerische Rokoko-Kirche," *Münchener Historische Studien, Abteilung Bayerische Geschichte*. Max Spindler, Editor, vol. 5. (Kallmünz: Lassleben), pp. 55–56. Recounted in Harries, op. cit., p. 4.

26. Plaster work imitating marble, granite, and so on.

27. Harries, op cit.

28. Harries, Karsten. 1989. *The Broken Frame*. (Washington, D.C.: The Catholic University of America Press), p. 68.

29. The reflectance of typical colors is illustrated on the back cover of Bernard R. Boylan, 1987, *The Lighting Primer*. (Ames, Iowa State University Press). A good source for information on paints is a local paint store, where some samples state the reflectance. Reflectance can be calculated by measuring the incident illumination in foot-candles on a surface and then, under the same lighting conditions, measuring the luminance in foot-lamberts of the surface. Reflectance is luminance divided by incident illumination: foot-lamberts divided by foot-candles.

30. Zambonini, Giuseppe. 1988. "Notes for a Theory of Making in a Time of Necessity," *Perspecta 24:* 3–23. Recollections of Eugejio De Luigi, a longtime collaborator with Scarpa, p. 9.

31. Carter, Brian, Editor. 1994. *Patkau Architects*. (Halifax, Nova Scotia: TUNS Press), p. 88.

32. Tanazaki, Junichiro. 1977. *In Praise of Shadows*. (New Haven, Conn.: Leete's Island Books), p. 18. Reprinted by permission of the publisher.

33. Interview by Marshall Meyers on August 11, 1972. Reported in Loud, Patricia Cummings. 1989. *The Art Museums of Louis I. Kahn*. (Durham, N.C.: Duke University Press), p. 156.

34. Personal communication from Peter McCleary in May, 1994 concerning his observations during a two-day visit to the museum.

35. Millin, Laura J., Editor. 1982. *James Turrell: Four Light Installations*. (Seattle, Wash.: The Real Comet Press), p. 18.

Formal Light: Monastery of Sainte Marie de La Tourette

Eveux-sur-l'Arbresle, near Lyon, France
1952–59

Atelier Le Corbusier
André Wogenscky, Studio Foreman
Iannis Xenakis and Gardien, Collaborators

The key is light, and light illuminates shapes and shapes have an emotional power.[1]
—LE CORBUSIER

The physical context for the Dominican monastery and church of La Tourette is a hillside site near the village of Eveux-sur-l'Arbresle west of Lyon in France. The monastery enjoys a broad prospect over the valley. The south and west sides open onto a sloped field, totally exposed to the light and the weather, while the north side emerges from the trees that are the boundary on the east side.

The religious context is an order of Dominican Brothers that fulfill their monastic duties by combining private study and devotion with service to the community. They have been described as preaching friars that live in "obedience, chastity and poverty"; their life is characterized by "exclusion of the world, the inviolability of the religious life, quiet study."[2] This duality of being extremely orthodox, and yet being constantly in contact with the public, has led them to be characterized as "the archsophisticates of dialectic."[3]

The complex to house them and provide a school for their seven-year course of study is made up of two distinct parts: the living quarters of the monks, and the church. A broad range of forms manipulating light are employed to express this dialectic—to express the Dominican conflict between working in this world and yet not being connected to this world. Colin Rowe has pointed out that this building represents an ultimate dialectic experience encompassing the two form expressions that were the passions of Le Corbusier's work: *megaron volumes*, "tunnel spaces compressed between vertical planes," derived from the Maison Citrohan; and the better-known (from the Maison Domino and the Villa Savoye) "*sandwich volumes* where the pressure of the horizontal planes is the more acute."[4] It is also an ultimate dialectic experience encompassing the expressions of light in the work of Le Corbusier: the contemplative darkness of the Chapel at Ronchamp; and the open lightness of many of the residences, such as the Villa Savoye in Poissy (1928–29).

The church and the residential quarters contrast with each other in plan, in elevation, in section, and in meaning and experience. The plan is reminiscent of a horseshoe being drawn to the bar of a magnet—the U-shaped living quarters approaching the rectangular shape of the church. The exterior walls of the living quarters are mostly glazed on the inner and outer perimeters, while the walls of the church are solid thick concrete with few penetrations. As shown in the photograph of the West side of the complex, the articulated façade of the living quarters displays patterns of light and shadow from the forms of the fenestration, while the façade of the church is a blank wall with the angular "saddle bag" of the organ enclosure protruding in the middle. In section, the living quarters are layered, sandwich volumes in which floor and ceiling planes are most defining, allowing the apparent space to continue on through the glazing. The church, on the other hand, displays the megaron volume of space sandwiched between solid high vertical walls, with few openings and no views through them.

The meaning of the order of building also has much to do with the duality of the individual and the collective: the individual devotion of each brother, and the collective life that they lead together.[5] The experience of each of these two parts is distinct, each experience defined by light.

The experiences of light result from the form. Light also drove the design process that shaped the form of the building. Light was at the beginning as well as at the end of the process—alpha and omega. Le Corbusier had, in 1923, published his statement that "Architecture is the skillful, accurate and magnificent play of masses seen in light; and contours are also and exclusively the skillful, accurate and magnificent play of volumes seen in light."[6] He used forms to reveal light, and light to reveal forms. His experience up to the point of designing La Tourette included his recording of light in cities and ancient monuments during his early travels.[7] He was also aware of the thermal role that light plays in buildings (see Chapter 1). His design for the Salvation Army Building (1929–33) in Paris and the later addition of brise-soleils (literally "sun-breakers") to solve the overheating problems, his projects for North Africa and South America, and his work in India had all contributed to his recognition of the twin roles that light and heat play. In La Tourette, conceiving of the forms, as well as the experience of them, depends upon light.

Each part of the monastery is defined according to the time of its light. The private cells for the monks face south, east, and west, so that each block of cells receives sunlight, or sees the sunlit landscape, at its own time of day. The refectory gets both morning and afternoon light, sunrise and sunset light. The passages that connect the parts of the monastery, the modern cloister, are adorned with sweeping patterns of light and shadow from the *ondulatoires*. These shadows act as gnomons to the attuned eyes of the monks, indicating the passage of the day and the seasons. The light is the ornament to the stark building forms, giving life to the daily ritual in the monastery.

Colin Rowe points out that what is important

> *… are the distinctions of emotional tone which the different levels of the living quarters support. These are affected by an orchestration of light. There is a movement from the brilliance and lateral extension of the refectory and chapter house, through the more somber tonality of the library and the oratory, up to the relative darkness and lateral closure of the cells. There are the progressive degrees of concentration and intimacy; …*[8]

In the passageways, which are the most communal and active spaces of the living quarters, the ceiling and floor planes—often sloping—contrast with the open views to the sides through ondulatoires. The ondulatoires, or "undulating glass panes,"[9] are vertical concrete casings, or mullions, that hold glass panels of varying heights that fill in the intervening spaces from floor to ceiling. The horizontal spacing of the concrete members was determined by Le Corbusier's collaborator Xenakis according to musical intervals with the underlying idea that the density of the *chiaroscuro* is similar to the density of sounds in music.[10] The ensuing patterns of light and shade therefore display a similarity with musical composition, especially on the west façade where there are three consecutive tiers of ondulatoires. On the uppermost of these three layers, the refectory and chapter house next to it are defined on the exterior façade by these ondulatoires and, on the façade facing the courtyard, by a three-tiered rhythmic pattern of glass and opaque panels. In the refectory, the closely-spaced vertical mullions act as baffles to the sky and the view outside, while the wide glass panels reveal them. On the opposite side, the panels create a strong pattern at the perimeter. Direct sunlight can penetrate during both morning and evening hours, and skylight floods in. The state of being in the middle, between the inner cloister and the exterior world, is clear. There is a presence of the time of day and of the seasons as the ondulatoires cast shadows, or form a pattern against the diffuse sky. At night, three rows of fluorescent lamps in shiny metal troughs reflect light off the ceiling, maintaining the sense of containment between the two horizontal layers of floor and ceiling.

The "sense of brilliance and lateral extension" is due to the daylight flooding through almost totally glazed façades and the horizontal floor and ceiling slabs sandwiching the space of the room. The form and the structure—integral—admit the light. The light then models the form and reveals the spatial enclosure.

In the Student-Brothers' Common Room and the Oratory, the light is more subdued. The Common Room is glazed only on the interior cloister side with a checkerboard pattern of glazed and opaque panels. The light is quieter, modulated by the interior surfaces of the courtyard. There is the beginning of a sense of refuge, of enclosure, where exposure to the light is optional rather than mandatory. The Oratory, a place for private prayer in the midst of the rooms for study, is separate and more isolated. There are three types of daylight openings. The first is the glazed south side of the connecting bridge between the Common Room and the Oratory. The second is two thin vertical strips of glazing at the outer corners of the volume, extending from approximately waist-height up to the point where the wall plane breaks to form the pyramidal roof. These glass strips have brightly colored panels placed beside them, reflecting colored light. The third type is an angled light-grabber that juts out from the east side (the entry side) of the pyramid-roof and casts its glow of diffuse skylight almost exactly over the area contained between the top and bottom of the two vertical glazing strips. There is a strip of fluorescent lighting fixtures along the back wall. One is secluded here, cut off from views of the monastery, but the daylight washes the rough stucco surfaces and reveals the altar clearly. It is not a dark room, but a separate room. The flood of daylight and the view at the bridge seems symbolic, as if one breaks connection with the outer world of the monastery when one enters, and then reestablishes contact upon leaving. It is a "somber tonality" in that the light is for the most part passive, revealing the surfaces but not actively playing over them. The room is filled with light, but one faces solid walls.

The individual cells for the friars are arrayed on the east, south, and west sides on the top two floors. The corridors leading to them run along the inside of the U-shaped monastery building, facing the cloister. There is a single band of horizontal glazing, interrupted by concrete blocks, at eye level running the length of these corridors. Here the visual connection to and from the larger community is regulated, the levels of illumination lower, the effect quieter and more somber. A rectangular baffled window terminates each corridor, the baffle both reducing the brightness seen through the window and blocking views of the exterior, emphasizing the inward-turning character of these communal hallways leading to the private cells. Intense colors, such as green flooring and yellow doors and door frames, provide visual interest and a sense of liveliness in this otherwise muted atmosphere.

The cells themselves open to the exterior at the end of

a long, narrow volume. Just inside the entry, farthest from the exterior, is the washing and storage area, in relative obscurity and absolute privacy. Next is the sleeping zone. The study desk is placed next to the window where there is ample light for reading and writing. Beyond that is the balcony. Open concrete blocks below the railing allow ventilation. Light and air enter through the fully open area above the railing. The "window" between the railing and the floor slab above frames the view. One is drawn to this balcony and to the light and world beyond it—a connection between the outer world and this most private inner world. The cells, compressed versions of the units at the Unité d'Habitation (1946–52) in Marseilles, condense the experience of moving between darkness and light into this one long narrow space where darkness defines the entry and light beckons us to the world outside. There is "relative darkness and lateral closure," and movement between the darkness and the light.

The dialectic of the light definition of the monastery and the church pivots with the large door that is the monk's entrance to the church. At this point, dark and light, sacred and profane, are clearly juxtaposed. To enter the church, the monks descend in the glass-sided passage of the cloister, the ondulatoires sending rhythmic bursts of morning light over the floor, or revealing mists, or shrouded in darkness. They pass from the glass-walled cloister to the vertical enclosure of the dark and narrow church with no view to the outside. Le Corbusier described this room as "d'une pauvreté totale."[11] This austerity, this emptiness, and this darkness do not distract, do not provide pretty images, and do not exalt, but rather force one into one's own depths, into one's inner being, to the essence, to a possible connection with the God within. Perhaps it is easier to make this transition to sacred darkness from the cloister than from the outer world, easiest if one's inner world is in harmony with it.

Whereas the living quarters were private,[12] the Dominican brothers came into contact with the public during services in the church. The church is entered by parishioners and the public from the northeast, climbing down a path along the tall north wall from the road that leads along the east side of the monastery. The entrance is unprepossessing, humble, a mere hole in the wall. Entering from outside, the church seems a stark cavern. It is shrouded in darkness. It stops you in your tracks—to adjust to the low light levels and to try to understand where you are—to comprehend the space. The contrast—the dialectic between inside and outside, sacred and profane, the outer world and this inner world—is pronounced.

The sheer size of the room in relation to the paucity of glazing assures a low level of illumination, relative darkness. But the placement of the glazing, and how it is integrated into the form of the church, shaping its space, are clearly important. The same amount of glazing sprinkled like salt over a plateful of food would have produced a uniformly tasteless room. As designed and built, the openings are precisely modulated and carefully positioned.

At the public entry in the east end, the darkness is punctuated by several openings: a large floor-to-ceiling baffled light slot; three *light-cannons* positioned over the north altar, the Chapel of the Holy Sacrament, and the altars below; two slots that separate the piano-shaped north chapel from the main body of the church; and three small punctures around the confessional. The slot at the junction of south and east walls is said by Xenakis to have been added by Le Corbusier late in the design process to boost the level of illumination, as was the slit between the west wall and ceiling.[13]

The burst of light from the three light-cannons over the Chapel of the Holy Sacrament is perceptually the brightest part of the church. The north altar with the tabernacle rests under the white light-cannon. As in a cave where a ray of light penetrates, the darkness deepens in contrast to this strong light.

The tall west wall of the church emerges from the shadows, illuminated by an angled skylight above. The slit at the top of the west wall, just below the sloped ceiling, signals the upper limit of the wall and the presence of the ceiling, otherwise concealed in darkness. Centered in the choir area, the skylight gathers light from the eastern sky and, during the morning, spills a moving shaft of light onto the west wall with its organ chamber. On a clear day, the patch of light is focused sunlight. On overcast days, a soft-edged scallop of light falls on the wall. In the afternoon, the wall is dark.

The monks sit on pews in the choir just below and in front of colored slots that angle through the thick concrete wall. One sees only the illuminated colored surface, and cannot see outside. The painted sloped sills of the windows color the daylight that enters the choir. The focus of deep colored light over the stalls was intended to provide light for the brothers for reading "without dazzling the opposite stalls."[14]

The altar in the middle is highlighted by its white surfaces of Bourgogne stone that stand out against the dark surround. It divides the congregation—seated in the light that spills from the Chapel of the Holy Sacrament—from the faintly colored luminescence of the monks in the choir stalls. The enclosure of the church is lost in darkness, the corners indiscernible and the perimeter lost to view. There is a sense, even in the daylight, that the darkness of the sanctuary is impenetrable. The sanctuary is high—how high? It is long—how long? As one sits and accustoms oneself to the light, these relationships begin to appear. But they can be hidden again behind the brightness of a glance into a skylight. The parts are delineated by light, but in a way that makes their perception sequential, as in viewing the parts of a painting. It is not possible to get a sense of the whole all at once. In this sense it is similar to the Gothic cathedrals with their sequential perception of spaces, even though the church *seems* to be a simple volume.

The sloped enclosure of the sacristy is dimly visible from both seating areas. Its form is revealed by the light spilling from seven *light-guns* oriented to allow direct sunlight into the nave at noon on the equinoxes, thereby joining the church "to the cosmos like the pyramids and other sacred edifices."[15] The walls of the sacristy—a room where the brothers prepare for services—do not extend all the way to the ceiling, but curve inward, suggesting a separate sculptural volume that is independent from the ceiling.

The light from the two sides of the nave—the sacristy on the south and the north chapel—forms the bar of the cross in juxtaposition to the long dark nave defined by a slit of light at either end. The main altar sits in shadow in the middle of the church, visible to the monks and parishioners alike, approached by them from different sides. The private altars for the senior friars on the lower level can be entered only through the red and black compressed space of the sacristy. From there, one descends a flight of steps, goes through a passage under the main altar, and emerges under the black light cannon at the bottom of a sloped ramp. Seven private devotional altars sit on level platforms against brilliantly colored walls, their sides canted in so that only the horizontal surfaces of altar tops and platforms receive the light from the light-cannons above. The interior surfaces of the light-cannons are colored black, red, and white. Are these colors symbolic—the black of this world, the red of the blood of sacrifice on the cross, and the white of attainment? Or are the colors meant to define planes in space, as in Le Corbusier's paintings? Or do they serve dual functional and symbolic purposes, softening the light in the entry to the lower altars and then progressing to a burst of white light at the end, literally and figuratively moving into light?[16] Perhaps all. Perhaps the answer is different for each of us.

The inner surfaces of the conical skylight well at the far end, at the top, are white, creating a brighter burst of light there than under the smaller red- and black-painted ones. The experience of entering this lower chapel—the most exalting experience in the church—is one of going from darkness to light, both literally and figuratively. The focus of light suggests that the unseen private altars below are the real heart of the church. The parishioners are not invited below to the private altars, and cannot see them from above. This part of the order of the light is not revealed to them.

These altars are the focus of the church, the apotheosis of the daily journey of light that each friar follows. Having left behind his dark cell opening onto the world, having departed from the communal light-filled domain of the living quarters, each friar is now connected through space and light to the public part of the church above, the preaching aspect of his mission. Yet each friar is alone in the light that leads him to spiritual renewal.

The forms and the light of La Tourette are a dialectical composition revealing the perpetual conflict between the sacred and the profane. Le Corbusier saw clearly the struggle between spirit and matter, and expressed it. The essential experience of the sacred revealed in light is in that which is left over from the darkness, that which is wrested from the dark material forms—the light of the spiritual world revealed through matter.

In the interior the essential takes place.[17]
—LE CORBUSIER, WRITING ABOUT LA TOURETTE

ENDNOTES

1. Petit, Jean, Editor. 1989. *Le Corbusier: texts and sketches for ronchamp.* (Switzerland: Association Oeuvre de Nôtre-Dame du Haut, Ronchamp).

2. Jordan, Robert Furneaux. 1972. *Le Corbusier.* (New York: Lawrence Hill & Co.), p. 145.

3. Rowe, Colin. 1991. "Dominican Monastery of La Tourette" in Palazzolo, Carlo, and R. Vio, Editors, *In the Footsteps of Le Corbusier.* (New York: Rizzoli), p 236. (Originally published June 1961 in *The Architectural Review* under the title "Dominican Monastery of La Tourette, Eveux-sur-l'Arbresle, Lyons.")

4. Ibid., p. 240. The descriptive term "megaron" is attributed to Vincent Scully in his 1961 book *Modern Architecture.* (New York: George Braziller), p. 42.

5. Curtis, William J. R. 1986. *Le Corbusier: Ideas and Forms.* (Oxford, England: Phaidon), p. 181.

6. Le Corbusier. Translated by Frederick Etchells. 1974. *Towards a New Architecture.* (New York: Praeger Publishers), p. 202. An imprint of Greenwood Publishing Group, Inc., Westport, Conn. Used with their permission. World rights granted by Butterworth-Heinemann, Ltd. The original edition was published in Paris by Editions Crès in 1923. The title in French is *Vers Une Architecture.*

7. Le Corbusier. Ivan Zaknic, Editor. 1987. *Journey to the East.* (Cambridge, Mass. and London: The M.I.T. Press).

8. Rowe, op. cit., p. 237.

9. Xenakis, Iannis. "The Monastery of La Tourette" in: Brooks, H. Allen, Editor. 1987. *Le Corbusier.* (Princeton, N.J.: Princeton University Press), p. 146.

10. Ibid., pp. 144–46.

11. Le Corbusier. W. Boesiger, Editor. 1965. *Oeuvre Complète,* 1957–65. (Zurich: Les Editions d' Architecture), p. 49.

12. The population of the monastery has dropped considerably from approximately 100 at the opening of the building in 1960. The building is now operated as a conference and study center by the small population of monks, so

the living quarters are open for tours as well as overnight visits.

13. Xenakis, op. cit., p. 146.

14. Ibid.

15. Ibid.

16. Cole, Raymond, Colleen Dixon, and Sherry McKay. 1993. *Le couvent de Sainte-Marie de La Tourette: A study of the passage of light*. (Vancouver, B.C.: School of Architecture, University of British Columbia), pp. 62-63.

17. Le Corbusier. 1971. *Le Couvent Sainte Marie de La Tourette à Eveux*. (Lyons, France: M. Lescuyer et Fils), p. 84, quoted in Curtis, op. cit., p. 86.

FIGURE B2–1 *The lighting condition of the Villa Savoye.*

FIGURE B2–2 *The lighting condition of Nôtre Dame du Haut at Ronchamp.*

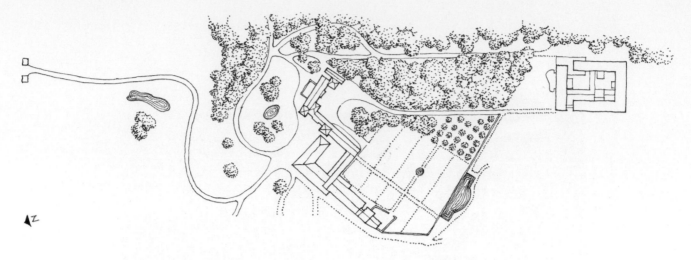

FIGURE B2–3 *Site plan, Monastery of Sainte Marie de La Tourette.*

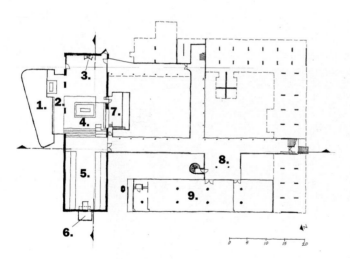

FIGURE B2–4 *Plan, Level 2, church level.*

1. Private altars
2. Chapel of the Holy Sacrament
3. Confessional
4. Main altar
5. Choir pews for monks
6. Organ
7. Sacristy
8. Atrium
9. Refectory

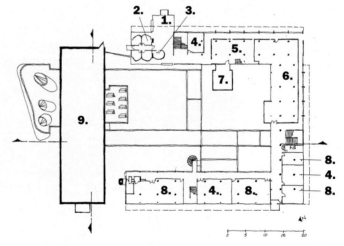

FIGURE B2–5 *Plan, Level 3, entry level.*

1. Entry
2. Parlor
3. Porter
4. Community rooms
5. Junior Brothers' Common Room
6. Library
7. Oratory
8. Halls
9. Upper part of sanctuary

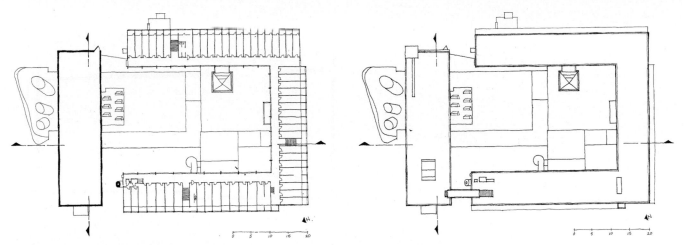

FIGURE B2–6 *Plan, Level 5, cell level.*

FIGURE B2–7 *Roof plan.*

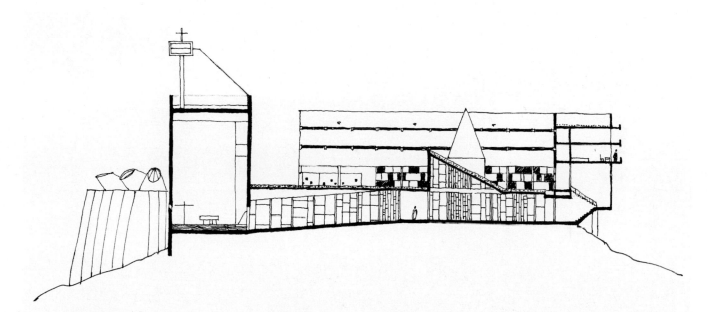

FIGURE B2–8 *Section of the monastery cut through the church (to the left), the Atrium, and cells (to the right).*

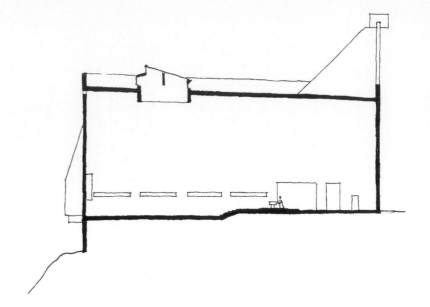

FIGURE B2–9 *Longitudinal section through the church.*

FIGURE B2–10 *View of the west façade, with the church to the left, and the living quarters to the right.*

FIGURE B2–11 *View of the interior courtyard with the pyramid of the Oratory.*

FIGURE B2–12 *View from an interior corridor through the courtyard and out to the countryside.*

FIGURE B2–13 *Corridor in sunlight with the patterns of the ondulatoires cast on the floor. Photograph by Virginia Cartwright.*

FIGURE B2–14 *Refectory, with the the west-facing exterior wall to the left and the wall to the courtyard to the right. Photograph by Virginia Cartwright.*

FIGURE B2–15 *Student-Brothers' Common Room with glazed wall toward the courtyard.*

FIGURE B2–16 *Oratory. Photograph by Virginia Cartwright.*

FIGURE B2–17 *Cell-level corridor with strip windows facing the court-yard. The end window is baffled with a concrete panel. Photograph by Virginia Cartwright.*

FIGURE B2–18 *Exterior view of concrete panel outside the end-window of a corridor.*

FIGURE B2-19 *Cell, view from entry to balcony. Photograph by Virginia Cartwright.*

FIGURE B2–20 *Cell, view to entry. Photograph by Virginia Cartwright.*

FIGURE B2–21 *This view taken between the church to the right and the living quarters to the left includes much of the formal vocabulary of openings for daylight. In the living quarters, view-slot windows open to the courtyard from the upper two cell levels. Below them is the checkerboard glass wall of the refectory and classroom levels. On the wall to the left, concrete panels block the views and glare at the ends of corridors. The seven light-guns over the sacristy and the full-height glazed light slot to the right admit light to the church.*

FIGURE B2–22 *Entrance to the church from the cloister.*

FIGURE B2–23 *Entrance to the cloister from the church.*

FIGURE B2–24 *View in the church from the west end, the choir end, to the east end where the public enters.*

FIGURE B2–25 *View from the east end to the west end. The exterior form of the sacristy on the left is obscure on an overcast day.*

FIGURE B2–26 *Sunlight entering through the angled skylight patterns the west wall with light. Photograph by Martin Schwartz.*

FIGURE B2–27 *View of the colored light slots over the choir pews for the monks. Photograph by Virginia Cartwright.*

FIGURE B2–28 *View of the exterior form of the sacristy with sunlight at noon near the equinox. Photograph by Virginia Cartwright.*

FIGURE B2–29 *The North Chapel of the Holy Sacrament near the public entrance, with the three light cannons.*

FIGURE B2–30 *The private altars for the senior friars on the lower level under the light cannons.*

LIGHT
REVEALING
SPACE

Space remains in oblivion without light. Light's shadow and shade, its different sources, its opacity, transparency, translucency, and conditions of reflection and refraction intertwine to define or redefine space. Light subjects space to uncertainty, forming a kind of tentative bridge through fields of experience.[1]

—STEVEN HOLL

The definition of architectural space is the definition of enclosure, in which light plays a major role. Our sense of space is dependent upon the way that light reveals the enclosure to us. A white room with one glass wall appears open and spacious when flooded with daylight; and mysterious at night with one candle burning, the corners and edges of the room obscured, the image of the candle reflected in the glass which appears to cover endless black space. Put a white curtain in front of the glass wall and the conditions change. By day, the daylight is diffused and muted. At night, the curtain catches and diffuses what little light there is from the candle, enclosing the room with its illuminated surface. We perceive these changes every day in our own homes and where we work and play. We open and close curtains, switch lighting fixtures on and off, and dim them, thereby changing the perceived nature of the room. When we manipulate light, we manipulate our perception of architectural space.

Space, as we experience it in architectural settings, is the result of our entire perceptual system: "One sees the environment not with the eyes but with the eyes-in-the-head-on-the-body-resting-on-the-ground."[2] As we walk through a room, our visual perceptual system tells us both about the invariant structure of the environment and also about our movement in relationship to it. The light is structured both according to its source and also by the surfaces of the environment, so that the resulting illumination of the room surfaces informs us about the room. A change in the lighting conditions means a change in our perception of the room. We perceive the physical structure of the room as unchanging even as we react to changes in the patterns of light.

Our perception of the space around us is based in part on experience and preconceptions. Our perceptual process is revealed more clearly to us when we are confronted with situations outside our normal range of experience, as James Turrell has shown through his works of art. The brain receives sensory cues, but how it interprets them to represent "reality" do not always match the reality of the physical form, particularly in low levels of illumination. Turrell has created installation pieces that at first seem to be flat planes, or "paintings," on the wall, but which in fact are three-dimensional "sensing spaces" that

> *... draw all their energy from the spaces just outside themselves, the spaces you stand in. In those sensing spaces, the energy (the light) diffuses throughout the entire space as it passes through the opening and becomes an expression of the space you're standing in.... (T)he light is diffused ... and the space size is coordinated with the color tone that enters. In this way, the light is made to reside in the space, not on the walls.[3]*

Iltar appears at first sight to be a flat gray canvas hung on the wall—but it is strangely luminous. In fact, it is a hole in the wall. The ambient room light from the "viewing space" has been balanced with the size and proportion of the "sensing space" to create this effect. "In *Iltar* the light tends to materialize something that's thought not to be there."[4] By revealing our reactions at the limit of our perceptual capabilities (very low levels of illumination are necessary for the illusions to work), he makes us aware both of the enormous power of our perceptual abilities, as well as the thin line of their limitations.

Definition of architectural space in light has many aspects. It is especially evident at the exterior wall where inside and outside meet; here light can be used to emphasize connection *or* separation between the two. Internally, the way that light and form interact can unify *or* differentiate the space. Light can also connect interior spaces, or separate them. And light is a powerful device in providing orientation in a building by providing focus or developing a hierarchy or suggesting movement.

LIGHT AT THE BOUNDARY

> *Since the inside is different from the outside, the wall—the point of change—becomes an architectural event. Architecture occurs at the meeting of interior and exterior forces of use and space. These interior and environmental forces are both general and particular, generic and circumstantial. Architecture as the wall between the inside and the outside becomes the spatial record of this resolution and its drama.[5]*
> —ROBERT VENTURI

Light defines for us the difference between inside and outside. We expect that the inside will shelter us from the glare of the sun and the dark of night and furnish us with an experience different from the outside. We expect that it will create a distinct form and environment that fosters participation in the activity that is sheltered there. But the sheltering function is complicated with respect to light. The other elements, such as heat, cold, water, snow, dust, and wind, often need to be excluded from the inside in order to make it comfortable for human habitation. Light, on the

FIGURE 3–1A Iltar *(1975), installation by James Turrell at the Center for Contemporary Art, Seattle, Washington, 1982. The photograph shows a view of the sensing space from the viewing space. Photograph courtesy of James Turrell.*

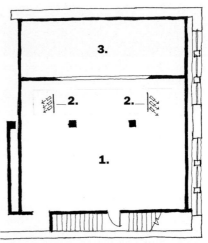

FIGURE 3–1B *Plan of exhibition room of* Iltar *for Seattle installation. Redrawn from Laura J. Millin, Editor. 1982.* James Turrell: Four Light Installations. *(Seattle, Wash.: The Real Comet Press). Used with permission of James Turrell.*
1. Viewing space
2. Lighting fixtures
3. Sensing space

other hand, is most often desired. This situation increases the complexity of the role that the wall must play. In some climates, as in hot-dry, its role is static—to reject heat and most of the light all of the time. This requirement most often leads to a regional expression of massive walls with high thermal capacity, such as adobe, with small openings for the passage of light and air. The resulting interior is usually dark and feels entirely separate from the exterior. However, the majority of climate regions are characterized by at least two conditions, often more, and these conditions can vary widely from hot and humid to cold and dry. Designing a wall that will provide comfortable luminous and thermal conditions inside, at the same time achieving the intended spatial definition is tricky.

Decisions about the relationship between inside and outside are not always based on achieving the most efficient building envelope, but it is important to include climate response in the equation or the inhabitants may be too uncomfortable to enjoy the view. There are glass buildings in northern locales that are exposed to the weather—for example, the heavily-glazed swimming pavilion at the University of Jyväskylä in Finland (Alvar Aalto Architect, 1967–75) and Philip Johnson's Glass House in New Canaan, Connecticut (1949). Clearly their relationship to the surroundings is above all spatial and visual rather than dictated by efficiency in response to climatic exigencies. It can be that the sense of free association between inside and outside is worth more to the client than the increased cost to maintain thermal comfort inside. All these factors must be weighed in the balance of light mediating between inside and outside.

At the two ends of the spectrum, interior space is presented either as a continuum of exterior space, or contrasted with it. Definition of the relationship between inside and outside occurs at several stages in setting the building form, from overall configuration down to fenestration details. Christian Norberg-Schulz introduced the concept of filter, connector, barrier, and switch to describe the physical control of energies that determine regional character,[6] and these analogies can be applied at all stages of the design process. The Italian window pre-

FIGURE 3–2 *Gamble House dining room window portraying trailing vine outside. Photograph used with permission of The Gamble House.*

sented in Chapter 1 as an expression of genius loci can serve as an example. (See Figures 1-9 and 1-10.) These window configurations appear all over Italy—and in similar forms in other southern countries—due to their success in offering a variable means of control to mitigate the luminous and thermal conditions there. In the Italian window, the shutters filter light between inside and outside while connecting air movement; the clear glazed panels connect the light between inside and outside but are a partial barrier to noise, air, heat, and cold; the curtains are a switch which can be open and connecting or closed and filtering; and the surrounding wall is a constant barrier to light, noise, air, heat, and cold.

The window is a major component of the "spatial record" between inside and outside. With its size relative to the solid wall, it determines the sense of separation from or connection to the outside. With its placement, it determines the direction in which attention is focused. With its details, it defines the transition between room and landscape.

The way that light is treated at the boundary, at the exterior wall, can connect *or* separate inside from outside. As Christian Norberg-Schulz has noted: "In general *openings* serve to concretize different inside-outside relationships. 'Holes' in a massive wall give emphasis to enclosure and interiority, whereas the filling in of a skeletal wall by large surfaces of glass 'de-materialize' the building and create an interaction between exterior and interior."[7] These definitions, as well as the details of the boundary conditions that transmit light, convey the intention that is embodied in the design.

The idea of light signifying a connection or a separation between inside and outside, as well as its meaning and its interpretation, differ among cultures, and also through time within a culture. Locally available building materials, construction methods, and prevalent climate conditions often determined the number, size, and type of connections between inside and outside. Dwellings in severely cold climates, such as northern Europe, tended to have few openings in massive walls, resulting in inward-focusing dim interior spaces. In locations where comfort was obtained by exposure to the breezes and shelter from the rain, such as Tahiti, walls were as open as possible under thatched roofs. When the experiences of inside and outside are contrasting (such as bright snowy landscapes and dark stave church interiors, or bright sunlit hills and cool shadowy interiors), separation is emphasized. When the experiences of inside and outside are similar, or aspects of outside are deliberately introduced into the inside, connection is emphasized.

In many contemporary public and commercial buildings, even in homes, we have separated the requirements for light from the "drama" of the wall between inside and outside by the overriding use of electric light. We have been able, through technology, to avoid the "resolution" of light from the outside to the inside and to separate and control the inside to suit our rational and emotional needs. The decision to use daylight or electric light in a new commercial building is often not even considered; electric lighting is most often assumed. Yet a decision to use daylight provides even greater benefits than energy savings.[8] In providing visual cues about the surroundings, daylight keeps us connected to our physical environment. In distinguishing inside from outside, daylight shapes the space. With a distinctive voice for both daylight and electric light, light enriches our experience of space.

Light connecting inside and outside

Dwellings built in the United States in the twentieth century have undergone a wave of changes in light connecting inside and outside. The homes built by Frank Lloyd Wright and members of the Prairie School in the early years of this century used larger areas of glazing than was usual at the time so that inside and

FIGURE 3–3A *Eames House, view from inside to outside.*

FIGURE 3–3C *Detail of juncture between inside and outside surfaces in light.*

FIGURE 3–3B *View of same corner from outside.*

outside were connected through carefully framed views. There were also fewer partitions inside so that interior areas were also connected with light. Later the Case Study Houses,[9] built in the 1940s and 1950s in the mild climate of southern California, used large areas of glazing that seemingly obliterated the visual barrier between inside and outside. Light signified the difference between connector (the glazing) and barrier (the wall).

Cultural attitudes toward the desirability and propriety of connecting inside and outside have changed along with fashions and social mores. In the early 1900s, the stained glass window above the built-in buffet in the Gamble House in Pasadena, California (Greene and Greene, 1907–08), was designed as a connection to the outside, recalling the trailing vine outside that window.[10] The real vine outside the window casts its shadow onto the glazing so that image and reality mingle. Clear-glazed windows in another wall furnish views to the garden, but this colored window presents an equally important symbolic image of the outside.

Later, in that same locale, connection between inside and outside demanded nearly total visual transparency, as in the Charles and Ray Eames House in Pacific Palisades (Charles Eames, 1949). Set into a hill facing south, the east, south, and west sides of the house are almost entirely glazed within an industrial steel frame. Curtains act as filters for the light, providing some thermal protection as well.[11] The Eames House repeats its connective message on several levels. For example, the detailing of the transition where one steps from inside to outside, or vice versa, is very carefully designed and built to intrude only minimally on the smooth transi-

FIGURE 3–3D *Shadows merge the shapes of the window frames with the shapes of natural forms inside and outside. Photograph by Eames Demetrios. Photographs a, b, and d courtesy of Lucia Eames Demetrios dba Eames Office, © 1994.*

FIGURE 3–4 *Entry lobby of the Yale Center for British Art in New Haven, Connecticut.*

tion between them. The level of illumination is only slightly reduced in the interior, so there is not a markedly different experience of light as one moves between inside and outside. That is perhaps the biggest "connector." The floor surface continues beyond the glass wall on the east side, reducing the separation between inside and outside to the thin plane of the glass. On the south side, a gravel strip separates the interior floor from the exterior boardwalk, but the surfaces are kept as nearly level as possible. The physical conditions underfoot and overhead do not change much when one steps outside or inside.

At a more subtle level, objects are deployed in the Eames House to catch and emphasize the quality of the light as it enters the house. A branch of tumbleweed is suspended in front of a white wall, catching the light filtered through the huge eucalyptus trees to the south and west, sending another shadow along the wall.

The culmination of light connecting inside and outside was Philip Johnson's Glass House (1949) in New Canaan, Connecticut, in the harsh climate of New England. The cost of maintaining thermal comfort inside was high, as was the cost of lighting the interior. It was illuminated indirectly by light originating from spotlights mounted on the underside of the exterior soffit and bounced from the surrounding pavement.[12] The interior was thus surrounded by a veil of light which lent its illumination to interior surfaces. It required much more energy than local lighting, as light decreases rapidly with distance, but maintained the illusion of an unencumbered pristine enclosure. So the house is an architectural oxymoron: its visual effect is one of maximum connection with nature, yet inhabiting it requires experiental separation and a large expenditure of energy. The Glass House is a folly, a celebration of the visual delights of nature without regard for the cost.

Even a subtle rendering of light in the interior of a building can make a statement that brings the outside inside. Revealing the presence of the light outside was necessary for Louis Kahn: "A space can never reach its place in architecture without natural light."[13] His office designed several museums—a building type that is very exacting in restrictions on the use of daylight. In the Yale Center for British Art in New Haven, Connecticut (1969–77, completed posthumously by Pellecchia and Meyers Architects), the distribution of daylight is controlled in the galleries (see Figure 2–33). Sunlight and daylight are allowed to enter the lobby directly, however, through clear glass skylights, bringing with them the moving patterns of sunlight and the changing light levels that indicate the weather conditions outside. One can see the sky directly through the skylight, but that is not the point; it is the play of light on the materials and forms, the *presence* of the natural light, that is important. It connects us to the larger whole beyond. This connection is indirect in the galleries, where the light is filtered through several layers, but the clear skylights in the lobby provide welcome bursts of sunlight to mark one's coming and going.

Walking through the corridors of the Literature Faculty of the University of Amsterdam (Theo Bosch, 1978–86) is an experience in which light constantly connects one to the cityscape and the sky outside. The meandering upper façade of the building seems to be the result of an exercise in sculpting the building so that every part is open to its surroundings. The volume of the building, stretched between a street and a canal, is eroded so that every room has light from at least two sides. Sometimes the light is "borrowed" through interior glass partitions, but it is always nearby. The resulting feeling is one of openness and lightness, two char-

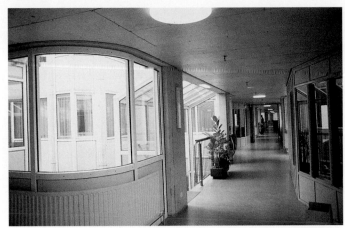

FIGURE 3–5A *Upper level corridor in the Literature Faculty of the University of Amsterdam. The side to the left faces the canal.*

FIGURE 3–5B *Façade toward the canal.*

acteristics prized by the Dutch, crowded as they are onto a limited area of land restricted by the sea. In the Literature Faculty, the lighting levels are higher and the experience of being connected to outside is more immediate in the corridors, where one is often walking next to a half-glazed wall. In classrooms there are additional layers of mullions and panels that block, filter, and dampen the light, filtering the light for this more concentrated activity.

Below the street level, a special effort has been made to admit daylight directly into an underground language laboratory. The site is constrained: the wall with the sloped glass block panels abuts the sidewalk, so the glazing must withstand abuse. Interior privacy is afforded by diffuse glass blocks. Horizontal panels of glass block are located just inside the windows, pulling additional daylight into this subterranean room. The study carrels are located directly under these light panels, allowing the daylight to be used for visual work. The light is physically filtered through glass blocks, but even without views, people in the room are connected to the outside through the presence of daylight, however muted. The connection to daylight is all the more valued since it is unexpected to find it in an underground room.

Using courtyards to modify both the luminous and thermal environments in hot climates is an approach that has been used for as long as we have evidence to see—examples being ruins of courtyard houses in ancient Rome and Pompeii and the existing Alhambra in Granada, Spain. The creation of such an environment in the midst of harsh conditions is a way to extend the space of the room to include the exterior courtyard space.

FIGURE 3–5C *Lower level language laboratory with glass blocks overhead.*

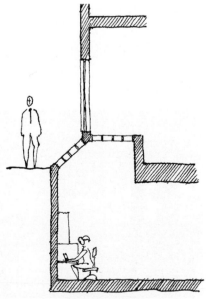

FIGURE 3–5D *Section showing the relationship of the underground language laboratory to the street facing the canal.*

FIGURE 3–6 *View from reading room to the enclosed courtyard at the Las Vegas Library in Nevada.*

This space in turn tempers the heat, the wind, and the light so that they become features of delight. The courtyard is a celebration of the elements rather than a denial of them.

In urban settings, openings for daylight can be concentrated around courtyards where the light (as well as other environmental factors) can be modified by means of geometry, materials, and plantings. The geometry controls the incident sunlight by means of the proportions of the courtyard in relation to the solar altitudes. The materials and plantings modify the light by selective absorption and reflection. Plantings can filter the light as well when they are encouraged to grow over windows. Heat is controlled as well as light. In the Las Vegas Library in Nevada (Antoine Predock, 1986–90), one entire wall of the reading room is glazed floor to ceiling. The walls and ground of the courtyard reflect sunlight and daylight into the room, softening the harsh desert light.[14] Eventually the leaves of the trees will filter the light, subduing it even more. The short bubbling fountains give a psychologically cooling effect, even though the building is air-conditioned. The glass is a visual connector and a thermal and acoustic barrier. The entire courtyard serves as a giant daylighting fixture, that reflects, filters, and colors the light.

In the more pastoral setting of the campus of the University of British Columbia in Vancouver, a similar technique is used in an addition to the Faculty Club (Erickson Massey Architects, 1968). Here in the Northwest marine climate the open-ended courtyard was designed to increase the access to daylight rather than to subdue the light. As Arthur Erickson put it: "In the North the problem has always been how to get enough light in, and in the South how to keep it out."[15] The reflecting pool outside the lower level dining room, in full sunlight at lunch time, furnishes the sparkle of reflected sunlight and a light ground surface that mirrors the sky. It supplies what Erickson calls the "right response to light" in the Northwest, and so is related to genius loci as described in Chapter 1. The reflecting pool at the Faculty Club brings the sky's brightness onto the earth. In doing so, it enlarges the space of the dining room to include not only the courtyard but also the sky. And since the sky vault of an overcast sky is brighter than that of a clear sky, the surface of the pool is brighter just when it is most needed to enliven the ground surface.

Plantings are also used to temper the daylight and provide a sense of connection between inside and outside at the Faculty Club. Vines hanging over the beam outside the glazing filter the light from above as well as blur the distinction between inside and outside. Although in this moderate climate there is no need to modify the elements thermally as is done by courtyards in hot climates, still the quality of the light has been enhanced by the use of water and plants.

FIGURE 3–7A *View from the lower level dining room to the courtyard and pond, Faculty Club at the University of British Columbia; late afternoon, summer.*

FIGURE 3–7B *View from outside to inside during a summer lunch.*

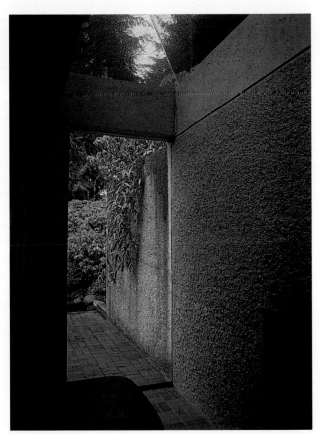

FIGURE 3–8 *View from inside to outside from the entrance lobby of the main lecture hall at Jyväskylä University in Finland.*

FIGURE 3–9 *View from inside the living room to outside along the fireplace wall in the Eppich House in Vancouver, British Columbia.*

The design and detailing of interior spaces adjacent to outside affect the sense of connection between the two. In the entrance hall to the main lecture theater at Jyväskylä University (Alvar Aalto Architect, 1951–57) in Finland, the view outside discloses the subtlety of the connection between inside and outside, revealed in light. The vertical tiling on the columns creates a pattern of light and shade that mimics that of the trees outside, so that the patterns of light and shade of the landscape continue right into the entrance hall. Looking outside from the lobby, it is more than just the light that connects—it is the *pattern* of light that connects. The interior space seems to extend continuously into the exterior because the defining patterns of light are consistent.

In the Eppich House in Vancouver, British Columbia (Arthur Erickson Architects, 1974), a connector between inside and outside is provided at the fireplace wall in the living room, a contrast to the focal warmth of the hearth. The light enters from both a skylight above the wall and from glazing set into the side wall. The pyramidal skylight overhead is fashioned of plexiglas without glazing bars. The vertical glazing is let into the walls and beam above in a reglet, and into a small framing member at the floor. All of these glazing details minimize the visual intrusion of the framing members. The brick floor surface continues outside the glazing. The overall effect is one of unbroken continuity between inside and outside, as the glazing details allow unbroken distribution of light over exterior and interior surfaces alike. The telling difference between inside and outside is that the exterior surfaces have weathered and taken on a patina while the interior surfaces are clean. This difference adds to the sense of the fragility of the protection that the thin sheet of glass affords. It is a simple but elegant statement about the relation-

FIGURE 3–10A *View from inside to outside, shell collection window at Taliesin East in Wisconsin.*

FIGURE 3–10B *View from outside to inside. Photographs used with permission of the Frank Lloyd Wright Foundation.*

ship of inside and outside made in light. It works due to very careful detailing.

Frank Lloyd Wright carried out many experiments with glazing details, many of which can be seen at Taliesin East in Wisconsin (1911–59). There is a distinct difference between windows framed in wood or metal, designed as window bands, and openings where the presence of the glazing is minimized. In the latter, the glass almost disappears, creating the illusion that inside space and outside space are continuous. In the early years of construction, the glass was cut to fit rough opening and the joints were not tight. During the design and building process of Falling Water in Bear Run, Pennsylvania, and Taliesin West near Scottsdale, Arizona, in 1935, the detail of a reglet with the glass let into a slot in the stone wall was devised. In the window of the garden room at Taliesin East, two stone walls frame a wooden shelf displaying sea shells. The glass part of the enclosure is three dimensional—a bay window attached to the outside of the stone walls so that the junction between glass and stone is not visible from the inside. There are no corner mullions; the glass pieces butt together at the corners. From the inside the shelf seems suspended in the space between the stone walls and between inside and outside. The glass is clearly framed into a wood frame at both the top and the bottom, but these details do not detract from the sense of connection. The lower frame looks like a lip to the shelf. One's attention is immediately drawn to the bright garden setting beyond. Although an uninterrupted ceiling plane would have increased the sense of connection, the brightness of the view outside attracts one's attention as much as do the details of the shells on the shelf. One's glance travels back and forth uninterrupted between inside and outside.

Electric lighting can connect inside and outside in certain situations. At dusk electric lighting allows us to look from the outside in and see the rooms that were hidden to us in the light of day. In the Netherlands, where there is a tradition of openness and display, large front windows are often left uncurtained. Then the street at night enlarges to include the living rooms that front on the streets and canals. Looking from the inside out at night, the view is usually of darkness. A view of the sparkling lights of a city or an illuminated garden outside a window at night extends the perceived boundaries of the room beyond the glazing and into the exterior.

Light separating inside and outside

The obvious separator of inside and outside at night is light: "The open fire yielded points of light in the night. This point was once the definition of a place, since the fire was a maker of a 'room,' the creator of private and intimate realms without interior walls. The 'room' beyond the light belonged to the night."[16] This poetic view of light defining space in darkness has been largely lost due to the widespread availability and use of electric lighting. Today electric lighting produces brightly illuminated interiors that defy the darkness, separating inside from outside by vast differences in quantities of light. Electric light now is more likely to combat the darkness through blatant disregard, overpowering it rather than affording a poetic counterpoint to it. At dusk on winter afternoons in the Mt. Angel Abbey Library in Mt. Angel, Oregon (Alvar Aalto Architect, 1963–70), electric light can be observed defining "rooms" in the twilight. The warm glow of incandescent light differs so much from the spectral distribution of daylight that it creates its own aura and separates inside from outside. The quality of the daylight in the library room is so fine and well-balanced that for normal usage only local lighting fixtures are turned on until it is quite dark outside. In the view shown, the reading lamp at the main desk defines the place of activity there. In the entrance lobby beyond the main desk, incandescent spotlights send a warm glow to paintings on

FIGURE 3–11 *View through the lobby of the Mt. Angel Abbey Library in Oregon at dusk.*

FIGURE 3–12A *Interior of the Rio Grande Nature Center and Preserve in Albuquerque, New Mexico. The windows are integral with the displays.*

FIGURE 3–12B *View out a window to the wetlands.*

the side walls. Beyond the entrance lobby is the fog-softened landscape of a winter afternoon. The incandescent light is seen in layers against the outside light. As in the Centraal Beheer office building (see Figure 1–21), the incandescent lighting defines specific places in the spatial layering of the building. The definitions furnished by the electrical lighting distinguish the inside spaces from the outside in the spirit of Fehn's remark that light is the maker of the room.

Daylight can separate inside from outside too. It seems paradoxical to think of daylight playing this role, but light can create a metaphorical separation between inside and outside even when there is a clear view to the outside. In the Rio Grande Nature Center and Preserve in Albuquerque, New Mexico (Antoine Predock, 1982), the windows are designed so that they appear to be display panels. Set in splayed wall niches, the windows are interspersed among back-lit display panels in which the flora and fauna of the surrounding marsh are presented and explained. Looking at the windows, it seems as if a picture of the surrounding wetlands has been cut out, framed, and hung on the wall—but the clouds are moving. The windows are displays too; they are stopping points on the tour of the museum, presenting an overall view of the wetlands to complement the detailed explanations of the parts seen on the display panels.

FIGURE 3–12C *Visitors at the fence between the Rio Grande Nature Center and the Preserve.*

The windows in the building are similar to the "windows" in the fence outside, which are located at different levels to frame particular views and to afford views to short, medium, and tall visitors. The fence is reminiscent of a construction fence, meant to keep people outside the site and thus safe, but allowing glimpses in to reveal the mysteries of the site. There is a sense of being allowed into a special place after having been able to glimpse it through the fence. The windows in the walls of the museum play a similar role, providing tantalizing views into the marsh but clearly restricting access to it. The windows emphasize separateness. The interior light quality is incidental; it is the view presented as part of the museum display that counts. As such, these windows where light separates inside and outside are indelibly tied to the specific context of the museum in which the surrounding environment is one of the displays.

Separation between inside and outside can be a means to mitigate the harsh glare of the light in hot climates. Light quality and comfort were major considera-

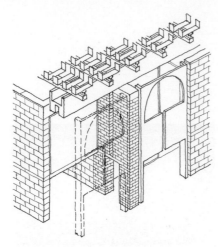

FIGURE 3–13 *Proposed wall and roof construction for the United States Consulate in Luanda, Angola (not built). Redrawn from original drawings in the Louis I. Kahn Collection, University of Pennsylvania and Pennsylvania Historical and Museum Commission.*

tions in Louis I. Kahn's unbuilt project for the United States Consulate in Luanda, Angola (1959–61). In Kahn's words: "I came to the realization that every window should have a free wall to face. This wall receiving the light of day would have a bold opening to the sky. The glare is modified by the lighted wall, and the view is not shut off. In this way the contrast made by separated patterns of glare which sky-light grilles close to the window make is avoided."[17] Kahn thought of it, poetically, as "wrapping ruins around buildings."[18] These "ruins" were not randomly appropriated and applied, however, but were carefully designed to solve the problem of glare so as to provide visual comfort for people inside. These "ruins" would have separated the interior light from the harsh exterior conditions.

In Kahn's proposed design, a very small courtyard exterior to the glazing acts as a lighting fixture, modifying the daylight. Daylight and sunlight, filtered by the shade roof structure riding on the beam above, would illuminate the inside of the outer wall, the *free wall*, thereby lessening the contrast between it and the view of the bright landscape beyond. Looking out from inside the building, one would see a wall bathed in filtered light and, through openings in it, the landscape beyond. The semicircular cut-out at the top would offer a view of the sky. This exterior buffer space would have been open to the sky above and to the sides as well, so that air could move freely through it, carrying off the heat. The thick brick pier between two outdoor minicourtyards would block views from the side but allow light and air to filter through the tall vertical slot and door-sized opening below. These surfaces too, then, would be revealed in gradations of daylight—incident, filtered, and reflected. This free wall and the interstitial space it formed would have

FIGURE 3–14A *View from the lobby through the verandah to the outside, Suhrawardy Central Hospital, Dhaka.*

FIGURE 3–14B *View along the verandah. Photographs by George A. Loisos.*

furnished the means to modify the light and the viewing conditions between inside and outside.

Although the Consulate building in Luanda was not built, the concept of "wrapping ruins around buildings" was used in later designs by Kahn including the buildings in Dhaka for the government of Bangladesh (1962–83). At Dhaka, in the Suhrawardy Central Hospital, the entrance verandah forms an interim buffer area similar to the concept as drawn for Angola. The forms for the openings are bold curved shapes, however, and there are no openings to the sky above. The verandah tempers the daylight and sunlight through absorption and interreflection before it reaches the lobby. Views outward from the lobby are framed by the outer walls that receive reflected light from the concrete floor and white ceiling and are therefore much lighter than the interior wall surfaces of the lobby.

Although the sunscreens of the High Court at Chandigarh (Atelier Le Corbusier, 1951–56) provided a precedent for the development of the form of the Luanda free wall,[19] Kahn's development of space between the interior and the free wall outside was new. He developed a totally new formal approach to the problem of glare—one that resolved several issues of environmental control at once: preventing glare, providing adequate illumination, furnishing shade, affording protection from the monsoon rains, and allowing free ventilation. The surfaces of Le Corbusier's brise-soleils form an interstitial space between the window and the sky, but one can still view the sky directly. The free wall, however, blocks the view of the sky, and the openings in it restrict one's view to the darker landscape. The free wall also forms another room outside the window, whereas the brise-soleil forms a screen. Both forms separate inside from outside with an interstitial space, but that space acquires a different meaning when it can be inhabited. At the Suhrawardy Central Hospital, it affords protection from the elements to all visitors—as well as more comfortable thermal and viewing conditions from the interior—as part of the experience of the building.

Both Le Corbusier and Kahn were deeply concerned with light as a design material, both produced buildings that are paradigms of light in architecture, and each had their own way of working with forms in light. (For a discussion of Le Corbusier's approach to light in a particular building, see Chapter 2, "Formal Light;" for Kahn's approach, see Chapter 4, "Sacred Light.") Le Corbusier tended to try to standardize certain aspects of form that he had determined to be correct, as indicated by the subtitle of his publication: *The Modulor: A Harmonious Measure to the Human Scale Universally applicable to Architecture and Mechanics.*[20] Le Corbusier's vocabulary of forms that controlled light quality was developed through years of observation and practice in hot climates, such as North Africa and India, where mechanical means of climate control were not prevalent. At the time of the design of one of his last buildings, the Carpenter Center for the Visual Arts (1961–64) at Harvard University in Cambridge, Massachusetts, Le Corbusier's vocabulary of architectural forms that modify light had been set down, and he was determined to use all of them.[21] They were: *pans-de-verre*, panes of glass stretching from floor to ceiling; *ondulatoires*, vertical mullions placed at varying intervals (according to the Modulor) between strips of glass; *brise-soleil*, large cross-baffles placed in front of the fenestration to obstruct direct sun; and *aérateurs*, solid pivoting doors for ventilation.[22] Referring to the vocabulary of environmental controls presented by Norberg-Schulz, this set of forms encompasses the whole range of connector/barrier/filter/switch. The pans-de-verre connect inside and outside with light, and are a barrier to heat, air, and sound. Ondulatoires and brise-soleil are filters for light, allowing it inside but modifying it in different ways. The brise-soleil distinguish between sunlight and skylight, blocking the former while filtering the latter. The aérateurs, inserted in the ondulatoires, are switches with respect to all the environmental forces: light, heat, air, and sound. The dynamism of these froms emerges from their use in response to climatic factors and their simultaneous manipulation of the spatial tension at the building's edge.

FIGURE 3–15A *Le Corbusier's vocabulary of window forms on the west façade of the Carpenter Center for the Visual Arts: pans-de-verre, aérateurs, and brise-soleil.*

FIGURE 3–15B *View from inside the north-facing studio showing ondulatoires and aérateurs. Photograph by Ronald Kellett.*

This palette of architectural forms was mixed and applied in the Carpenter Center to support Le Corbusier's aesthetic vision and also to fulfill the building's circumstantial requirements. The ondulatoires developed for La Tourette (see Chapter 2, "Formal Light") were at first intended to be used "everywhere" in the Carpenter Center, but in the end were used only on the curved north wall of the second-floor studio. The ondulatoires (in French literally "undulatory" or "wave") clearly limit the interior space. They form an implied visual barrier that defines the limit of interior occupation while still allowing full floor-to-ceiling views both from inside out and from the outside in. The large expanse of glazing gives a wide view and much light, but both the view and the light are interrupted. They are an architectural oxymoron, a form that says "connection" and "separation" at the same time, an example of Le Corbusier's continual expression of dialectics, of opposing forces.[23]

LIGHT AND SPACE

Light contributes to the definition of space. Our only clue to the vastness of outer space is the presence of the visible stars in the galaxies. There may be much more beyond what we can see, but we can only know what we can perceive with our own perceptual system or by extending it with instruments. Starlight defines the extent of our perceptible habitat. Likewise in the desert, in the woods, in the countryside, in cities, and in buildings, light defines the spaces we inhabit.

Just as the "room" was first created by the presence of fire, rooms are still created by the presence and arrangement of light, whether that be daylight, fluorescent light, or candlelight. The way in which light and form interact defines the spaces that we perceive as habitable and comfortable or inhabitable and uncomfortable. That definition of comfort has changed over time, varying according to culture and circumstance.[24] Light revealing space has changed along with evolving spatial definitions, but in the most powerful instances they work together.

Le Corbusier, writing in 1923 about his experiences in the Green Mosque in Broussa during his travels in the Orient in 1911, described and sketched the space according to the rhythm of the light in the mosque:

FIGURE 3–16 *Sketch of the Green Mosque in Broussa by Le Corbusier, 1911. Reprinted from: Le Corbusier. Translated by Frederick Etchells. 1974.* Towards a New Architecture. *(New York, N.Y.: Praeger, Publishers), p. 168. An imprint of Greenwood Publishing Group, Inc., Westport, CT. World rights granted by Butterworth-Heinemann Ltd.©1996 Artists Rights Society (ARS), New York/SPADEM, Paris. With permission of the publisher and the Fondation LeCorbusier, Paris.*

> *You are in a great white marble space filled with light. Beyond you can see a second similar space of the same dimensions, but in half light and raised on several steps (repetition in a minor key); on each side a still smaller space in subdued light; turning round, you have two very small spaces in shade. From full light to shade, a rhythm. Tiny doors and enormous bays.... You are enthralled by a sensorial rhythm (light and volume) and by an able use of scale and measure, into a world of its own ...[25]*

Light unifying space

In the Byzantine Church of Sta. Maria in Cosmedin (eighth century) in Rome, the simple volume of the church is symmetrically illuminated by daylight. Deep clerestory windows set under the ceiling cast light onto the enclosing surfaces of the walls and the ceiling. Daylight enters from both sides. Both the space and the light are symmetrical. Slight variations in shadow depth from one side to the other indicating the location of the sun. The windows are located high in the wall directly under the ceiling, so the ceiling receives light reflected from the deep windowsill and from outside surfaces. The distribution of daylight from these high windows is recorded on the floor plane, and it is fairly even by the time it reaches there. Candlelight furnishes spots of brilliance, including patterns of reflected light

FIGURE 3–17 *Sta. Maria in Cosmedin, Rome. Photograph by Catherine Jean Barrett.*

on the floor. Daylight defines the enclosure, and candlelight highlights the ritual.

An inversion of this lighting scheme can be seen in Christ Church Lutheran (Eliel Saarinen, 1949) in Minneapolis, Minnesota, where daylight is admitted through the lower walls. In both churches, the light from two sides reveals both sides of the enclosure equally, creating unified enclosures. Admitting the light at the bottom, however, demands more means of control so that parishioners can focus on the cross (see Figure 2–10) without being distracted by light and views at the sides. The particular way in which the forms are detailed in Christ Church Lutheran produces the effect of a unified whole, a softly illuminated, simple high brick volume. The lighting details have been developed to express this unified whole. In the lower and wider volume, wood-covered piers and windows form a muted boundary that admits light without destroying the sense of enclosure. Direct views of the exterior are prevented by the geometry of the lower piers and through the use of obscure glazing. The piers are formed so that views to the exterior are blocked from the pews. The filtered light admitted through these windows

FIGURE 3–18 *Christ Church Lutheran, Minneapolis, Minnesota. Interior view from the aisle with daylight and electric lighting.*

does not distract from the two points of focus at the front of the church: the baptismal font under the low ceiling at the left, highlighted by the daylight washing the brick wall behind it; and, the major focus, the cross.

The upper brick walls contain a darker space, channeled toward the altar and the cross. The electric lighting reinforces this organization. Recessed incandescent downlights cast light evenly over the lower surfaces of the church while uplights from the left cast light onto the upper room surfaces, emphasizing the wall directly above them and reinforcing the asymmetry of the focal lighting. Light and form reveal the space of the church as a unity which is complemented by asymmetrical emphasis on the baptismal font and the cross.

Aalto used a specially-shaped vessel to enclose space in the Parish Church in Seinajoki, Finland (1958–60). The Lutheran interior space, separated from the worldly exterior, is expressed as a unity.[26] Although upon first glance the space seems to be a simple volume, in fact the enclosure is very specifically shaped and molded in light to achieve that impression. Both plan and section narrow toward the altar, the walls converging and the ceiling sloping downwards. These converging forms, not the light, create a focus on the altar and the cross behind it. The window forms respond to the shape of the enclosure, merging light and space into a seamless unity. Tall slots of clear glazing are centered between the columns at the side, the columns for the most part baffling views from the congregation to them. At the top, the glazing widens to span between the columns, following the curve of the cross vaults at the top so that daylight washes over these surfaces. From the outside, these glazing forms express the interior structure and organization. From the inside, the entering light illuminates the forms nearest it most strongly, casting shadows that are softened by the light coming from the opposite side. The white surfaces of the interior accept and reflect this light, so that in the end it is coming from all directions, from all the white surfaces. This even light with subtle variations unifies the interior space. The forms do not stand out as strong shapes for their own sake, but contribute to the unity of the enclosure.

A very different definition of unified interior space for Lutheran worship was created with light in the Kaleva Church in Tampere by Reimi Pietilä and Raili Paatelainen (1959–66). Here the plan is convoluted while the section describes a

FIGURE 3–19A *Parish Church in Seinajoki, Finland. Interior.*

FIGURE 3–19B *Interior window elevation with columns between the T-shaped openings.*

FIGURE 3–19C *Exterior, Seinajoki.*

simple volume with the intrusion of ceiling baffles for sound control. The glazing is located between the tall concrete piers so that it is mostly hidden from view, and daylight entering the church falls on the curved wall segments. The ceiling is dark, shaped in inverted channels, and so blocks light from traveling along it. Attention is thereby displaced to the walls. The surface of the wall segments is raw concrete and the floor brick, both light-absorbing. The wood pews and organ casing stand out as light and warm against this muted background. In the Kaleva Church, the

FIGURE 3–20A *Kaleva Church, Tampere, Finland. Interior view down center aisle.*

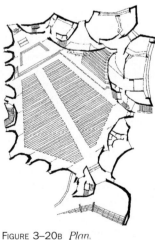

FIGURE 3–20B *Plan.*

FIGURE 3–20C *Section.*

FIGURE 3–20D *Exterior, Kaleva.*

FIGURE 3–21A *Exhibition gallery in the museum Historial de la grande guerre, Péronne, France. Photograph by James T. Tice.*

FIGURE 3–21B *Gallery with curved wall. Photograph by Virginia Cartwright.*

walls, bathed in muted light, clearly protect the interior space from the outer world. The wall surfaces form the effective enclosure revealed in light as opposed to the dominant ceiling plane leading toward the altar in the Seinajoki Church.

Directly washing walls with light reinforces the effect of enclosure. In the Historial de la grande guerre (Henri Ciriani, 1987–92) in Péronne, France, both daylight and electric light are used to highlight wall surfaces. Daylight from above washes the flat wall surface that serves as backdrop for the exhibits. Incandescent light washes the curved wall. The electric lighting fixtures have been carefully selected so that they provide an even wash of light on the walls and are not themselves obtrusive.[27] The ceiling, not directly illuminated, is perceptibly darker than the walls, with the result that the walls, bathed in light, define and unify the space.

Light differentiating space

Light can define distinctly different places within a large area. In the Rovaniemi Library in Finland, (Alvar Aalto Architect, 1963–68) five areas—all visually and physically accessible from each other—are nevertheless defined in light as separate "rooms." Exhibits on a display wall of the corridor are illuminated by fluorescent fixtures suspended from the wall above them. Two parallel lines of fixtures—one line of round "saturn rings" and one of fluorescent "disk" fixtures—define the circulation corridor. A large rectangular skylight draws attention to both the stairs descending to the lower floor and to the circulation desk, while a denser pattern of the "disk" fixtures accentuates the circulation desk. In the main hall, perimeter book stacks are flooded with daylight from a clerestory and scoop. Lower down in the center of the main hall, book stacks lining a reading area are highlighted from fixtures mounted at the top of the stacks, the yellow glow standing out against the crisp white light in the main hall beyond. These spaces flow smoothly one into the other, and yet are differentiated by their light. It is easy to find one's way: each area is visible from the others. The hierarchy of both kinds of light—daylight and electric—and the arrangement of the lighting fixtures (including the "daylighting fixtures") accentuates the divisions of the free-flowing space.

Light can also define a vertical separation of space. This layering occurs when electric lighting fixtures are suspended below the ceiling, forming an implied ceiling plane. Two layers of light are also produced, one directed down into the room and one defining the upper reaches of the room. By limiting the amount of light

FIGURE 3–22A *Rovaniemi Library, interior view showing areas differentiated by light.*

FIGURE 3–22B *Section, Rovaniemi Library.*

1. Corridor
2. Circulation desk
3. Main library hall
4. Sunken reading area

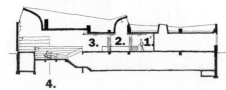

FIGURE 3–23 *Council Chamber, Oulunsalo Town Hall, Finland.*

FIGURE 3–24 *Meeting room, Martin Luther's Church, Halmstad, Sweden. Photograph by Peter Cohan.*

emitted upwards from the fixtures, the upper part of the room can be left in relative darkness, thereby changing the perceived space of the room between daytime and nighttime. This effect is created using suspended fixtures in the Council Chamber of the Oulunsalo Town Hall in Finland (K. and R. Niskasaari, 1982) in the main chamber and also over the balcony. The enclosing forms of the room create one definition of spatial enclosure, while the definition created by the distribution of light creates another. The upper and lower parts of the rooms are differentiated in light.

Light slices the room in half in a meeting room in Martin Luthers Church (Bertil Engstrand and Hans Speek, 1970) in Halmstad, Sweden. Of the two shallow vaults that form the ceiling, one is glazed and the other is opaque, so that the sense of enclosure differs drastically from one side to the other. Light is related to function, as bookshelves are gathered together under the skylight, identifying that side of the room as a place for reading. It is a room with two quite different characters depending upon where one is seated. One is seated either "under the sky" looking into a "cave" or "in a cave" looking out toward the "sky." The spatial division between light and dark, expansion and compression, is quite distinct. It is clearly one room, and a small one at that, but light differentiates between the use and the experience of the two sides of it.

Light disintegrates the spatial enclosure of the dining room at Maximilien's in the Market, a French bistro at the Pike Place Market in Seattle, Washington. It does so through its multiple reflections in mirrors. Covering all interior walls that are not glazed, the mirrors reflect the sky and Elliott Bay, creating a crazy-quilt of reflections that challenge one's perceptions of the edges of the room. For diners seated facing a mirror-covered wall, the mirrors, reflecting the view, become their windows. Space seemingly extends beyond the walls in all directions.

FIGURE 3–25 *View of window and mirrors, Maximilien's in the Market, Seattle, Washington.*

FIGURE 3–26 *View of the administrative offices, Weisman Museum of Art, Minneapolis, Minnesota.*

Light connecting inside spaces

Within a building rooms can be separated from one another physically, thermally, and acoustically, and yet be connected by light through the use of glass partitions. The light is often "borrowed" from a perimeter space with direct

FIGURE 3–27A *Communal hall, Apollo Montessori School, Amsterdam, The Netherlands.*

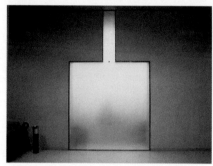

FIGURE 3–28 *Only light is exchanged between the corridor and office space in the addition to the Banco Popolare (Carlo Scarpa, 1973–81) in Verona, Italy. The obscure glass maintains visual and acoustical privacy for office workers. Photograph by Lucy Carter Sloman, ©1996.*

FIGURE 3–29 *Division of light between the foyer and a fourth-floor gallery in the Yale Center for British Art, New Haven, Connecticut.*

FIGURE 3–27B *View of window in stairwell.*

access to daylight and "delivered" to an interior room. The interior space then has visual access to the perimeter, and so the sense of available space is expanded. Daylight from perimeter areas can then be utilized in internal areas of the building, obviating the need for electric lighting and thereby conserving energy.

But light from any area can spill into another. Light can be "borrowed" from an area with relatively high levels of illumination—such as offices—for areas where low levels of illumination are adequate or preferable—such as corridors. In such a case, no additional electric lighting may be needed for the corridor, thereby saving energy. Visual privacy can be provided by locating glass high in the wall or using obscure glass.

At the Weisman Museum of Art (Frank O. Gehry and Associates, 1991–93) in Minneapolis, Minnesota, the administrative reception office is nestled inside the actively-shaped volume of the façade (see Figure 2–18). This reception area has no exterior walls. It is, however, light-filled due to the glass walls between it and the west gallery and the north lobby as well as the skylight overhead. It also participates in the spatial dynamism of the western lobby space.

In the Apollo Montessori School (Herman Hertzberger, 1980–83) in Amsterdam, The Netherlands, glazed partitions between perimeter classrooms and the interior central hall exchange both light and views. Large panes of glass at the top of the walls joining classrooms and the central hall transmit light and views both ways, so that the central hall has light around its edges and the classrooms have light from all sides. Children playing in the central hall can see into the classrooms and vice versa. The lower glazing at door height serves more directly for visual communication at the classroom entries. A passage for light is repeated at a smaller scale in the stairway. A hole in the concrete wall accommodates four glass blocks as well as a small incandescent lamp shielded behind frosted glass. The small "window" at the level of the stair tread is located where children can appreciate it. It creates a special connection—a special window to the daylight and a special place of light on the stairs.

Light separating inside spaces

The quality of light in adjacent rooms can, on occasion, separate them. In the Yale Center for British Art (Louis I. Kahn Architect, 1969–77, completed posthumously by Pellecchia and Meyers Architects) in New Haven, Connecticut, the galleries open onto the light-filled foyer (see Figure 3–4). As discussed in Chapter 2, the skylights in the galleries are specially constructed to prevent direct sunlight from reaching the paintings (see Figure 2–33). The level of illumination in the galleries is therefore lower than that in the foyer to which it opens, and the quality of the light is softer, more diffuse, and less active. The human perceptual system easily accommodates these changes, but one is left with a clear lighting cue as to the different nature of these two spaces.

Only one skylight has been used to define two distinctly different adjacent spaces in the Männistö Church (Juha Leiviskä, 1992) in Finland. Upon entering the lobby, one is immediately confronted with the wall that separates both the skylight and the two spaces of the coat room and lobby. Although a wall separates the two rooms, the quality of the light in each does as much to separate them as does the wall. The light establishes a different character for each room. In the coat room,

FIGURE 3–30C *The lobby. Photographs by Virginia Cartwright.*

FIGURE 3–30A *Division of light between the coat room and lobby, Männistö Church, Finland.*

FIGURE 3–30B *The coat room.*

FIGURE 3–30D *Section through the skylight shared by the two rooms. The corridor is to the right, the lobby to the left.*

only a narrow aperture allows daylight to be reflected from the wall behind the coat rack. The white surface of the wall stands out in contrast to the dark brick wall opposite it. The cool daylight is also clearly differentiated from the electric light, golden-colored due to the brass fixtures. Daylight is let in as a background light. In the lobby, however, daylight defines the wall as the dominant feature of the room. On this side, the daylight aperture to the sky is much wider, and daylight is invited in directly to highlight the wall and spill over into the rest of the room.

LIGHT THAT DIRECTS

Humans are phototropic; we respond to light. The brightest spot in a scene usually attracts our attention first, whether it be a patch of sunlight in the forest or an illuminated billboard in Times Square in New York. Light is a practical and poetic means of providing orientation at all scales of the built environment. It can define a focus, reinforce a hierarchical organization of space, or encourage movement along a path or through a space.

Light to create a focus

At the urban scale, brightly illuminated monuments are focal points and attractions in major cities—the Arc de Triomphe in Paris, the Brooklyn Bridge in New York, Trafalgar Square in London, and the Piazza Navona in Rome, to name only a few. These historical markers serve as guideposts for the city, marking events in the nighttime experience. Smaller structures without historical significance can also serve as focal points for a neighborhood. In Barcelona, a café space is created at night on the Ramblas by the simple technique of lighting a curved trellis overhead. The enclosure is largely symbolic since it prevents neither rain nor dust nor noise from entering the sheltered area, but it does define the "enclosed" space in light and provide a visual focus for this area of the street.

FIGURE 3–31 *The Fountain of the Four Rivers (Gian Lorenzo Bernini, 1648–51) in the Piazza Navona, Rome, at Christmastime. The lights in the fountain create a focal point for the activities in the surrounding market stalls erected at this time of year. Photograph by Dennis Tate.*

FIGURE 3–32 *In Barcelona, a café space is created on the Ramblas by illuminating a curved trellis overhead. The trellis becomes a focus for activity and a symbolic enclosure, visually separated from the surrounding traffic.*

Creating a focus with daylight requires precise siting and orientation as well as careful use of materials. In Orvieto, Italy, the Cathedral is a strong focus at the end of the Via Maitani. The church's west façade (Lorenzo Maitani, constructed during the fourteenth to seventeenth centuries) glimmers in afternoon sunlight while the walls fronting the Via Maitani are in shadow. The façade is highly modeled and articulated, presenting a rich play of light and shadow. Its stone is a light golden yellow that stands out against the darker colors on the adjacent street. Gold mosaics sparkle in the sunlight. Differences in form, material, color, and orientation between the façades of the church and its neighbors focus attention on the church in the afternoon sunlight.

It might seem easier to create focus through light inside a building since the environment is more controlled, but it is often a challenge to balance all the forces that are involved. It is not just a matter of punching one hole in a wall and leaving everything else dark: that situation creates glare. There must be balanced light; but the focus, to be effective, must seem to be brighter. In the apse of St. Peter's in Rome, the sculpture of St. Peter's Chair (Bernini, 1667) incorporates a stained-glass sunburst that attracts attention by its gold color and through its luminosity in contrast to the shadowed sculpture below. Daylight also enters the space from windows at the same level and higher up, providing ambient illumination. The sunburst, however, is set apart by its coloring and by its small size and circular form. The golden-colored light that enters through it plays on the bronze forms of the surrounding sculpture, creating a composition in chiaroscuro. It holds within it the image of the

FIGURE 3–33 *The western façade of the Cathedral in Orvieto, Italy. Photograph by Catherine Jean Barrett.*

FIGURE 3–34 *St. Peter's Chair in the apse of St. Peter's in Rome. Photograph by Catherine Jean Barrett.*

Figure 3–35a *View of the crosses, altar, and pulpit in the Church in Vuoksenniska, Imatra, Finland.*

Figure 3–35b *View of the light sources for the altar and crosses.*

dove, the symbol of the Holy Spirit: the light that enters through this window symbolizes divine light. It is the golden burst of light that first draws one's attention to the sculpture, but it is the many levels of detail that keep it there. Form, material, and color provide the contrasts that focus attention on the sunburst.

Almost three centuries later, the altar and cross of Christ Church Lutheran (Eliel Saarinen, 1949) in Minneapolis, Minnesota, were made the foci of the sanctuary with a completely different set of forms revealed in light. In Chapter 2, the way the form of the cross is delineated in light was described (see Figure 2–10). Earlier in this chapter, the way that light unifies the simple volume of the space was described (see Figure 3–18). These two sets of lighting strategies together create the focus on the crosses at the front of the church. The concept and the intention of the design were brought together by lighting forms to create particular spatial relationships.

The altar and three crosses were made the focal point in the Church in Vuoksenniska, Imatra, Finland (Alvar Aalto Architect, 1956–58), in quite a different way. This composition is one made up of subtle changes in value. The altar is white marble with (at the moment of the photograph) an altar cloth of light gray; the crosses are white; and the surrounding walls and ceiling are white. It is an effect of chiaroscuro, but a quiet one, one in which light plays a larger role than shadow. A light cannon protruding through the roof grabs light from the sky and aims it at the altar and crosses, casting shadows behind the crosses even when the sky is cloudy. Two light niches in the north wall to the right of the altar direct light from the side toward the altar and crosses and, through the cut-out in the wall to the left of the altar, to the pulpit. Even though the entire interior is bathed in light, the focus on

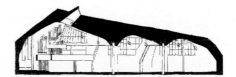

Figure 3–35c *Longitudinal section through the church showing the relationship of the skylight to the crosses and altar.*

FIGURE 3–36 *A gallery in the museum Historial de la grande guerre in Péronne, France. Photograph by Virginia Cartwright.*

FIGURE 3–37 *In a shop in Barcelona, a trio of incandescent globe fixtures not only shed useful light on the cash register but also draw attention to the tiny shop itself.*

the necessary elements to a Lutheran church—altar table, cross, and pulpit[28]—is achieved.

Electric lighting emphasizes and repeats this focus. Two small hooded incandescent fixtures are mounted on the top of the altar table, casting a warm glow on its top as well as throwing shadows of the crosses on the wall. The light niches each have two incandescent fixtures made of brass that contribute warm light from the side. These gentle gradations of light and shadow create their own subtle high-key chiaroscuro to complement the daylight composition.

Focus is often desired in the daytime in museums to attract attention to displays. In the museum Historial de la grande guerre (Henri Ciriani, 1987–92) in Péronne, France, electric light is used in some galleries to provide focus on the displays while daylight plays a background role. The glazing above the floor and at the end wall allows a view out to the enclosing wall ruins—a historical reminder—and also allows daylight to wash over the floor and wall surfaces. It is electric light, however, from PAR lamps[29] that precisely highlights certain displays. The color and intensity of the electric light, as well as the precise pattern that it takes, distinguishes it from the more evenly distributed daylight and draws attention to the objects it illuminates.

The brightness of electric lighting fixtures themselves attracts attention, so they can be used as focal points. Their

FIGURE 3–38 *It is people that inhabit architecture, and to whom attention should be drawn. In a café in Stuttgart, lighting fixtures are located to focus on the customers. Photograph by Dennis Tate.*

luminance must be controlled, however, so that it is not uncomfortably bright. Light can provide focus, either through its source or through the surfaces that it illuminates. Awareness of this guiding potential of light is an aid to using light that directs.

Light to develop a hierarchy

Light aids in orientation when it adds cues that help us negotiate an established spatial hierarchy. As mentioned earlier, monuments and special parts of a city are lighted at night to make them focal points in the nightscape. They then become part of a spatial hierarchy that defines the city as a whole. An example of a special district that has its own hierarchy within a city is Ghirardelli Square (original renovation by Wurster, Bernardi, and Emmons, with Lawrence Halprin and John Matthias, 1962–67) in San Francisco, California. A huge lighted sign on top of the building announces its presence and establishes its location in relationship to the rest of the city. A hierarchy of lighting fixtures was developed to reinforce the spatial organization of the complex. The lighting theme is a variation on carnival lights: small incandescent lamps are used in lines and groups to delineate special areas. The "Ghirardelli" sign is made up of these small lamps (although they are too far away in the photograph to be seen as separate lamps), as are the lighting standards that line the stairway from the street to the square. In these lighting fixtures, bands of the small lamps are arranged in a radial pattern to form a globe. These fixtures indicate the transition from the street below—with its two fixtures with plain diffusing globes—up the stairway to the delights of the square above.

The interior of Stockholms Sodra in Stockholm (completed 1989) displays an elegant hierarchy of light. The atrium is topped by a curved vault of glazing and the end wall is fully glazed. Daylight provides all the light necessary on a bright summer day. Electric lighting fixtures stand by, however, for the long dark winter. White saucer-like fixtures are suspended down the center. The light sources are concealed in the lower hemispheres, illuminating the upper "saucers" which become focal points and suggest separation of the lower lobby from the upper reaches of the space. On the ground floor white globes are grouped on short street-lighting standards, four globes to a post, giving a sense of human scale to this vast room. On the first balcony, fluorescent wall sconces direct pools of light to the ceiling. On the second and third balconies, cylindrical fixtures focus light on planters. Above the top row of interior windows, indirect lighting fixtures illuminate the upper surfaces and the skylight. The rendition of the atrium by day and by night are totally different, but

FIGURE 3–40 *Interior view of the atrium, Stockholms Sodra in Stockholm.*

in each version the hierarchy of the space is defined. In daylight, the grading of light from top to bottom reveals the order. By night each area is defined with its own particular light. The vertical organization of the building and its spatial hierarchy are reinforced by the design of the lighting with both daylight and electric sources.

Horizontal divisions of space are defined in the Resurrection Chapel (Erik Bryggmann, 1939–41, renovated 1984) in the Turku Cemetery in Finland. The mourners sit in the pews to the left, and the casket is

FIGURE 3–41 *The Resurrection Chapel in the Turku Cemetery in Finland.*

FIGURE 3–42 *Communal hall, Apollo Montessori School, Amsterdam, The Netherlands.*

FIGURE 3–43 *Main stairway in the Stockholm Public Library.*

placed under the low ceiling in the light of the windows to the right. The altar and cross form another area of focus. Daylight furnishes the major definitions, washing the altar and cross with light from the side and flooding the low-ceilinged area with light from two sides. High windows on the right sprinkle light into the high-ceilinged seating area, with a few small windows on the left affording more a view of the trees outside than adding significant amounts of light to the room. The areas for mourners, the coffin, and the cross are distinct one from the other in both enclosure and light. Electric lighting fixtures continue the differentiation. Suspended brass fixtures (see Figure 2–45) float over the seated mourners and direct pools of light downward. Brass fixtures mounted on the low ceiling of the lateral area direct light to the ceiling as well as downward. At the altar, candles both large and small glimmer even in the daylight. Each area has its distinctive light relating it to the whole.

In the Apollo Montessori School (Herman Hertzberger, 1980–83) in Amsterdam, The Netherlands, light defines use. The communal hall is topped by skylights and borrows daylight through side openings. The classrooms have fluorescent lighting fixtures for ambient light in addition to daylight from large windows. At the classroom entry, fluorescent lamps hidden behind yellow plexiglass cast warm pools of light onto the wood surfaces of the private work place. There are three levels of lighting organization that are consistently applied: ambient daylighting for the communal hall, overhead fluorescent lighting and perimeter daylight for the classrooms, and local lighting for special individual areas. The spatial hierarchy of the school, from communal areas to private retreats, is reinforced by its lighting.

Light and movement

Procession can be encouraged by light. We tend to follow light. Light can beckon us down a path, through the woods to the open fields, to the end of the tunnel. The brightest objects or points of light attract us most, so relative brightness is important. If one wants to suggest a direction of movement in the dark countryside, the light need not be bright. If one wants to foster movement in Times Square, the light needs to be very bright.

Movement is encouraged by light at the destination. At the Stockholm Public Library (Erik Gunnar Asplund, 1918–27), the main staircase leads up between dark gray walls to the daylit rotunda above. The hovering glass bowl of a lighting fixture catches the daylight, becoming a daylighting fixture in addition to its role as an

FIGURE 3–44A *Corridor in the Camino Real Hotel in Ixtapa, Mexico.*

FIGURE 3–44B *Another corridor by night.*

FIGURE 3–45 *Main shopping arcade in the Pike Place Market in Seattle, Washington.*

FIGURE 3–46 *Movement is clearly encouraged in a fast-food restaurant in Raleigh, North Carolina—movement right up to the ordering counter. The strips of neon, whose image is reflected in a mirror above and behind the counter, swoop into the distance, drawing one along with them.*

electric lighting fixture. It marks the destination and distributes light both by day and by night.

In the corridor of the Camino Real Hotel (Ricardo Legorreta, 1981) in Ixtapa, Mexico, a screen of yellow-painted open concrete blocks creates a clear perspective and a differentiation between the outside wall and the inside wall. The alternation of light and shadow also creates a sense of movement by the rhythm it suggests. The light patterns produced by the yellow screen suggest a *staccato* rhythm that accompanies one down the corridor. The pattern of light changes rhythm beyond the doorway where it takes up the longer interval of a colonnade. An enclosed corridor at the same hotel is made into an event by the spacing of incandescent lamps in low boxes that create patterns of light on the ceiling and floor. These rhythms are regular beats, like a bass accompaniment, steady and repetitive. The light patterns, seen in perspective at constant intervals, mark off the distance already covered and yet to go, registering one's movement.

Four rhythms of light mark the variation of movement in the Pike Place Market in Seattle, Washington: the continuous wash of daylight from the side; the steady beat of the dark green enamel industrial fixtures with incandescent lamps spaced evenly between columns, highlighting the goods for sale; the faster rhythm of the bare incandescent lamps outlining the edges of the ceiling over the center walkway; and intermittent loud accents of neon signs announcing special attractions (just visible in the background). The daylight provides the ambient background light. The industrial fixtures demarcate the "stop and look" areas, where people who have escaped from the current of the central corridor gather in eddies to sample the goods. Reinforcing the natural perspective of the columns and the ceiling, the lights also reflect the relative speed of movement in the market.

The arcade at the court level of the Salk Research Institute (Louis I. Kahn, 1959–65) in La Jolla, California, displays a rhythm of light and dark in daylight and at night as well. The clear alternations between sunlight and shadow, and light and dark, define the receding perspective. The light, coming from the side by both day and night, draws one out into the court. Repeating the direction of the daylight with electric light connects the two situations in one's memory. One is simultaneously drawn both down the arcade and to the light.

FIGURE 3–47 *In the Kalevala Church in Finland, the structure, the light, and the form are integrally bound together in a syncopated rhythm that defines the perimeter of the sanctuary. Movement along the benches is encouraged by the movement toward the light. One is presented with light as a goal upon entering the church, when taking one's seat, and again when facing the altar and pulpit (see Figure 3–20). Light accompanies movement.*

Figure 3–48a *Arcade at the lower level of the Salk Research Institute in La Jolla, California. Day.*

Figure 3–48b *Night.*

All of these ways of expressing space in light—defining the boundary between inside and outside, defining spatial enclosure, and directing movement—enrich our experience in buildings. When light is used purposefully to reveal the spatial definition intended by the architect, then form, space, and light are joined together to create experiences rich in light.

ENDNOTES

1. Holl, Steven. 1989. *Anchoring.* (New York: Princeton Architectural Press), p. 11.

2. Gibson, James J. 1986. *The Ecological Approach to Visual Perception.* (Hillsdale, N.J.: Lawrence Erlbaum Associates, Publishers), p. 205.

3. Millin, Laura J., Editor. 1982. *James Turrell: Four Light Installations.* (Seattle, Wash.: The Real Comet Press), p. 19. Reprinted with permission of James Turrell.

4. Ibid., p. 20.

5. Venturi, Robert. 1966. *Complexity and Contradiction in Architecture.* (New York: The Museum of Modern Art), pp. 88–89. Venturi devoted an entire chapter to "The Inside and the Outside," the formal resolution of the difference between inside and outside and the richness of the complexity possible in the resulting forms.

6. Norberg-Schulz, Christian. 1965. *Intentions in Architecture.* (Cambridge, Mass.: The M.I.T. Press), pp. 112–27.

7. Norberg-Schulz, Christian. 1984. *Genius Loci.* (New York: Rizzoli), p. 67.

8. Energy savings result both from less electrical power consumed by lighting fixtures and also from lower cooling demands. Two watts of lighting require approximately one watt of cooling to offset the heat gain. Incandescent lamps add more heat to a space than do fluorescent lamps for the same amount of light delivered. Since most office buildings in most climates are cooled most of the time, saving lighting energy has a significant effect on overall energy use.

9. McCoy, Esther. 1977. *Case Study Houses 1945–1962.* (Los Angeles: Hennessey and Ingalls).

10. Bosley, Edward R. 1992. *Gamble House: Greene and Greene.* (London: Phaidon Press).

11. The mild climate of southern California requires little protection from the cold. In this coastal location on the sea cliffs, morning fog is the norm, preventing overheating inside the glass house. The line of eucalyptus trees to the south shades the major glass façade.

12. Nicholson, Arnold. 1958. "Mr. Kelly's Magic Lights." *Saturday Evening Post*, July 5, 61.

13. Wurman, Richard Saul, Editor. 1986. *What Will Be Has Always Been: The Words of Louis I. Kahn.* (New York: Access Press and Rizzoli), p. 257.

14. The photograph here was taken on a rainy day, so some effort of imagination is needed to fill in the "harsh desert light."

15. Erickson, Arthur. 1975. *The Architecture of Arthur Erickson.* (Montreal, Quebec: Tundra Books), p. 33.

16. Fjeld, Per Olaf. 1983. *Sverre Fehn: The Thought of Construction.* (New York: Rizzoli), p. 50.

17. Wurman. op. cit., p. 9.

18. Ronner, Heinz, and Sharad Jhaveri. 1987. *Louis I. Kahn: Complete Work 1935–1974.* (Basel, Switzerland: Birkhäuser), p. 127.

19. Brownlee, David B., and David G. De Long. 1991. *Louis I. Kahn: In the Realm of Architecture.* (New York: Rizzoli), p. 68.

20. Le Corbusier. 1968. *The Modulor.* (Cambridge, Mass.: The M.I.T. Press), first published in France in 1948.

21. Curtis, William. 1986. *Le Corbusier: Ideas and Forms.* (Oxford: Phaidon Press Limited), p. 220.

22. Griffin, Fritz, and Marietta Millet. 1984. "Shady Aesthetics," *Journal of Architectural Education.* 37 (3 & 4): 43–60.

23. Frampton, Kenneth. 1991. "Le Corbusier and the Dialectical Imagination" In Palazzolo, Carlo, and R. Vio, Editors. *In the Footsteps of Le Corbusier.* (New York: Rizzoli), pp. 243–49.

24. Rybczynski, Witold. 1986. *Home: A Short History of an Idea.* (New York: Penguin Books), pp. 217–32.

25. Le Corbusier. Translated by Frederick Etchells. 1974. *Towards a New Architecture.* (New York: Praeger Publishers), pp. 167–69. An imprint of Greenwood Publishing Group, Inc., Westport, CT. Used with their permission. World rights granted by Butterworth-Heineman Ltd.

26. Pietilä, Reimi. 1983. "A 'Gestalt' Building" in *A + U: Alvar Aalto.* May 1983 Extra Edition, 12–13.

27. If the wash of light on the curved wall were not even but patterned, then those patterns would attract attention and interfere with the sense of a continuous enclosing plane, as do reflections on the lower glass panels.

28. Pietilä, Reimi, op. cit.

29. PAR is an acronym for parabolic reflector. The silvered reflector behind the filament is shaped to throw a particular pattern of light ranging from a very narrow spot to a wide flood. The relationship between the filament and the parabolic reflector is crucial to achieving the distribution, as is the treatment of the glass lens of the lamp.

Spatial Light: Mt. Angel Abbey Library

Mt. Angel, Oregon, U.S.A.
1963–70

Alvo Aalto Architect
Vernon DeMars, Associate Architect
Eric Vartiainen, Project Coordinator
from the Aalto office

After I have developed a feel for the program and its innumerable demands have been engraved in my subconscious, I begin to draw in a manner rather like that of abstract art. Led only by my instincts I draw, not architectural syntheses, but sometimes even childish compositions, and via this route I eventually arrive at an abstract basis to the main concept, a kind of universal substance with whose help the numerous quarreling sub-problems can be brought into harmony.

When I designed the city library at Viipuri (I had plenty of time at my disposal, five whole years) for long periods of time I pursued the solution with the help of primitive sketches. From some kind of fantastic mountain landscapes with cliffs lit up by suns in different positions I gradually arrived at the concept for the library building. The library's architectural core consists of reading and lending areas at different levels and plateaus, while the center and control area forms the high point above the different levels. The childish sketches have only an indirect connection with the architectural conception, but they tied together the section and the plan with each other and created a kind of unity of horizontal and vertical structures.[1]

—ALVAR AALTO

The "abstract basis to the main concept" of a library that Aalto discovered through his design process for the Viipuri Municipal Library (1927–35) was used again and again in the library designs by the Aalto office. The architectural con-cept that Aalto developed was comprehensive, combining ideas that range from landscape associations to the notion of one person and a book. This relationship between a person and a book in light, which is the essence of a library, was explored by Aalto in his study sketches for the Viipuri Library. (See Figure 1–50 and discussion in Chapter 1.) The "cliffs lit up by suns" became the basic generating idea for much of his lighting: light reflected from a surface before it travels to the receiver, either a book or an eye. That surface can be a wall, a skylight well, or reflectors in a lighting fixture. These diagrams represent an architectural idea, in this case focused on the relationship between form and light to create a space for reading. The idea represented is comprehensive. It relates a person to a book in light as well as to the room.

The technical aspects of these studies are interesting in that they demonstrate Aalto's concern for using available technology to make comfortable places.[2] More interesting is the integration of these technical aspects into his formal and spatial vocabulary over time. The diagrammatic section of the Viipuri Municipal Library is the conceptual basis for all Aalto libraries, each one having been adapted to its own location, landscape, views, and program. The essence of this diagram is the intersection of horizontal and vertical activity zones— "a kind of unity of horizontal and vertical structures"—with a light-delivery system. The spaces are connected visually but experienced concentrically. In the Viipuri Municipal Library, the visually-connected horizontal activity zones are the reading room and the main library room. The vertical activity zone is comprised of the two levels of the main library room, both lined with bookshelves. The light-delivery system is a series of deep conical skylights, approximately six feet in diameter, evenly distributed throughout the ceiling. Diagrammatic analyses showing spatial enclosure, visual connection between activity zones, daylight entry, movement, and light distribution in four libraries—Viipuri, Seinajoki, Rovaniemi, and Mt. Angel—reveal the progressive modulation and combination of these elements. In Seinajoki, the light-delivery system drives the section of the building. At Rovaniemi, the distribution of light becomes more varied. The interrelationship among all these elements is most sophisticated at Mt. Angel where the intersection of horizontal and vertical activity zones and the light are all concentrated under the curved clerestory. This mezzanine area is also the hub of the paths of movement.

The Mt. Angel Abbey Library is Aalto's final library. It is situated on the campus of a Benedictine monastery school that tops a butte in the otherwise flat farm country near Salem, the capital of the state of Oregon. The site is located in the damp marine climate of the coastal Northwest, quite different from the more northern climate of Finland or northern Europe for which the Aaltos normally designed. The quality of light, with which he was so concerned, is obviously different from that of Finland. In Oregon, the shift between short winter days and long summer days is not so marked; the altitude of the sun is higher; there are more overcast days; and there is not usually snow on the ground in the winter to reflect the light.

The library is located in the middle of the northeast side of the monastery quadrangle, which is surrounded by trees and simple brick buildings, the chapel at the head. One enters the buildings under a cantilevered canopy that extends over the sidewalk and part of the driveway to shelter those arriving on foot and by automobile. The metal canopy seems to extend the canopy of the trees filling the quadrangle as daylight filters past its framework at the edges. The central portion of the canopy is solid—a practical consideration in this rainy climate. It also has the effect of lowering the lighting level as one approaches the entry. The transition into the entry lobby is then easy: the levels of illumination outside and inside the glass entry doors are seemingly equal. One moves gradually from under the open canopy of the tree to the metal canopy framework, then under the solid ceiling of the canopy, through the glass doors, and under a ceiling with solid walls on the side. There the horizontal extension causes one to pause and look around. A curved wood-slat partial-height partition to the left forms an enclosure for the coat room, borrowing light from the lobby through the spaces between its slats. Opposite the entry doors, four skylights straddle the glass partition separating the lobby from the library. The skylights attract our attention more by the brightness of their sloped sides than by the light cast through them onto the floor, especially when it is cloudy outside (which it usually is). Through the glass partition, one is presented with a view clear through the library room to the northeast beyond, to a bright perimeter that lures one beyond the low wood slat ceiling above the main desk.

One might guess at the library's character of expanding space by first viewing both its frontage on the quadrangle—low, single-story, unassuming—and its explosion of three-story height and curvilinear form in back at the edge of the butte. There is clearly a transformation from the low rectilinear frontage to the high curved back. This transformation takes place within the library proper, the fan-shaped room that starts at the neck of the interior entry by the curvilinear main desk and then expands both horizontally and vertically. Light defines this expanding space, providing connections between the core and the perimeter and between the upper and lower levels.

Entering the library room, one descends three steps to the main level. The oval circulation desk anchors the two levels together both by its placement and by the wood slat ceiling that hovers over it, a dark plane that, along with the movement down the steps, contributes to a sense of compression. Two skylights over the outer part of the circulation desk add more light to the desk top and draw attention to that area due to the bright surfaces of the white skylight wells. At the outer edge, the floating wood ceiling radiates spokes against the curve of the white ceiling above it, following the curve of the clerestory recess.

Following the spatial compression one experiences proceeding through this entry sequence, there is an expansion that follows when one moves beyond the edge of the wood slat ceiling and sees the curved clerestory opening above and the mezzanine and lower level opening below. There is a subsequent compression, though less intense than at the entrance, through the radial stack area, followed by the final expansion at the perimeter. At this perimeter, the ceiling slopes up to high clerestory windows. The daylight reflected from the sloped ceiling bounces back to the outside wall and the carrels along it, providing good reading light as well as a bright surface that encloses the space.

This account of a journey through the library room is not entirely accurate, for one cannot walk straight across from entry to perimeter, but must go around the central curved lower mezzanine. This route, along which one views the library from many angles, adds to the spatial complexity that one experiences. The clear elucidation of the forms in light prevents confusion or disorientation, however. The organization of the library, from central circulation desk to outer perimeter, is clearly structured, and its order is one of light, centered on the curvilinear clerestory. Looking across the room from any vantage point, this order is clear because the forms, the space, and the light are working together. The unity is especially clear when descending to the mezzanine and then on to the lower floor via skewed stairs that turn back on themselves, taking one on a visual tour that encompasses views in every direction. One descends under the clerestory in the highest space that also extends down to the lower floor, incorporating the entire height of the room. As one descends, there are views out horizontally between the layers of ceiling and floor, always bounded by light: either the outer perimeter light, or daylight visible through the glass wall at the library entry, or daylight coming from the southeast-facing window wall of the Periodical Room. Light always defines the extent of the space and its hierarchy.

On the lower level, the sequence of space and light are different, proceeding from a dark inner convex core to a light perimeter. The light from the curved central clerestory and light from the perimeter bound the space. There are individual study carrels all along the outside wall. They are enclosed in glass to allow the perimeter to be defined in light and the daylight to reach the book stacks. The glass partition wall is a beautiful example of "borrowed light"— light connecting two inside spaces, allowing daylight to penetrate through an area where acoustic separation is needed. The glass is obscure up to the height of the door tops and clear above, providing visual privacy below and a clear view to the sky above.

The experience of the library is one of space and light. Even though the light is active in defining the spatial sequences, it is in fact a muted light (and not only due to the climate) that allows the spatial complexities to work without competition. The curved clerestory captures almost all entering direct sunlight within its well, except on a few days of high summer. The surfaces of the well scatter and diffuse the light, sometimes picking up the reflected color of the red gravel on the roof. The conical skylight wells also trap the sunlight within them, diffusing it to the room below. Light from the windows on the periphery is muted by external vertical louvers, spaced differently according to their location. They are similar to the white ones used at the Seinajoki Library, but here they are all dark wood, reminiscent of the bark of the trees outside. Indeed the effect they have is to block and absorb the light at the north perimeter, acting as a sort of screen of branches outside the windows.[3] The light from the three view windows is softened by interior splays. One is presented with light from many sides, filtered past louvers and bounced off interior surfaces. All the light is modified by external or internal devices, sometimes both.

A richly modulated luminous environment has been created by means of the shape of the enclosure; the location, size, and shape of the glazing; and the treatment of the openings, such as the use of louvers and splays. Each area of the library room is defined by its own quality of light and its relative intensity. There is visual contrast between the areas, but since the light is mostly indirect—bounced around by the white upper surfaces—visibility is very good. The experience of the library fulfills Aalto's statement made when he addressed an audience of local practitioners and students during a site visit to the Mt. Angel monastery: "I try to get light which spreads in the room so that no matter at which angle you hold the book there will never be hard reflection in your eyes."[4] It is a clear lesson in the importance of the quality, not the quantity, of the light.[5]

In the evening, the landscape analogy used by Aalto in his development of Viipuri Library still holds. In the dark we sense people moving in the landscape by observing the light from flashlights that they carry. As darkness gathers in the library, the lights in the carrels and the reading lights along the counters reveal the locations of readers, as do flashlights in the landscape. When night has fallen and the general (as opposed to the specific reading lights) electric lighting is turned on, the surfaces of the room are illuminated somewhat differently than in daylight, and so the spatial experience changes. The curved clerestory surfaces and the perimeter sloped ceiling are both lit by fluorescent lighting fixtures. Their roles of providing a sense of expansion and also reflecting light to surrounding surfaces are therefore maintained. But the ceiling that stretches between them is illuminated by fluorescent fixtures mounted on top of the stacks, bouncing light indirectly off the ceiling and diluting

the sense of compression that was formed in daylight by the relatively darker ceiling surface. The daylight at the edges is, of course, gone, replaced by the black of night, so the central focus on the curved mezzanine and clerestory is not as clearly balanced by the perimeter, even though the walls are illuminated. The circulation desk stands out as a darkened hub at the center of the white wheel of the library, its dark surfaces washed by recessed incandescent downlights in the wood slat ceiling above it. Incandescent cylinder lighting fixtures are suspended over the skylights, at least symbolically replacing the daylight at night, making the skylight wells glow.

Of the six libraries designed by the Aalto office between 1958 and 1970,[6] the spatial definition seems most dynamic at Mt. Angel in large part because the lighting reinforces the spatial moves. From each vantage point, your eye is drawn through a space that compresses to an expansive space that opens up with light, and sometimes through another sequence as well. The modulation of the light reinforces these sequences. The sense of compression at the library entry is reinforced by the darker ceiling and lower levels of illumination. The sense of expansion in the mezzanine area is increased by the light-filled curvilinear clerestory above. Beyond the clerestory, the flat ceiling of the stack area does not receive direct daylight and is therefore darker. In contrast to the total openness of the mezzanine area, the stacks channel views as well as the flow of light.

The spatial hierarchy of this library room is revealed in light. The central area is clearly the mezzanine reference area and writing area, where the burst of light and space occurs. One moves around the central light horizontally and through it vertically. The other areas are deployed around it: the upper and lower stacks and, at the perimeter, private carrels and study rooms. There is a corollary hierarchy of light that follows a similar progress in the vertical dimension. It starts with the light-organizing space of the central curved clerestory, is echoed in the reading places defined by individual electric lighting fixtures along the counters of the mezzanine, and ends with the individual study rooms at the lower perimeter.

The effects of light are achieved with only a few materials of quite different nature: the white painted plaster of the walls and ceilings, reflecting and diffusing light; dark gray carpeting, absorbing light and "grounding" the room; black countertops, also light-absorbing; and wood, a warm contrasting note to the neutrals, used on the vertical surfaces of the stacks and the main desk, in the low ceiling over the circulation desk, and for trim and furniture. Here each material has a clear role to play in describing the enclosure and modulating the light.

The library is a model of energy conservation: the daylight is so well-distributed that the electric lighting is turned on only at dark. Even on dark winter afternoons there is enough light to see clearly, and readers turn on just the lights they need, such as the fixtures in the carrels or the hooded fixtures ringing the upper reading counter and the mezzanine. In such a situation, the meaning of "a place for reading," of one person with a book in light, becomes abundantly clear.

When I stood in the library hall and felt the combined effect of space and light, I knew that we had designed a good building.[7]
—ELISSA AALTO

ENDNOTES

1. Aalto, Alvar. Edited by Göran Schildt. 1978. *Sketches.* (Cambridge, Mass.: The M.I.T. Press), p. 97.

2. In the Viipuri Library, the heating, cooling, and ventilation system was integrated with the building form and construction as well. See Fleig, Karl, Editor. 1963. *Alvar Aalto. Volume I, 1922–1962.* (Zürich: Les Editions d'Architecture Artemis), pp. 44–59.

3. Similar vertical louvers do not work so well on the south side of the building where they cover the windows to offices. Here they cast disconcerting patterns of sunlight and shadow over the desks.

4. Canty, Donald. 1992. *Lasting Aalto Masterwork.* (St. Benedict, Oreg.: Mount Angel Abbey), p. 29.

5. For Aalto's comments on the importance of light quality, see his 1935 lecture "Rationalism and Man" (pp. 47–51) and his 1955 lecture "Between Humanism and Materialism" (pp. 130–33) in Aalto, op. cit..

6. The library in the Wolfsburg Cultural Center in Germany (1958–63); the library in Scandinavian House, Reykjavik, Iceland (1962–68); in Finland, the libraries in Seinajoki (1963–65), Rovaniemi (1963–68), and at the Institute of Technology in Otaniemi (1964–69); and in the United States, Mt. Angel Abbey Library.

7. Remark written by Elissa Aalto following her 1980 visit to the library. Alvar Aalto, who died in 1976, never saw the library. Reported in: Canty, op. cit., p. 30.

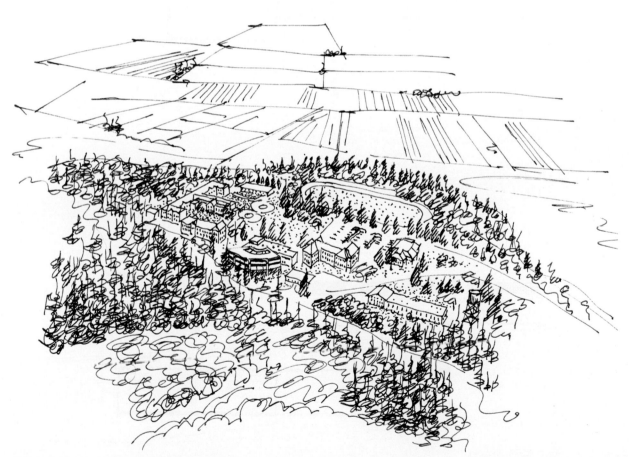

FIGURE B3–1 *Mt. Angel Abbey Library, aerial view.*

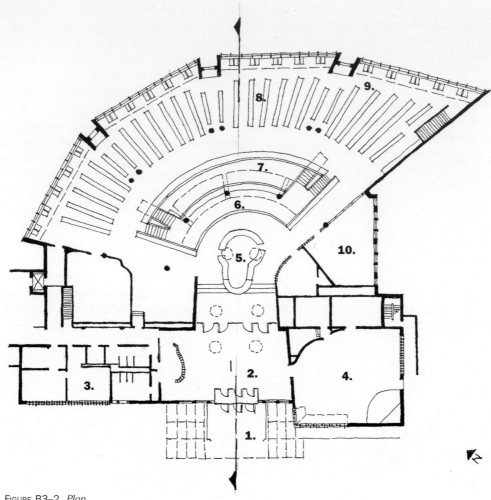

FIGURE B3–2 *Plan.*

1. Entry
2. Lobby/exhibits
3. Offices
4. Auditorium
5. Circulation desk
6. Mezzanine
7. Open to lower level
8. Book stacks
9. Reading Carrels
10. Periodical room

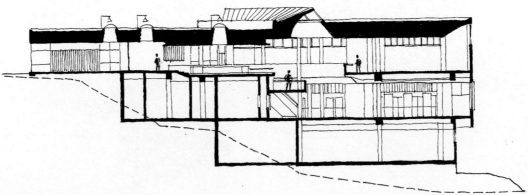

FIGURE B3–3 *Section.*

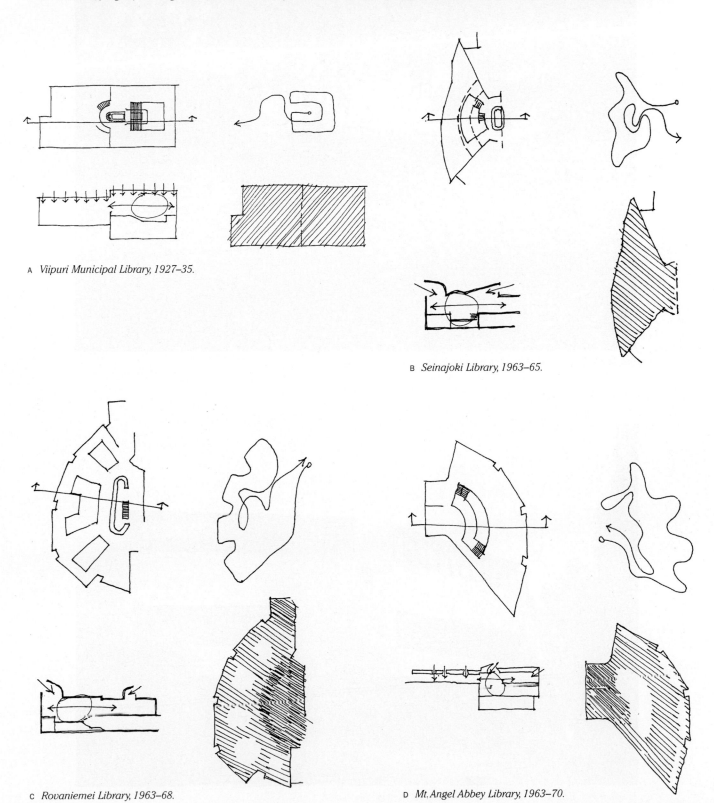

FIGURE B3–4 *Diagrammatic analysis of four Aalto libraries. Top left: plan diagram showing section cut. Bottom left: section diagram indicating the visual connection of horizontal activity zones by a horizontal line with arrowheads, the vertical connection by a loop, and light delivery system by small arrows. Top right: plan diagram of movement through the library. Bottom right: lighting diagram of relative levels of daylight illumination.*

A *Viipuri Municipal Library, 1927–35.*

B *Seinajoki Library, 1963–65.*

C *Rovaniemei Library, 1963–68.*

D *Mt. Angel Abbey Library, 1963–70.*

FIGURE B3–5 *Exterior view of main entry to library from quadrangle.*

FIGURE B3–6 *Exterior view of faceted library façade from the Northwest.*

FIGURE B3–7 *Interior view of the entry lobby. Entry doors from outside are to the left; doors into the library are to the right.*

FIGURE B3–8 *The view from the circulation desk encompasses the entire breadth and depth of the library.*

FIGURE B3–9 *View back to the circulation desk through the central curved mezzanine reference area.*

FIGURE B3–10 *A similar view with the addition of the electric lighting.*

FIGURE B3–11 *The entire height of the library is included under the curved clerestory.*

FIGURE B3–12 *Slivers of sunlight enter the library through the curved clerestory on a summer afternoon.*

FIGURE B3–13 *The lighting is subdued in the perimeter reading carrels on a winter afternoon.*

FIGURE B3–14 *Three view windows with beveled surrounds afford views to the valley below. The beveled sides catch the daylight entering through the window, softening the contrast between views of interior and exterior surfaces.*

FIGURE B3–16 *View from the lower level up into the curved central clerestory.*

FIGURE B3–15 *View from one of the view slots back to the circulation desk. The layering of the light and the dominance of the curved central clerestory are evident.*

FIGURE B3–17 *View from a stairwell to the perimeter of the lower level.*

FIGURE B3–18 *The perimeter study carrels on the lower level with glazed inner partitions providing borrowed light.*

LIGHT REVEALING MEANING

For it is through symbols that man finds his way out of his particular situation and 'opens himself' to the general and the universal. Symbols awaken individual experience and transmute it into a spiritual act, into metaphysical comprehension of the world.[1]

—MIRCEA ELIADE

A particular symbol system and the world view that supported it may have disintegrated, but the natural language of sky and earth, light and dark, order and mass, support and load, vertical and horizontal, remains available to the architect to create buildings that . . . will speak of the promise of an ideal dwelling.[2]

—KARSTEN HARRIES

The natural language of light and dark is a powerful one with which to express meaning in architecture. Light, in revealing architecture, simultaneously reveals the meaning in the building, be it sublime or banal.

Light symbolizes that which is beyond our normal comprehension. This symbolic role of light is recognized in everyday homilies, such as "the light at the end of the tunnel." It is revelatory, as in "seeing the light." It is connected with creation—"let there be light." In all religions, special meaning is accorded to light, and it is interpreted in many different ways.

Light has the capacity to move us.[3] A sunrise, the colored mosaic of light moving across the surfaces of a Gothic cathedral, the darkness of a Nordic stave church, or a disco light glittering over a crowd of dancers—all convey a certain meaning to us which differs according to our momentary state of being. When we are moved, we may extend our awareness beyond our current physical state into the realm of the unknown, the unfathomable.

Darkness—the absence of light—is part of our experience of light. Just as black is necessary to complete the definition of white, so darkness is necessary to complete the experience of light. Light can reveal *or* suppress. Darkness, in suppressing visual perception, represents the unknown, provoking many responses. Fear is a particular and strong reaction to darkness, as described by Washington Irving in *The Legend of Sleepy Hollow*:

> *What fearful shapes and shadows beset his path amidst the dim and ghastly glare of a snowy night!—With what wistful look did he eye every trembling ray of light streaming across the waste fields from some distant window!—How often was he appalled by some shrub covered with snow, which, like a sheeted spectre, beset his very path!—...*
>
> *All these, however, were mere terrors of the night, phantoms of the mind that walk in darkness; and though he had seen many spectres in his time, and been more than once beset by satan in divers shapes, in his lonely perambulations, yet daylight put an end to all these evils;...* [4]

A metaphysical look at the meaning of life is another response to darkness, as in this poem written by Rainer Maria Rilke:

> *You darkness, that I come from,*
> *I love you more than all the fires*
> *that fence in the world,*
> *for the fire makes*
> *a circle of light for everyone,*
> *and then no one outside learns of you.*
>
> *But the darkness pulls in everything:*
> *shapes and fires, animals and myself,*
> *how easily it gathers them!—*
> *powers and people—*
>
> *and it is possible a great energy is moving near me.*
>
> *I have faith in nights.* [5]

Darkness as well as light is rich in associations and carries with it the potential for expressing meaning. Its effects can induce a mood, a feeling, or a state of mind. Appreciation of darkness can lead to a contemplative light. Festive light, on the other hand, celebrates a holiday or a place. Theatrical light dramatizes a setting or an event. Metaphorical light suggests comparison with another place or concept. Symbolic light represents something else, often something even more immaterial than itself, such as the abstraction of infinity. The light then gains meaning through association with that which is symbolized. Divine light is a special aspect of symbolic light that represents the deity.

CONTEMPLATIVE LIGHT

The Mexican architect Luis Barragan was sensitive to the need for relief from high levels of illumination that define most of our contemporary environments. Barragan advocated "half-light":

> *Architects are forgetting the need of human beings for half-light, the sort of*

FIGURE 4–1 *An interior view in Kusakabe Mingei-kan in Takayama, Japan. Photograph by Patricia Emmons.*

FIGURE 4–2A *View of the living room in the Schindler House.*

 — top right plan

FIGURE 4–2B *Plan showing integration of the landscape and the building. The light is filtered and softened through plantings in small exterior courtyards.*

light that imposes a tranquillity, in their living rooms as well as in their bedrooms. . . . We should try to recover mental and spiritual ease and to alleviate anxiety, the salient characteristic of these agitated times, and the pleasures of thinking, working, conversing are heightened by the absence of glaring, distracting light.[6]

Junichiro Tanizaki, in his booklet *In Praise of Shadows*, describes the sense of tranquillity that accompanies darkness in traditional Japanese culture:

. . . when we gaze into the darkness that gathers behind the crossbeam, around the flower vase, beneath the shelves, though we know perfectly well it is mere shadow, we are overcome with the feeling that in this small corner of the atmosphere there reigns complete and utter silence; that here in the darkness immutable tranquillity holds sway.[7]

The house on Kings Road that Rudolf Schindler built for his family and the Clyde Chase family in Hollywood in 1921–22 alludes to the Japanese sense of light

FIGURE 4–3A *Interior of the Council Chamber in the Säynätsalo Town Hall in Finland. View to the corridor on the south from the rear of the chamber.*

FIGURE 4–3B *View to the front corner of the chamber, showing the large shuttered window in the north wall and the small louvered window behind the President's desk.*

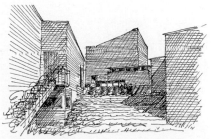

FIGURE 4–3C *Exterior sketch view. The small window behind the President's desk is seen on the left of the west face of the Council Chamber block, which is located in the middle.*

FIGURE 4–4 *Certain activities are associated with certain levels of illumination, such as dark nightclubs and bright workplaces. In the Centraal Beheer office building (Herman Hertzberger, 1968–72) in Appeldoorn, The Netherlands, there is an employee café area that looks and feels like a nightclub. The lighting is intimate and warm and kept low to the tables except for circular coffers that offer highlights of incandescent warmth. The intention was to create a relaxed state of mind in contrast to the work place, and to signal it in the arrangement of furnishings and the lighting. Perhaps not quiet enough for contemplation, still the café offers a distinctly different atmosphere than do the working quarters.*

FIGURE 4–5 *Gallery in the Louisiana Museum in Humlebaek, Denmark.*

FIGURE 4–6 *Corridor in the museum Historial de la grande guerre, Péronne, France. Photograph by Virginia Cartwright.*

without slavish copying of the forms. It contains muted light and the character of peaceful repose of Japanese dwellings. The landscaping around the house contributes to this effect, with screening shade plants near the windows that filter the light before it enters the interior. The configuration of the windows with respect to the rooms is a creative adaptation of the feeling of a Japanese room to the southern California climate without copying any of the forms, such as *shoji*. Certain walls are almost entirely glass, but the effect of the bright southern California light is muted by exterior plantings. Other walls have limited openings, such as the vertical slots in the living room. The wall finishes are matte, softening the California sunlight. The dark wood ceiling absorbs the light and darkens the room. Pieces of shiny metal, such as the copper fireplace hood, reflect light, providing subtle glimmering accents.

Contemplative light is a condition of one of the most powerful rooms designed by Alvar Aalto, the Council Chamber in the Säynätsalo Town Hall (1950–52). In contrast to the many large, airy white rooms one is accustomed to seeing in buildings designed by the Aalto office, this room is dark and seems to have been roughly hewn out of the landscape. The intention seems to be to remind the town council members of their close ties to nature and their dependence upon it. But the darkness is not a complete darkness; it is a balanced dimness that allows one to see the people and papers necessary for the pursuit of government. Daylight spills in from high clerestory windows in two adjacent walls: above the stairway and entry corridor to the south; and above the public gallery on the west side at the back of the room. Daylight is also admitted, seemingly reluctantly, through a huge window on the north side of the chamber. This window offers a potential connection with the outside, but it is shuttered with wood louvers, set within the window mullions, that color, warm and mute the daylight.

Behind the President's desk at the front of the room, at the same level as the desk top, is a small window shuttered so that the presence of the daylight is detected only by means of the light that is reflected by the shutters to the brick wall. There is a definite sense of separation from the world outside and a turning inward for contemplation. This sense of separation is heightened by the absorptive surfaces of the room: the rough-textured brick walls, the black desk tops, and the warm polished wood of furnishings and shutters. For much of the year the daylight is only seldom present, and for those long dark days the electric lighting fixtures provide pools of light on the black desk tops of the council members. The fixtures themselves—black cylinders suspended from the ceiling on long cords—disappear in the darkness at the top of the room. The focus is always on the council members, not the room containing them.

Contemplation is an aspect of certain other activities as well, such as visiting museums and considering their contents. One function of light in museums, that of viewing the objects, was discussed in "Light and the Task" (Chapter 1); another purpose, that of recreating the experience of a particular place to enhance a collection, was discussed in "Experiential Light" (Chapter 1). The idea of light fostering contemplation in museums is yet another aspect of its role, one that was briefly mentioned with regard to Kahn's approach to the viewer and the art which will be taken up again in "Sacred Light" at the end of this chapter. One approach to supporting concentration and contemplation has been to remove museum interiors from the experience of everyday life. The inside of the resultant white box is another world, symbolically removed from the material presence of strong colors and textures that might distract one from observing the pure harmony of the art itself, that might distract one from "the myth of the eternality and transcendence of pure form."[8] Especially in modern museums and art galleries, we are often presented with a neutral container for works of art. This sense of removal from ordinary space and time is further accomplished by a diffuse light that has been filtered through reflectors and diffusers until it has lost its character. In the Louisiana

Museum (Jorgen R. Bo and Vilhelm Wohlert, 1959–82) in Humlebaek, Denmark, modern art is displayed in a series of deftly designed airy pavilions. Light is admitted in different ways, from the side (see Figure 1–54) and from overhead, directly or through layers of louvers and baffles. When the daylight is diffused and baffled it does not create patterns that conflict with viewing the paintings and sculptures. Contemplation is nourished by lack of distractions, either in the container or in the light that reveals both it and the art.

A similar effect is produced in a corridor in the museum Historial de la grande guerre (Henri Ciriani, 1987–92) in Péronne, France. With a gleaming wall and floor and deep light baffles, all off-white, the effect is somewhat antiseptic, decidedly neutral, and empty in contrast to the detailed and moving exhibits in the galleries (see Figures 3–21 and 3–36). Contemplation is encouraged by the neutrality of the light, the color, and the forms. This corridor offers a transitional contemplative light between the emotional impact of the gallery exhibits and the outside world.

Certain paintings demand a particular light. In contemplating a Rothko painting, the light in the room should be background light so that the light in the painting can be revealed. A special setting has been designed for paintings by Mark Rothko in the Museum of Contemporary Art in Los Angeles (Arata Isosaki, 1981–86) that limits the amount of light so that the room seems dim and the paintings luminous. The low levels of illumination require one to stop and allow one's eyes to adjust in order to see clearly; this dimness also causes one to stand close to the painting. The design of the Rothko Gallery makes it intentionally dim due to the very small skylight aperture in relation to the volume and wall surface of the

FIGURE 4–7A *The Rothko Gallery in the Museum of Contemporary Art in Los Angeles, California. View of the splayed skylight wells.*

FIGURE 4–7B *The room and paintings as viewed upon entry.*

FIGURE 4–7C Untitled, *Mark Rothko, 1955, oil on canvas, 81½ by 43 inches. Collection Walker Art Center, Minneapolis. Gift of Judy and Kenneth Dayton, 1991.*

room, the distance of this light source from the paintings, and the deep ceiling coffers that accept the entering daylight on their surfaces and in turn distribute it to the room below. Contemplating a Rothko painting in sympathetic light, one can lose oneself the same way one can lose oneself in a dark room. It is an experience that leads to symbolic light—light that leads one to contemplate life beyond the finite and temporal.

FESTIVE LIGHT

Festivals and festive activities are often accompanied by special light: candles on Christmas trees; *farolitos*[9]; lights that festoon city streets all over the world for special festivals; lights that outline rides and features at Tivoli Gardens in Copenhagen and Disneyland in California; and lights in Las Vegas, to name a few. The light is almost always presented as pinpoints of light that disclose a shape, such as the outline of a building or pictorial elements. They are celebrations of the night, pushing back the darkness in a festive display that defies the fearful nature of the darkness. The origin of festive lights may well have been connected with the imitation of starlight, the heavenly constellations that were the evidence of humanity's relationship with the greater macrocosmic order as well as the basis for the practical aid of navigation. Fire itself is another possible origin—fire that offered human beings some protection in the night, some control of the nighttime environment. When that fire can be controlled to small flames that do not threaten to burn down the surroundings, the element of fire is controlled to the point of eliciting delight. It seems plausible that the dual associations of the taming of fire and the outlining of shapes that define a place—as the stars do the heavens—would provoke intuitive primal responses to festive light.

The city of Victoria is the capital of the province of British Columbia in Canada. It is also a vacation resort, attracting visitors with magnificent gardens, museums, and quaint shopping streets. One of the attractions by night is the government buildings themselves. Outlined in pinpoints of light and framed by decorative street lamps with hanging baskets of flowers, they make a festive backdrop for a stroll along the waterfront.

At Tivoli Gardens, as at amusement parks around the world, festive lights

FIGURE 4–8 *Lines of small clear incandescent lamps outline the Government Buildings in Victoria, British Columbia, adding to the festive atmosphere of the capital, which also serves as an attraction in this vacation resort.*

FIGURE 4–9 *Pinpoints of light outline features of a building at Tivoli Gardens in Copenhagen, Denmark. Representations of fireworks are also part of the display. Photograph by Dennis Tate.*

FIGURE 4–10 *The "Parade of Lights" at Disneyland in Anaheim, California.*

announce that this area is a world apart: this area is for play, not for work. Features of a building make a fanciful pattern that is outlined in lights under a "Tivoli" sign. A delicate framework has also been added that holds lamps outlining an explosive pattern of fireworks, an image in lights that reinforces the celebratory character of Tivoli Gardens. The lighting sets the stage for the recreational activities that Tivoli offers, and differentiates it from the everyday working world. The lighting creates the ambiance for a world of escape and illusion that borders on, and can include, theatrical light.

The festivities at Disneyland in Anaheim, California, are completed each day with a spectacular "Parade of Lights" that verges on theater. Accompanied by real fireworks, fantastic electrically illuminated "floats" are presented, such as a dancing, smoking dragon, and a clock tower surrounded by dancing girls in costumes with patterns outlined in "fairy lights." The celebration is expressed in festive light—light that catches the mood of play—presenting a fantasy in which all are invited to participate.

Technological advances have presented the laser, a lighting tool that has replaced strings of light for certain festive occasions. Motoko Ishii, a Japanese lighting designer with a renowned international practice, has created several laser art performances that carry festive light over into the realm of theatrical light.

THEATRICAL LIGHT

Theatrical light adds drama by creating illusion. Lasers and fireworks add theatrical light to festive light. Lasers are relatively new, but people have grown up with fireworks in many cultures. Although fireworks can be invested with different cultural meanings, they are usually connected with the joy of a celebration such as the Fourth of July in the United States, Guy Fawkes Day in Great Britain, or Bastille Day in France. Some of these celebrations have their origins in battles in which there were "bombs bursting in air," in the words of the United States anthem, which produced a far different state of mind than joy. The association of fireworks with joy and celebrations is an acquired one, judging from the fear and terror of young children upon their first exposure.

FIGURE 4–11 Son et lumière *at the El Castillo pyramid at Chichen-Itza in the Yucatan, Mexico.*

FIGURE 4–12A (LEFT) *View of the Wonder Wall at the New Orleans World Fair of 1984.*

FIGURE 4–12B (ABOVE) *Detail view of "leaves" of a tree in the Wonder Wall, showing the calculated use of materials to reflect and model light. Photographs © Alan Karchmer.*

Illusion can be created quite easily through the manipulation of light since we are phototropic beings. Our attention is attracted by light, and we assess form and space by the way it is rendered in light. That is why illusion depends upon darkness and control of the light, as in the theater and in "horror houses" and rides at Disneyland. In the theater, careful manipulation of lighting effects can change our perception of the time of day or the season, or take the scene from inside to outside.

As in the theater, lighting is used to create specific luminous conditions during *sons et lumières* (sound and light shows) at famous monuments throughout the world. At Chichen-Itza, a Mayan temple complex in the Yucatan in Mexico, red lights are arranged to reproduce the effect of the "snake shadow" that occurs on the side of the stairway of the Great Pyramid, *El Castillo*, an hour before sunset at the equinoxes.[10] Here a natural event with cultural meaning is reproduced nightly with theatrical light for tourists in order to dramatize the event and to convey information about the temple complex and the culture that created it.

World fairs and expositions are festivals that celebrate a diversity of cultures and achievements and offer a glimpse of the future. Some of them are presented with theatrical lighting that nudges the experience of the fair into the realm of delightful fantasy. The Wonder Wall (Perez Associates with Charles Moore, lighting designed by Richard Peters, sculpture by Joy Wulke) that surrounded the New Orleans World Fair of 1984 was intended to do just that. Using numerous light sources and techniques, the Wonder Wall was intended to reinforce the fantasy theme of the fair. The lower portions

FIGURE 4–13 *View of the passage between concourses at the United Airlines Terminal at O'Hare Airport in Chicago, Illinois.*

of the Wonder Wall housed man and place, such as shops; the middle regions represented an ethereal, mystical world; and the top areas suggested a celestial realm.[11] The lighting of the wall was controlled through a computer to which Richard Peters had remote access, enabling the lighting levels and sequences to be changed. The themes the lighting suggested, along with the constantly shifting patterns of moving lights, played a major role in establishing the illusion of a world apart. The lighting was also certainly festive, but it went beyond festive to enter the realm of fantasy and illusion where lighting creates the drama of something that is actually not there.

The drama of movement fits the hustle and bustle of air travel, and theatrical lighting creates a sense of movement in the tunnel connecting the two concourses of the United Airlines Terminal at O'Hare International Airport (Murphy/Jahn Architects; Sylvan R. Shemitz Associates, lighting consultant; neon ceiling sculpture by Michael Hayden; 1983–88) in Chicago, Illinois. The light, in concert with music played through speakers placed sequentially along the route, accompanies one through the tunnel in waving patterns of colored neon. The separate pieces of neon turn on and off sequentially, creating the effect of a wave of colored light sweeping through the tunnel. The neon shapes are mounted on a reflective ceiling surface so that their effective image is doubled. The side walls are composed of translucent wall panels illuminated by fluorescent light reflected from colored walls behind them. These colored panels are punctuated by "columns" defined by white light that fan out into ceiling elements that reach to the central undulating neon. The effect is theatrical, illusionistic, frenetic, and disconcerting to some, especially those people who have bad eyesight or are infirm and unsteady in their movements. The effect in the tunnel is one of moving light, and that light removes you briefly from the world of reality, of dashing from one flight to the next, to be enveloped in theatrical light.

Theatrical lighting has moved into merchandising, perhaps illustrated nowhere better than in Nike Town, Nike's flagship store in downtown Portland, Oregon (Nike, Inc.; Robert Dupuy and Mark Ramsby, lighting consultants; 1991). Entering the store is rather like walking into a "ride" at Disneyland. The store furnishes entertainment, as does a theater, a space museum or an amusement park. The shopper does not so much browse as explore, enticed from the central entry hall by the lights of the surrounding "attractions." The theatrical experience begins in the entry lobby, which seems to be a center stage, surrounded on two levels by entries to visibly brighter attractions. The major lighting technique used is spotlighting, traditional to theaters. The fiber-optic billboard advertising "Nike" is similar to an illuminated scoreboard in a baseball park. The environment for the American pastime of shopping has finally been raised to the level of theater, or at least amusement parks.

FIGURE 4–14 *View in the entry lobby to Nike Town in Portland, Oregon, showing the Nike "billboard" and the entries to the surrounding "attractions."*

METAPHORICAL LIGHT

Metaphorical light suggests that it reveals something other than physical reality. It may reveal an association with another place, as discussed in "Light as Image of Nature" (Chapter 1), or with an idea than is obviously apparent. In this sense, many paintings are metaphors since they represent a concept beyond that which they literally depict. Edward Hopper uses light as a metaphor in his paintings, pushing the role of light beyond that of merely revealing form. Light reveals the message of the painting. Hopper sets the scene with dominant light: strong shafts of sunlight, limpid pools of incandescent light, or the contrast of bright interiors to the dark of night. In *New York Movie*, the two worlds of the movie theater—the soft-edged illusion in which the movie-watchers are bathed, and the hard-

Figure 4–15 *Edward Hopper,* New York Movie, *1939. Oil on canvas, 32¼" x 40⅛" (81.9 x 101.9 cm). The Museum of Modern Art, New York. Given Anonymously. Photograph © 1996 The Museum of Modern Art, New York.*

edged reality surrounding the usher—are defined by the light. The movie-watchers are in a dream world. The usher is in a reverie, too, but her illusion is inside, not touched by the clarity of the wall sconce or affected by the scenes of the movie. She is caught in a separate world. Hopper used the nuances of everyday lighting conditions, investing them with meaning, so that light becomes a metaphor for the worlds of illusion and reality.

In the movies, as well as in theater, light and color are used to create an illusion. Directors have used color and lighting in strongly metaphorical ways, suggesting places and concepts beyond the direct images on the screen. In *The Cook, The Thief, His Wife and Her Lover,* director Peter Greenaway used distinctly different color schemes and lighting conditions in each of the settings in the movie. The restaurant kitchen was high, cathedral-like, dim, and mysteriously illuminated by light with a greenish cast. The restaurant dining room, in contrast, was garish, red, and harshly illuminated. The ladies' restroom was white—all white—with a scintillating light that breaks up forms. Her Lover's apartment was brown, and the only room illuminated with the light of day. This clear delineation of the different settings by decidedly different coloring and lighting suggests that each environment is a metaphor for a different symbolic set of conditions, defining the activities there. The settings are included as characters in the drama through their metaphorical light.

Metaphorical light in architecture rests on expressing an idea or a concept and therefore cannot always be readily perceived. Steven Holl has written about his theoretical approach to building, and in it can be found references that accord with the physical realization of the D.E. Shaw Company (Steven Holl, 1991–92) in New York City. The lighting in the reception area emerges from Holl's way of perceiving architecture: "If we consider the order (the idea) to be the outer perception and the phenomena (the experience) to be the inner perception, then in a physical construction, outer perception and inner perception are intertwined. From this position experiential phenomena are the material for a kind of reason-

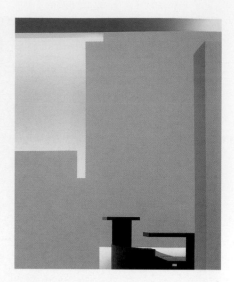

ing that joins concept and sensation."[12] The D.E. Shaw Company exists due to the high technology of electronic information systems and international trading. The office "works" 23-hours a day—as long as a stock exchange is open in the world. It is a high-stakes cerebral game. Information does not arrive directly from one person talking to another—it is transmitted by electronic signals.

The reception room of the container that houses these activities has no direct physical connection to the outside, to the hustle and the bustle of the city, to the populace, or to the daylight. There are no views out, and light does not enter directly—it is reflected and colored by an interior wall located parallel to and inside the exterior wall. Cutouts in the interior wall are offset from the windows in the exterior wall so that the light that enters the room is first reflected from the exterior surface of the interior wall, which is painted a fluorescent yellow.

The idea, the "outer perception," is electronic information transfer. The experience, the "inner perception," is reflected light. The cutouts refer to a higher geometric order, "a spiritual need in architecture that transcends rudimentary function.…Outer perception (of the intellect) and inner perception (of the senses) are synthesized in an ordering of space, light, and material."[13] Light is the metaphor that connects the two.

SYMBOLIC LIGHT

Symbolic light extends further than metaphorical light in that it represents a generally well-known idea or concept, such as life, death, or infinity. A special aspect of symbolic light is divine light, which will be discussed separately in the next section. We recognize symbolic light when we hold a candlelight vigil, or see universal meaning in a sunrise or the marking of seasonal change, such as the solstices and equinoxes. Symbolic light can be the sunlight streaming through the clouds, or a shaft of light in a dark interior, particularly a specially-shaped container such as the Pantheon (ca. A.D. 120–27) in Rome.

Daylight becomes symbolic light when it is captured in a certain way, or reflected from glossy surfaces so that they merge into the light. Light becomes part of the wall at the Vietnam War Memorial, designed by Maya Ying Lin and completed in 1982 in Washington, D.C. The reflected images in the wall remind one of the ephemeral and fleeting nature of our world. The clouds, the trees, and the puddles

FIGURE 4–17A *View along the wall of the Vietnam War Memorial, Washington, D.C.*

FIGURE 4–17B *Direct view of the wall.*

are all reflected in the polished face of the black granite between the incised letters of the names of the dead. The names of the dead are inscribed in the granite; the living are reflected in it. The life of the day is laid over the representations of the dead. The surroundings become part of the tribute to them. Thoughts about mortality are aroused by a visit to the memorial. They are strengthened by the symbolic role that light plays in conjunction with the surface of the polished black granite.

The electrical lighting fixtures are designed so as not to intrude upon the experience of the wall by day. They are discreetly located in small, closely spaced wedge-shaped blocks of stone that do not interrupt the starkness and isolation of the wall. Inside each block is a miniature lamp and a reflector shaped to spread the light up and across the surface of the wall. The fixtures perform their technical task quietly and unobtrusively and do not disturb the experience of the symbolic light.

Water in itself abounds with symbolic meaning, and when light interacts with it, the effect can be intensified. At the Salk Institute (Louis I. Kahn Architect, 1959–65) in La Jolla, California, a strip of water extends down the middle of the courtyard seemingly to blend with the sea in the distance to the west. The surface of the narrow channel of water reflects the sky, as does the surface of the sea, and suggests a continuum from the channel to the sea to the sky. It suggests infinity. It is a simple yet profound gesture that sets one's mind to searching beyond the known and expected, just as the researchers there are reaching beyond current knowledge in their work. The channel of water—its placement and its relationship to the immediate buildings and their larger setting—renders the daylight symbolic.

Antonio Gaudí has created symbolic light in the vaulted cupola over the central hall of the Palacio Güell (1885–89) in Barcelona by representing there the starry vault of heaven. The symbolism goes beyond mere effect: "For him the

FIGURE 4–18 *Salk Institute courtyard in La Jolla, California. Photograph by Martin Schwartz.*

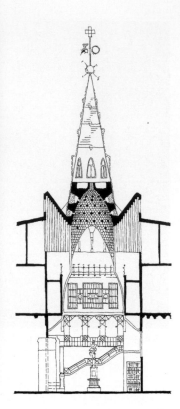

FIGURE 4–19A (RIGHT) *Palacio Güell, Barcelona, Spain, interior of central hall.*

FIGURE 4–19B (FAR RIGHT) *Section of central hall. Redrawn from Collins, George R. and Juan Bassegoda Nonell, 1983.* The Designs and Drawings of Antonio Gaudi. *(Princeton, N.J.: Princeton University Press), Plate 28, drawn for the Paris exhibition at the Société Nationale des Beaux-Arts, 1910. Cat. 24.8.*

architect seemed to be the humble instrument of a divine Power, and he considered each form he used to be fraught with mystical symbolism."[14] What seem to be stars in the dark sky are bright points of daylight, daylight that has been funneled through the thick roof. At night, incandescent lamps located between the inner and outer layers of the roof provide the light.[15] There are practical advantages to the dim interior—the relief from the heat and bright light of the street—but this central salon also offers an allegorical reference to the heavenly vault. As Eliade points out, "The regions above man's reach, the starry places, are invested with the divine majesty of the transcendent, of absolute reality, of everlastingness."[16] For Gaudí, the hyberbolic paraboloid of the vault even more specifically represented the Trinity of Father, Son, and Holy Ghost,[17] important in the Catholic church of which he was a devout worshipper. The combination of the symbolism of the shape of the structural support and that of the stars in the vault of heaven carries symbolic meaning beyond the mere representation of a natural phenomenon.

Symbolic light adds meaning that reaches beyond our visible world, and reinforces the introduction of that meaning both outside and inside buildings.

DIVINE LIGHT

The sky provides the connection to divine light: "…even before any religious values have been set upon the sky it reveals its transcendence. The sky 'symbolizes' transcendence, power and changelessness simply by being there. It exists because it is high, infinite, immovable, powerful."[18] Light has long been connected with the spiritual aspects of life and with the forces that symbolize the sacred and the divine. Certain aspects are closely related to experience as defined in the first chapter, but with more cosmic connections. For example, the sacred aspect of temporal change is expressed in special places such as Stonehenge and the solar temple of the Mnajdra temple complex on Malta.[19] Sacred places are often different and notable in ways that provide comfort in contrast to exterior conditions, such as dark, cool churches in the bright, hot villages of Mexico and Africa; the cool blue mosques of Istanbul; and the glittering warmth of St. Mark's in Venice in winter.[20]

Sacredness is expressed through many qualities; a major one among them is the quality of light. Light can lead us beyond the finite and temporal, beyond our known experience in space and time. *Where* it may lead us depends upon each individual, but it *can* lead us to wonder what lies beyond the world we know as mortals. When we are moved to wonder about our place in the universe, when we are pushed to ask what our role is in the greater whole that must exist, it may be a particular light that prompts us. It may be that beyond our personal experience lies universal truth. Although we may not have personal experience of the light of this knowledge, we can desire to attain it.

The divine is itself changeless, but the representation of the divine through light can be seen to change through time. If one accepts the metaphor of a divine immortal light that approaches humanity, and an earthly mortal light (such as the light of reason) that approaches the divine, then the construction of sacred places in light symbolizes the meeting of these two lights: "... the irruption of the sacred ... opens communication between the cosmic planes ..."[21] The expression of this intersection—how one sees and experiences the revelation of divine light in earthly matter—depends upon the period, the culture, and the spiritual approach to life.

A few examples will serve to briefly sketch the evolution of expression of divine light without trying to be comprehensive. Obviously light is but one of the many means of expressing the divine, and tomes have been written describing both religious practices and the buildings in which worship takes place. The intention of this short narrative is only to glimpse a few of the many approaches to expressing meaning in architecture through divine light.

The dates of the Great Pyramid of Cheops at Giza are not accurately known, but it is conjectured that it was built in the third millennium before Christ.[22] Originally covered with a thick skin of limestone, it would have glowed in the sunlight, especially at sunrise and sunset when the horizontal rays of the sun would have touched it and left the surrounding desert dark. Most obelisks and pyramids were topped by a pyramid-shaped capstone of precious metal. There may well have been a practical use for the glowing capstones: when obelisks and pyramids were used as astronomical instruments, a glowing tip would make it easier to see, both from a distance and in relation to celestial bodies passing overhead. The purely visual effect of these capstones glowing in the dawn or sunset light, or starlight and moonlight, must have been ethereal.

FIGURE 4–20 *Great Pyramid of Cheops (Third Dynasty, ca. 2570–2500 B.C.), Giza, Egypt. Photograph by Norman J. Johnston.*

This external visual effect is the one the majority of the population would see. But the Great Pyramid modeled all the physical measures and forces at work on this earth, including all the light that contributes to the order of this earth: the sun, the moon, the stars. It also functioned, as did the star temples, oriented to frame a rising star along an axis, thus marking the coming of a solstice or equinox. Reflective materials may have been used, as in the star temples, to respond to the starlight:

Herodotus describes two pillars of gold and green stone in the temple of Tyre which shone at midnight. According to Lockyer, 'there can be little doubt that in the darkened sanctuary of an Egyptian temple the light of Alpha Lyrae, one of the brightest stars in the northern heavens, rising in the clear air of Egypt, would be quite strong enough to throw into an apparent glow such highly reflecting surfaces as those to which Herodotus refers.'[23]

FIGURE 4–21A *View of the surrounding landscape, now the city of Athens, from the porch of the Propylaia (Mnesikles, 437–432 B.C.) on the Acropolis in Greece. Photograph by Thomas L. Bosworth.*

FIGURE 4–21B *The Parthenon (Iktinos and Kallikrates, 447–432 B.C.).*

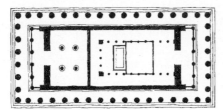

FIGURE 4–21C *Plan of the Parthenon.*

FIGURE 4–22 *View of the mosaics, S. Marco, Venice, Italy. Photograph by Dennis Tate.*

This line of thought is important in suggesting that there are many aspects of the meaning of the temples and pyramids related to light that go far beyond mere appreciation of a geometrical form in the desert sun. We may have lost access to the knowledge that related the divine and material worlds by means of these great structures, but we can still appreciate the magnitude of the connection. The Great Pyramid of Cheops, as a model of the universe, can be seen as connecting earth with the heavenly spheres through light: starlight, moonlight, sunlight. Its empty sarcophagus may have been empty not because it had been ransacked but because, as theories recounted by Peter Tompkins suggest, it was an Arc of the Covenant, acting as some type of resonator for cosmic energies. The pyramid may have been a transformer, mediating between the divine light—invisible—and the earthly light—visible. It not only *represented* the divine made manifest in this world, it *was* the presence of the divine light in this world.

The Greek temples were based on a similar set of principles, modeling the universe, but expressed in a rectilinear geometry.[24] An obvious difference in expression is the encasing of the innermost sanctum. In the pyramids, it was a void in the middle of a solid. In the Greek temples, it was a walled enclosure surrounded by colonnades. The walled enclosure represented the dwelling place of the god.[25] The difference between the inner sanctums of the pyramid and the temple in their relationship to the surrounding sky and the celestial bodies is quite striking, particularly as experienced by the general populace. If we assume that only initiates entered the innermost sanctuaries of the pyramids, then the perceived appearance of the pyramids to the general populace would have been simply as solid geometric forms. In the Greek temples, however, the colonnades allowed the worshipper to approach the walled sanctuary, visually from a distance and physically by walking through them. The colonnades mediated between the sanctuary and the landscape, between the inner divine light and the outer worldly light. Only a relatively thin stone wall separated the inner chamber from the sky. Connections with the surrounding environment were potentially more immediate, and could be made by puncturing holes in these walls or in the roof.

The screen of columns around the sanctuary both connects (by being penetrable) and separates (by presenting a visual barrier) the light of the sanctuary from the landscape and from the people. What is active in this colonnade is the light of the earth. A connection between the mortal and the immortal light may have come at sunrise on the deity's feast day. For temples in which the entry to the sanctuary is oriented to the east, the role of the rising sun has been suggested to be that of making interior gold or stone statuary luminous at sunrise. Again we find a joining of the metaphors of earthly and divine light: the earthly light of the sun causes the statue of the deity to emanate light—divine light—from the sanctuary.

In Medieval Christian churches, the cosmology led to a different symbol system in which daylight and candlelight revealed the representation of the stronghold of God, the Heavenly City. All the arts together defined the physical church, as in the Byzantine Church of S. Marco (ninth century; rebuilt 976–8 and in the eleventh century; mosaics eleventh century through the fifteenth century) in Venice, Italy. Here the sanctuary is located inside a building that the worshippers are free to enter. The interaction between the divine light and the earthly light now occurs within the building for all to experience. The church interior is dim, separated from the city outside. The gold mosaic tiles reflect the light, seeming themselves to glow and be the source of light. The representation of the divine, which is

FIGURE 4–23A (BELOW LEFT) *Interior view of the stained glass windows, Nôtre Dame de Chartres, France. Photograph by Grant Hildebrand.*

FIGURE 4–23B (TOP RIGHT) *Detail view of a stained glass window.*

FIGURE 4–23C (BOTTOM RIGHT) *Patterns of colored light cast by the stained glass windows onto the stone floor and column base.*

Figure 4–24 *Interior view of the dome, Sant' Ivo della Sapienza, Rome. Photograph by Wilmot G. Gilland.*

literal in the figures of the mosaics, is shown in such forms as the cross, Christ, the twelve apostles, and the dove—symbol of the Holy Spirit. Ruskin described the visible temple as being "in every part a type of the invisible Church of God."[26] Not only the images, but also inscriptions describe the process of sanctification. The light reflected from the gold mosaics flickers around the interior spaces of the domes, disintegrating any clear spatial separation of the parts by its glimmering mistiness. Ruskin noted that under these conditions, "... the man must be little capable of receiving a religious impression of any kind, who ... remains altogether untouched by the majesty of the colossal images of apostles, and of Him who sent apostles, that look down from the darkening gold of the domes of Venice."[27] The light inside S. Marco is divine light, scintillating and reflecting from the gold and brightly colored mosaic tiles, seemingly emanating from the mosaics, seemingly the light from heaven itself.

For the twelfth and thirteenth centuries light was the source and essence of all visual beauty.... To the medieval thinker beauty was not a value independent of others, but rather the radiance of truth, the splendor of ontological perfection, and that quality of things which reflects their origin in God. Light and luminous objects, no less than musical consonance, conveyed an insight into the perfection of the cosmos, and a divination of the Creator.[28]

Otto von Simson's description of the meaning of light to the medieval mind leads us to understand that this light in S. Marco, reflected from the surfaces of the mosaics, was seen as divine light.

During the same period as mosaics were being applied to S. Marco, divine light was being revealed within the cathedral of Nôtre Dame de Chartres (1194–1220) in France through the medium of stained glass windows. The light of day is transformed by passing through the colored glass, becoming not only the representation of divine light, but, to the perception of the worshippers, divine light in reality. The entire atmosphere of the interior is colored by the light. Even the materials are made to seem ephemeral by the patterns of glowing colored light that flow over them. The cathedral is mysterious—it is not revealed in one glance, but must be explored. Although lighter than the interiors of earlier basilicas and churches, it is still dark, inviting introversion and inner exploration. The symbolic stories told in the stained-glass windows carry the double meaning of both the story and the light that reveals it. All who enter the cathedral can bathe in this divine light.

In Baroque churches, the light still represents the divinity, but it becomes more ethereal, more indistinct and vague. As Karsten Harries states, "The sensuous is no longer used as a step in the soul's gradual ascent to the divine.... Instead such art points to the sacred by expressing the desire which relates man to the sacred not as to something known but as to something unknown."[29] The physical presence of light does not denote the divine; rather one is presented with the desire to know

something that is as yet unknown, one is led toward the light. This mystery is presented in Sant'Ivo della Sapienza (Francesco Borromini, 1642–60) in Rome. It is as if the church is the intermediary for the divine light that is itself ephemeral. There is a dialectic struggle between the sense of enclosure provided by the undulating walls and the sense of movement that is implied by the axial organization[30] as well as by the drawing of attention upwards by the light. The direct connection of light with the divine is gone, and in place of this analogy the light draws one's attention to a mysterious place beyond, above the dome, where the light resides, to which one can aspire.

According to Karsten Harries, the revelation of divine light in churches ends with the rococo: "The Bavarian rococo marks a last successful attempt to build churches as signs of the invisible Church. The playful way in which this sign character is established shows that this is indeed a last attempt."[31] In the Augustinian Priory Church (1732) by Johann Michael Fischer in Diessen, Germany, heaven is again represented pictorially, this time in frescos. Painting, sculpture, and architecture merge to create illusions that carry the symbolism of heaven intermixed with the history of the priory, merging time into timelessness.[32] Indirect light, modulated by the luminous zone between inner and outer shell, is used here both to reveal the frescos and to imbue the while walls and pillars of the church with an immaterial presence. "Light and matter fuse as stone and stucco are transformed into an ethereal substance."[33] This dematerialization of the forms adds to the illusions of light, the veils of mystery that fall between the worshipper and divine light. The earthly light and divine light are intermingled in an epiphany of images melting one into the other.

Today the relationship between the individual and the cosmos is approached in a manner more open to personal interpretation. In the recent history of church buildings, attention has been concentrated more and more on the personal vision of the architect as the source of the symbolism of light. Le Corbusier's personal vision clearly shaped his ecclesiastical works (see Chapter 2, "Formal Light"). The chapel of Nôtre Dame du Haut (Le Corbusier, 1950–55) at Ronchamp, France, seems to be a contemporary interpretation of Chartres, a pilgrimage chapel where the effects are similar but the means are different. Each is appropriate for a different population at a different time. Henry Adams' comment about Chartres also applies to Ronchamp: "We must take ten minutes to accustom our eyes to the light, and we had better use them to seek the reason why we come to Chartres rather than to Rheims or Amiens or Bourges, for the cathedral that fills our ideal."[34] Are

FIGURE 4–25 (LEFT) *View of the Augustinian Priory Church in Diessen, Germany. Photograph by Claus Seligmann.*

FIGURE 4–26 (RIGHT) *Detail of the Abbey Church of Neresheim, Germany (Johann Balthasar Neumann, begun 1750), showing the interdependence among the forms and the colors of the architecture, the sculpture, and the paintings to create the envelope of light at the perimeter. Photograph by Claus Seligmann.*

FIGURE 4–27A *Interior view toward the deep south wall, Nôtre Dame du Haut at Ronchamp, France.*

FIGURE 4–27B *Detail of a low deep-set window in the south wall.*

FIGURE 4–27C *Sketch of exterior.*

there similarities between the light in Ronchamp and the light in Chartres that make them both fill our ideal of a pilgrimage church?

In both Chartres and Ronchamp, the light is dim. There is a sense of mystery; it is not possible to see everything from one vantage point, even though the chapel at Ronchamp is one seemingly small room. In both, one must move around to look into the side chapels, and to get different views of all the windows. There exists paradoxes of clarity and yet disorientation; a simplicity of enclosure, yet complexity of form. The inside is very much separated from the outside. In the chapel at Ronchamp, there are white walls throughout, but the interior seems dark. On the other hand, it seems to be suffused in light. The effect of colored air in the space is similar to Chartres. Colored light creeps over the interior surfaces in both (although in different patterns), resulting in patterns of colored light that surprise and delight. The deep wall pocketed with openings is a symphony of shape and color and meaning, a modern interpretation of the effect of stained glass windows.

A different sense of the sacred underlies the white containers of light designed by Aalto in Finland, such as the Vuoksenniska Church in Imatra (1956–59). One clearly sees the light of day here. No images, no colors, intercede between the worshipper and the light. The light reveals the spare, though gentle and subtle, forms. The shape of the spatial enclosure, however, is complex with a double shell making layers of connection between the outer light and the inner light. The wall slopes down behind the cross, a continuous plane that connects the earth and the sky. The cross is simple and bare, illuminated by a skylight aimed toward it and by slanted side windows at the front that wash the wall with side light, making shadow-crosses behind the material crosses. The layers of light between inside and outside separate the sacred interior from the profane exterior. Aalto's design approach was essentially humanist, no less for churches than for other buildings. He said in 1957: "Architecture has an ulterior motive, which always lurks, so to speak, around the corner: the thought of creating a paradise.... Each house, each product of architecture that is worthwhile as a symbol is an endeavor to show that we want to build an earthly paradise for people."[35] The church should be a place where everyone can feel comfortable and welcome, where

Figure 4–28A *Interior view of Vuoksenniska Church in Imatra, Finland.*

Figure 4–28B *Sketch of exterior.*

everything is revealed and nothing is hidden. The divine light is there; it is up to each one to meet it.

Another personal interpretation of sacred space revealed in light is the Bagsvaerd Church (1973–76) near Copenhagen, Denmark, designed by Jörn Utzon. The metaphor concerns being on the earth under the sky.[36] Separated as we have been from building imagery since the advent of the functionalist approach, still we have the basic experience of inhabiting the earth on which to rely. Utzon's preliminary sketches for the church evoke this basic relationship. One sketch shows a group of people in the landscape looking to the horizon under dramatic clouds. The other sketch is similar, but shows built form interceding by means of side columns, smooth rounded planes overhead, and a cross at the horizon between earth and sky. Christian Norberg-Schulz has written about these sketches: "In general, the two sketches show that Utzon started out from a spatial vision, and that the space was intended as an *imago mundi,* that is, a built replica of man's basic existential situation."[37] He sees this situation as one of being between earth and sky, but aiming for the altar and the cross, the locus between earth and sky. The combination of forms and light in the Bagsvaerd Church suggests the experience of being under clouds, under the sky, with the cross that stands between the two revealed in light that changes as it washes over the white folds of the concrete ceiling. The light reveals the entire interior, including all the worshippers, the whole group under the sky, oriented to the cross. The light establishes the place, suggesting the landscape. How much farther it leads depends upon the individual and the group.

The Swedish architect Sigurd Lewerentz worked with a different image of divine light. In the church of St. Peter's at Klippan (1962–66), the use of light responds to that part of Scandinavian heritage that accepts the darkness. The response of the church at Klippan to the Nordic darkness is to deepen it. The effect of the glare of light from the small windows set in the dark wall is similar to a shaft of light in a mine: the surroundings look even darker. Electric light does not reveal much more. The effect of the electric lighting fixtures is reminiscent of stars, the heavens at night.

Colin St John Wilson likens the darkness of St. Peter's to a "haunting metaphor":

In a rare moment of explanation, Lewerentz stated that subdued light was enriching precisely in the degree to which the nature of the space has to be

FIGURE 4–29B (ABOVE) *Sketch of exterior.*

FIGURE 4–29C (RIGHT) *Preliminary sketch for the Bagsvaerd Church by Jörn Utzon showing the existential situation of being on the earth and under the sky.*

FIGURE 4–29D (FAR RIGHT) *Preliminary sketch translating the concept into a rough building enclosure. Sketches reprinted courtesy of Utzon and Associates.*

reached for, emerging only in response to exploration. This slow taking possession of space (the way in which it gradually becomes yours) promotes that fusion of privacy in the sharing of a common ritual that is the essence of the numinous.[38]

The light, made more apparent in the darkness, begins once again to become the symbol of divine light revealed in darkness. The expression of light that we can see causes us to look inward to our center, there to search once more for connection—a personal connection—with the divine light.

The vision of the architects who deal with light as a building material transcends the typical material and formal connections to this earth. They approach

FIGURE 4–30A *Interior view toward the altar in St. Peter's at Klippan, Sweden.*

FIGURE 4–30B *Interior view from the altar. Photographs by Peter Cohan.*

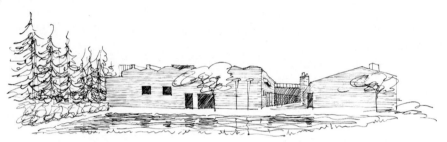

FIGURE 4–30C *Sketch of the exterior.*

the sublime in their conception of forging a connection between human experience and spiritual ideals. They eschew the traditional, not for invention for its own sake, but because of a higher and more encompassing vision. At the same time this vision is smaller and simpler. It incorporates the relationship between one human being and the surrounding universe, mitigated by the room, connected by light.

ENDNOTES

1. Eliade, Mircea. 1961. *The Sacred and the Profane.* (New York: Harper Torchbooks), p. 211.

2. Harries, Karsten. 1988. "Representation and Re-presentation in Architecture," *VIA 9*, p. 20.

3. Physically, light affects the pineal gland in the middle of the brain, which is in turn connected to all our glandular, hence emotional, centers.

4. Irving, Washington. 1984. *Two Tales: Rip Van Winkle and The Legend of Sleepy Hollow.* (Orlando, Fla.: Harcourt Brace Jovanovich, Franklin Watts Publishers). p. 30. Reprinted with permission of the publisher.

5. Bly, Robert, Editor and Translator. 1981. *Selected Poems of Rainer Maria Rilke.* (New York: Harper & Row), p. 21. Copyright 1981 by Robert Bly. Reprinted with permission of HarperCollins Publishers, Inc.

6. Banford-Smith, C. 1967. *Builders in the Sun: Five Mexican Architects.* (New York: Architectural Book Publishing Co.), p. 74.

7. Tanizaki, Junichiro. 1977. *In Praise of Shadows*. (New Haven, Conn.: Leete's Island Books), p. 20. Reprinted with permission of the publisher.

8. O'Doherty, Brian. 1986. *Inside the White Cube*. (Santa Monica, Calif.: The Lapis Press). Introduction by Thoman McEvilley, p. 12.

9. *Farolitos* are candles set in sand in brown paper bags. They are used to line the tops of houses, walls, and curbs, outlining the forms of the city in pinpoints of light. Among other places, farolitos are set out traditionally in Sante Fe, New Mexico during the Christmas season.

10. Rivard, J. 1970. "A heirophany in Chicken-Itza," *Katunob* 7 (30):51-55. Excerpt from pp. 49-50 quoted in Anthony F. Aveni. 1980. *Skywatchers of Ancient Mexico*. (Austin, Tex.: University of Texas Press), p. 285.

11. Richard Peters, personal communication to the author, September 1994.

12. Holl, Steven. 1989. *Anchoring*. (New York: Princeton Architectural Press), p. 11.

13. Ibid., pp. 7 and 11.

14. Collins, George R. 1960. *Antonio Gaudi*. (New York: George Braziller, Inc.), p. 8.

15. Ibid., p. 15.

16. Eliade, Mircea. 1958. *Patterns in Comparative Religion*. (New York: Sheed and Ward), p. 39.

17. Collins, op. cit., p. 122

18. Eliade, 1958, op. cit., p. 38.

19. Kostoff, Spiro. 1985. "Ch. 2, The Cave and the Sky: Stone Age Europe" in *A History of Architecture: Settings and Rituals*. (New York and Oxford: Oxford University Press).

20. Ruskin, John. 1885. *The Stones of Venice, Vol. 2*. (New York: John Wiley and Sons), p. 73.

21. Eliade, 1961, op. cit., p. 63.

22. Information on the Great Pyramid has been taken from: Tompkins, Peter, and Livio Stecchini. 1971. *Secrets of the Great Pyramid*. (New York: Harper & Row), pp. 1–4, 159–75, 201–13, 287–382.

23. Ibid., p. 165.

24. Ibid., pp. 355–61.

25. Lethaby, William Richard. 1975. *Architecture Mysticism and Myth*. (New York: George Braziller), p. 42.

26. Ruskin, John. 1885. *The Stones of Venice*, Vol. 2. (New York: John Wiley and Sons), p. 111.

27. Ibid., p. 101.

28. von Simson, Otto. 1965. *The Gothic Cathedral*. (New York: Pantheon Books), pp. 50–51.

29. Harries, Karsten. 1968. *The Meaning of Modern Art*. (Evanston, Illinois: Northwestern University Press), pp. 14–15.

30. Norberg-Schulz, Christian. 1984. *Genius Loci*. (New York: Rizzoli), p. 153.

31. Harries, Karsten. 1983. *The Bavarian Rococo Church*. (New Haven, Conn., and London: Yale University Press), p. 8.

32. Ibid., pp. 160–70.

33. Ibid., p. 73.

34. Adams, Henry. 1985. *Mont-Saint-Michel and Chartres*. (New York: Gallery Books), p. 63.

35. Aalto, Alvar. Edited by Goran Schildt. 1978. *Sketches*. (Cambridge Mass.: The M.I.T. Press), pp. 157–58.

36. Norberg-Schulz, Christian. 1988. *Architecture: Meaning and Place*. (New York:

Electa/Rizzoli), pp. 223–30; and Futagawa, Yukio, text by Christian Norberg-Schulz. 1981. *Jorn Utzon: Church at Bagsvaerd.* (Tokyo: A.D.A. Edita).

37. Norberg-Schulz, ibid. p. 223.

38. Wilson, Colin St. John. 1992. *Architectural Reflections.* (Oxford, England: Butterworth Architecture), p. 124.

Sacred Light: The Kimbell Art Museum

Fort Worth, Texas, U.S.A.
1966–72

Louis I. Kahn Architect
Marshall D. Meyers, Project Architect
Preston M. Geren and Associates,
*   Associate Architect*
Frank H. Sherwood, Project Coordinator
Richard Kelly and Edison Price,
*   Lighting Consultants*

Inspiration is the feeling of beginning at the threshold where Silence and Light meet. Silence, the unmeasurable, desire to be, desire to express, the source of new need, meets Light, the measurable, giver of all presence, by will, by law, the measure of things already made, at a threshold which is inspiration, the sanctuary of art, the Treasury of Shadow.[1]
—LOUIS I. KAHN

Sacred light connects us with a higher order of things, with the essential, with the immutable truth. Sacred light is not tied to revelation of a particular deity, or to a particular religion, or even to a typical religious place, such as a church. Rather sacred light reminds one, whenever one comes into contact with it, that a higher order exists, whatever it may be called.

According to Eliade, when the sacred is made manifest, "...there is not only a break in the homogeneity of space; there is also revelation of an absolute reality, opposed to the nonreality of the vast surrounding expanse."[2] Kahn's intentions in designing and realizing buildings were clearly connected to higher aspirations, to revealing an absolute reality. He termed this absolute reality *silence*. *Silence* possess a *will to be* which is satisfied through *design*, "which means an embodiment of the inner order."[3] Kahn's means of expression of an absolute reality have been described as stemming from a combination of Neoplatonic tradition,

German Romanticism, Jewish mysticism, and Egyptian hieroglyphics.[4]

In designing the Kimbell Art Museum, Kahn started with a vision of the *silence*—the unmeasurable—that would be revealed by *light*—the measurable. He pursued this vision throughout the process of design and construction, working with each element to develop it fully until it fulfilled his vision. With natural light, one of the aspects of the measurable, Kahn created a setting for the art collection of Kay and Velma Kimbell that goes beyond making the works of art visible. The Kimbell Art Museum introduces us to *silence*, the unmeasurable, through its confluence of form, materials, space, and light. From the main entry through a grove of trees, through the porch and lobby and through the galleries with glimpses of enclosed courtyards, the experiences and sequences of light suggest that this is a special place, a place apart. Through sacred light, it suggests a timeless place and presents us with the "revelation of an absolute reality."

The site for the Kimbell Art Museum is in the Will Rogers Memorial Park, serving Fort Worth as its recreational and cultural center. The area in general is flat and boundless, exposed to the light and the heat of the sun. Each park, fountain, and building is isolated, surrounded by a network of large roads.

The architectural program for the Kimbell Art Museum was thoroughly developed by its director, Richard F. Brown, who described the feeling of the space that he envisioned.[5] His primary emphasis was on the viewing of the works of art, the relationship between visitor and art work.

Natural light should play a vital part in illumination....The visitor must be able to relate to nature momentarily ...to actually see at least a small slice of foliage, sky, sun, water. And the effects of changes in weather, position of the sun, seasons, must penetrate the building and participate in illuminating both art and observer....We are after a psychological effect through which the museum visitor feels that both he and the art he came to see are still part of the real, rotating, changeable world.[6]

The Kimbell Art Museum consists of six bays of 104'–long concrete cycloid shells,[7] divided crosswise into three equal sections. On the west entrance side, two of the central bays have been removed, and one enters the museum here. On this side, the outermost bay is an open portico. On the main floor are located the galleries, an auditorium, refreshment area, entry lobby, and bookstore, with the library above on a mezzanine. On the lower floor, level with the east parking lot, are the offices and laboratories, shipping and receiving, shops, mechanical space, and the lower entrance lobby from the parking lot.

The entrance to the Kimbell Art Museum is a transition

between the vast, intense, bright, hot world outside and the contained, restrained, dim, cool world inside. The entrance from the west side was named the "Entrance of the trees" by Kahn in a letter and sketch sent to Mrs. Kimbell.[8] This entrance was intended to be the main one, as evidenced by references made by both Kahn and Brown in their correspondence.[9] Few people enter this way, however, since most arrive by car and walk directly from the parking lot to the door into the lower level lobby.[10] But the experience of following the intended entry sequence is a necessary part of the experience, the orchestrated withdrawal from the profane light of this world to enter the sacred light of the interior.

On the lawn, beyond the "Entrance of the trees," the Texas sun is hot, even on a February day. The shade of the trees dotting the lawn and lined up parallel to the building is welcome. From the trees, which have slowed one's pace, one ascends the platform and passes the pools of water. The movement of the water, spilling over the edge of long shallow pools at either side of the entry platform, provides active contrast to the grove. The water reflects and accentuates the sparkle of the sunlight while also offering cooling effects, both psychological and physical. As one ascends the steps to the entry platform, a phalanx of smaller trees, trimmed so their lower branches are all at the same level, protrudes from the entry court. Clearly this is no random natural grove of trees, but one that has been planted to provide modulated containment as well as shade. It furnishes respite from the heat and the harsh light and enclosure in a columnar order. It prepares one for the light of the building. Entering the portico, described by Kahn as an "offering," a "presentation of its spirit," there is more and deeper shade, as the light is further blocked and the air cooled. Along with these visual and thermal sensations go tactile and auditory ones, such as the feel and sound of walking on grass, gravel, and concrete, along with the sound of the water and sometimes the rustling of leaves.

Passing through the doors in the glass wall of the entry lobby, further transition in light quality and quantity takes place. The glass wall on one side of the lobby maintains connection with the light outside, while the interior light, modeled by the building form, begins to assert itself. This light is the sacred light, the light that identifies a special place apart from the everyday world, that connects us to the unmeasurable. The sacred light emerges from the meeting of daylight and structure.

Kahn stated his definite preference for daylight many times and in many ways, for example.

Artificial light is only a single little moment in light. . . . I can't define a space really as a space unless I have natural light. And that because the moods which are created by the time of day and seasons of the year are constantly helping you in evoking

that which a space can be if it has natural light and can't be if it doesn't. And artificial light—be it in a gallery be it even in an auditorium—loses one a great deal.[11]

He goes on to connect the light of day with the making of structure and the form of the building:

I think that the way a space is made is almost made with the consciousness of possibilities of light because when you have a column you see, you are saying a column is there because light is possible. A wall does not say it's possible . . . but when you have a column or a vault or an arch, you're saying that light is possible. So therefore the means of making a space already implies that light is coming in . . . and the very choice that you make of the element of structure should be also the choice of the character of light that you may want . . . and that I think is truly an architectural demand.[12]

In the Kimbell, the "way a space is made" means that the vault and the light are one. Vaulted gallery spaces were portrayed by Kahn in the very earliest of the conceptual design sketches. Perhaps the most telling document is the freehand sketch done by Kahn in March of 1967. There is no clear indication of the structural form, but the intent of the interaction of the form and light is evident. The light is activating all the surfaces, as it does in the completed building. But when the design was undertaken, the use of daylight in the gallery spaces was a revolutionary approach. The current standard for museum lighting, set by the Museum of Modern Art in New York, was electric lighting, affording both dependability and control. Richard Brown departed from the then-accepted norm by including the use of daylight as a major requirement of the program as well as by engaging Kahn as the architect.[13]

The design process of the vault and its "lighting fixture" was prolonged, extending from Kahn's earliest sketches in March 1967 to almost the last construction approval, that of the light reflector, in February 1972.[14] The form concept remained stable: vaults oriented on a north-south axis with light entering from above. The sizes of the vaults, their number, and the light modifier within them were studied continuously.

Drawings to the same scale adapted from Kahn's original sketches trace the development of the vault and the reflector. Very early sketches show the concept of integrating a daylighting fixture and electrical lighting fixtures between two vaults. In this study section (see Figure B4-7A), daylight and sunlight would presumably be gathered in the bell–shaped protuberance above the junction of the two vaults and then be reflected onto the underside of the curved ceilings by the wing–shaped reflector below it. A dual concern is expressed here: the desire to reveal the structure in daylight; and an attempt to control the quality and level of the light for the art by reflecting it from the ceiling. Rays of light seem to be traveling straight down under the light-catcher as well. Electric lighting fixtures are indicated mounted on the room side of the "wings" to focus light on the paintings on the walls. The vault, approximately 18 feet high, is unobstructed; the "lighting fixture," however, is quite large, and would require either special focusing equipment or reflectors or both. The idea of spreading light from a small aperture over a large surface, particularly suitable for this hot sunny climate, is introduced.

This idea of a lighting device at the intersection of vaults was further explored in other sketches from March 1967. A two-vault section is shown as approximately 40 feet high, with a large V-shaped trough taking up more than half the width (see Figure B4-7B). Due to the overlap of the trough and the curving roof, there would be no direct view of the sky. It seems as if the section were being checked for cut–off angles that would prevent direct sunlight from striking the lower part of the wall where paintings would be hung. The top sides of the trough become the reflectors; several profiles were sketched. Further sophistication was added by changing the top and bottom profiles of the light fixture: the top profile could do the work of distributing the daylight, and the bottom profile could do the work of shaping the room. One sketch suggests light filtering through the reflector.

Included in the first scheme that was presented to the client in March, 1967 is a section drawing showing a V-shaped trough carrying ductwork under a thirty-foot high angular vault (see Figure B4-7C). The drawing includes cut-off angles showing that sunlight could not strike surfaces below the top of wall panels. Glazing is tilted inward, which would deflect the heat of the sun. The top surface of the trough below the roof aperture is flat; it would reflect sunlight and skylight to the underside of the flat part of the ceiling. Diffuse light would illuminate the sloped sides of the vault, and the sides of the trough itself would receive the least daylight. It is interesting to speculate how these rooms would have "felt." Here the central reflector seems to divide the room in two, so that it becomes like two steeply roofed spaces. The light on the sides of the vault would mark it as different from the darker surface of the wedge of the trough. The space seems high and monumental, and the light on the ceiling would add to this effect. These characteristics were ones that Brown did not want. Although he admired the structural integrity of this scheme, he reminded Kahn that ". . . somehow we also must achieve the warmth and charm I spoke of in the program."[15]

In July 1967 a lower and rounded vault appears with what seems to be a wide concave reflector under a glazed slot at the apex of the vault (see Figure B4-7D). The glazed area under the slot captures the daylight within the building envelope and also seems to provide a location for electric light sources. Directions of the light are not indicated. The mechanical ducts have migrated to the interstitial spaces between vaults. Here much of the vault is obscured from view from the gallery space, with the reflector providing the sense of enclosure at the top of the room—unless one could see through it.

In fact Kahn's intention was to be able to see through the reflector. This idea for a "beam-splitter" is described by Meyers as it was presented in a sketch he made for Kahn in September 1967 showing a lower profile for the vault. He used the analogy of a partially mirrored prism in a single-lens reflex movie camera for the "beam-splitter"; but in the Kimbell the intent was "to give the illusion of dematerialization and transparency so you could see through it. By doing this it was hoped to avoid the heaviness of the conventional opaque reflector where its dark underside is seen highly contrasted against a brightly lit surface."[16]

A September 22, 1967, presentation sketch represented this idea with a wide flattened reflector (see Figure B4-7E). The daylight is expected to be reflected from its top surface and bounced across the vault. It also appears that electrical lighting fixtures will be located at the edges of the reflector. The ducts are now located in a channel between the vaults. Once again, much of the vault is obscured from view from the gallery space. However, in Kahn's words from a November lecture, the reflector is planned to be "mirrored glass shaped to spread natural light on the sides of the vault. This light will give a touch of silver to the room without touching the objects directly, yet give the comforting feeling of knowing the time of day."[17]

The *immeasurable* had been conceived, but the *measurable* had not yet been fully realized. Even though the outline specifications of December 1967 included "information on the 'glass reflector and lighting fixture,'"[18] it was not yet designed. The shape of the curve of the roof vault as a cycloid, obtained by tracing the moving point of a circle the height of the vault, was determined in December 1967. The structural engineer August Komendant was consulted on its construction, and Edison Price was asked to advise on the reflector shape. Richard Kelly and he had already been asked to work on the project, although Kelly was not consulted by Kahn until November 1968, following the proposal and acceptance of the third design scheme in September 1968. In January 1969 Kelly recommended that plastic be used for the reflector rather than glass. He also proposed vault and reflector curve shapes to optimize reflectance of the daylight to the underside of the ceiling. A significant change occurs here: the reflector, now biwinged, gathers the light from the skylight slot and scoops it to both sides with curves calculated to spread it evenly over the surface. The reflector is smaller and higher under the cycloid, less of an imposition on the space of the room[19].

The final realization of the form is present here, but not yet the materials. During the course of the discussions concerning costs, Kelly recommended using aluminum instead of plastic for the reflector, since it could achieve transparency through perforation as well as control the reflection of the light to the ceiling. A prototype of Kelly's design was installed in one of the skylights in January 1970, and later revised by Kahn, who widened the reflector to "achieve a more sweeping curve."[20] Kelly also suggested using track lighting integrated with the reflector, and Edison Price sent information on fixtures to Kahn's office in January 1970. At one point Kelly proposed a linear indirect light source at the center of the reflector. Although it has been suggested that it was eliminated for reasons of cost,[21] it would seem likely that Kahn would have wanted the source of daylight and the source of electric light to be distinctly different from each other, especially since he preferred not to have the latter at all.

In June 1971 Kahn and Kelly traveled to Fort Worth to view another mock–up of the reflectors, one in which two types of perforated aluminum were compared. Meyers reports that the more open perforations allowed direct sunlight onto south-facing gallery walls for a few minutes at noon, which was unacceptable to Brown. The more opaque material was unacceptable to Kahn, however, not reflecting light to his satisfaction. Frank Sherwood, the Project Coordinator, suggested a compromise solution: to use two reflector types, one made entirely of perforated aluminum in the lobby, bookstore, dining area, library, and auditorium, where protection from daylight was not an issue; and another one in the galleries with an opaque section directly under the skylight slot to block direct sunlight. This approach was welcomed by both Kahn and Brown; in fact they saw in it the addition of a subtle light variation between galleries and other areas as well as the desired glimpse of the sky through the all-perforated reflector.[22]

It was not until September 1971 that the gauge of aluminum and the perforation pattern were selected. The aluminum was to be .040 inches thick due to the curvature and the span. With the hole diameter about the same dimension as the thickness and the holes closely spaced, "the reflector itself would be able to provide a 45-degree cut-off for certain angles of the sun's rays."[23] For the fifth and final mock-up, a .050-inch hole spaced on 3/32-inch staggered centers was tried and worked, bathing the vault in light while allowing a veiled view of the sky. The light reflector was only given final approval in February 1972. Four months later, in June, the staff was moving in and the first informal openings were being held. To work out the details to realize the concept had consumed essentially the entire period of design and construction of the building.

The vault and reflector are usually the focus of attention in the Kimbell, but they are only parts of the whole. Kahn described the lighting concept for the building in a talk he gave at the New England Conservatory of Music in November 1967: "Added to the skylight from the slit over the exhibit rooms, I cut across the vaults, at a right angle, a counterpoint of courts, open to the sky of calculated dimensions and character, marking them Green Court, Yellow Court, Blue Court, named for the kind of light that I anticipate their proportions, their foliation, or their sky reflections on surfaces, or on water, will give."[24] The pattern of light courts within the museum—greater in quantity and type in early versions of the building—provides a counterpoint of active light to the muted light from the reflectors. They furnish the profane light of day to contrast with the sacred light from the vaults.

The use of courtyards is traditional in hot countries both for its cooling effect, especially when water is included, and also to modify the light before it enters the building. Kelly advised the use of foliage "to control light in the courtyards,"[25] and this advice has been followed in an elegant way by stringing a fine grid of wire trellis horizontally over the courts. This trellis supports a variety of Pin Oak, a deciduous tree noteworthy for not discarding its dead leaves until the new spring foliage forces them off, thereby providing shade to the courts and the interior all year long in this hot climate.

The vault lighting is quiet, providing a luminous background for viewing the art. The light of the courtyards is active, viewed either directly through glass walls or indirectly as a shaft of light cutting into a vista. The direct light from the sun is complementary to the indirect cool light bounced off the aluminum reflectors and concrete vaults. These two influxes of daylight establish the point-counterpoint of the gallery spaces. Together the different light sources form a balance between inside and outside, sacred and profane.

Other detailed aspects of the lighting received particular attention from Kahn as well. Daylight is also admitted to define the structure: the plexiglas lunettes at the ends of the vaults and the thin strips at the outboard edges under the beams show where continuous wall support is *not* required for the concrete cycloid shell structure. These "lightbands," as Kahn called the lunettes, were planned to be between two and four inches so as not to cause a sensation of glare. Since the end elevation of the shell roof does not follow the cycloid curve exactly due to the addition of an edge diaphragm, Kahn was faced with changing the shape of the lightband, which had originally reflected the cycloid curve. Kahn's decision was to "honor the engineering"[26]: the opening follows the curve of the structural diaphragm on the upper edge and the cycloid curve on the lower edge, varying from six to nine inches in width.

The presence of these openings also stems from a feeling that light should enter a museum in a variety of ways. They provide the multiplicity of sources of which Kahn spoke in 1959 as desirable in a good museum:

If I were to build a gallery now, I would really be more concerned about building spaces which are not used freely by the director as he wants. Rather I would give him spaces that were there and had certain inherent characteristics. The visitor, because of the nature of the space, would perceive a certain object in quite a different way. The director would be fitted out with such a variety of ways of getting light, from above, from below, from little slits, or from whatever he wanted, so that he felt that here was really a realm of spaces where one could show things in various aspects.[27]

Peter McCleary, in his article on the structure and construction of the Kimbell, argues that rigorous engineering principles are in fact not expressed in the final realization of the coincidence of structure, light, and room for which Kahn was striving. Whereas Kahn envisioned the area under one "vault" to be the "room" defined by the structure and the light, in fact the structural module was determined by the beam and extended from the middle of one "vault" to the middle of the next. McCleary's report on Kahn's response when he discussed this relationship with him is significant: ". . . he remarked that the quality of light and place in the then partially completed museum was sufficiently beautiful that for the moment, he was willing to sacrifice the truth of the structural principle."[28] The quality of light greatly influences our recognition of this museum as a sacred place. Dana Cuff, in a critique of the Kimbell Art Museum, notes that "The Kimbell's spiritual quality is most powerful when an individual with a single work of art, light, and ritual mingle."[29] It is the quiet wash of daylight over wall and painting that invites this mingling. Without the wash of daylight on the concrete shell, the interior loses its mystique and becomes uninteresting, even oppressive. Most daylight (except for that admitted by the lunettes and the horizontal strip openings below the edge of the shell) is blocked from the galleries for certain traveling exhibitions. When that happens, the comparison between the galleries with daylight and those without it is startling. In the daylit galleries, the enclosure is revealed by light. In the galleries with electric lighting only, the enclosure is lost, the structure and the rhythm gone. In this building, light from the sky and light from electric lamps are not equal. Daylight furnishes the light for the building as well as the art, and electric light provides supplementary light for the art when needed.

It is not the technical feat of washing the cycloid shell with light that is so remarkable, but the quality of that light, the softness that it imparts to the concrete, and the nobility that it imparts to the room. Since the reflector is specular aluminum, the changing spectrum of the daylight is reflected onto the concrete, becoming, in the process, ephemeral. There is a sense of the immutability of the building punctu-

ated by the views of moving sunlight and water and leaves in the courts—the eternal connected to the present.

Much of the description in this narrative has been directed to the technical realization of the lighting of the cycloid shell, because it was ultimately important to the realization of sacred light. The gentle wash of daylight on the underside of the shell creates a glowing background surface that removes the concrete from the realm of earthly matter, just as the surfaces in Gothic cathedrals are transformed by the light that has been filtered and patterned by the stained glass. The fact that Kahn was willing to pursue the realization of this new lighting concept that was beyond his own experience in building, just as he was willing to pursue a new structural approach that stretched the experience of his office and the structural engineer, attests to his search for an expression that reveals something higher, the *non luminous light*. Without a clear and correct resolution of the technical aspects of the vault reflector, the "revelation of an absolute reality" would not have been realized.

The poet is one who starts from the seat of the unmeasurable and travels towards the measurable, but who keeps the force of the unmeasurable within him at all times. As he travels towards the measurable, he almost disdains to write a word. Although he desires not to say anything and still convey his poetry, at the last moment he must succumb to the word after all. But he has traveled a great distance before he uses any of the means, and when he does, it is just a smidgen and it is enough.[30]

—LOUIS I. KAHN

ENDNOTES

1. Lobell, John. 1985. *Between Silence and Light: Spirit in the Architecture of Louis I. Kahn.* (Boston, Mass.: Shambala), p. 20.

2. Eliade, Mircea. 1961. *The Sacred and the Profane.* (New York: Harper Torchbooks), p. 21.

3. Norberg-Schulz, Christian. 1988. *Architecture: Meaning and Place.* (New York: Electa/Rizzoli), p. 201.

4. Burton, Joseph. 1983. "Notes from Volume Zero: Louis Kahn and the Language of God." *Perspecta 20:* 69–90.

5. Unless otherwise noted, all information on the design and construction process of the Kimbell Art Museum was taken from: Loud, Patricia Cummings. 1989. *The Art Museums of Louis I. Kahn.* (Durham, N.C.: Duke University Press).

6. Meyers, Marshall. 1979. "Masters of Light: Louis Kahn," *AIA Journal,* 68 (11): 60–61. Reprinted with permission of the publisher.

7. The structure is technically a shell, as pointed out by Peter McCleary in his article: McCleary, Peter. 1987. "The Kimbell Art Museum: Between Building and Architecture," *Design Book Review 11* (Winter): 48–51. Conceptually, however, it was thought of, and is usually described as, a vault.

8. Letter and sketch sent to Mrs. Kimbell dated Wednesday, June 25, 1969. In Kahn, Louis. Compiled by Nell E. Johnson. 1975. *Light Is The Theme.* (Fort Worth, Tex.: Kimbell Art Foundation), pp. 63–65.

9. Loud, op. cit., p. 137.

10. Apparently about fifteen percent of visitors enter by the "Entrance of the Trees," the remaining eighty–five percent from the parking lot. Suisman, Doug. 1987. "The Design of the Kimbell: Variations on a Sublime Archetype," *Design Book Review 11* (Winter): 36–41. From the parking lot, one enters through a door that leads into the lower level and then up one of two symmetrically placed stairways that attract one by light to the upper level entrance lobby.

11. Kahn, Louis I. 1961. "Louis Kahn," *Perspecta 7*: 14. Reprinted with permission from *Perspecta 7: The Yale Architectural Journal,* 1961.

12. Ibid. Reprinted with permission from *Perspecta 7: The Yale Architectural Journal,* 1961.

13. It is interesting to note that Kahn's approach had changed since his work on The Yale Art Gallery, where there was connection to the outside through large walls of glass but electric lighting was required both to illuminate the works of art and to counteract the high contrast between the interior and exterior.

14. The process is described in Patricia Loud's book and in Marshall Meyer's article, both previously cited.

15. Loud, op. cit., p. 111.

16. Meyers, op. cit., p. 61. Reprinted with permission of the publisher.

17. Kahn, Louis I. 1969. "Space and the Inspirations," *L'Architecture d'Aujourd'hui* 40 (Feb.–March): 15–16. From a talk Kahn gave at the New England Conservatory of Music in Boston in November 1967. Reprinted with permission of the publisher.

18. Loud, op. cit., p. 119.

19. In the building, daylight is admitted through a double layer of clear plexiglas in the skylight slot that runs the length of each bay at the apex of the shell structure and diffused by the biwinged reflector below it. Seymour, A.T. III. 1984. "The Immeasurable Made Measurable: Building the Kimball Art Museum," *Via 7:* 76–85.

20. Loud, op. cit., p. 148.

21. Cialdella, Philip, and Clara D. Powell. 1993. "The Great Illuminator," *LD+A,* 23 (5): 65.

22. Meyers, op. cit., p. 62.

23. Ibid. Reprinted with permission of the publisher.

24. Kahn, 1969, op. cit. Reprinted with permission of the publisher.

25. Loud, op. cit., p. 139.

26. Jordy, William. 1974. "The Span of Kahn," *Architectural Review 155* (928): 332.

27. Loud, op. cit., p. 261.

28. McCleary, op. cit., p. 51.

29. Cuff, Dana. 1987. "Light, Rooms, and Ritual," *Design Book Review 11* (Winter): 45.

30. Lobell, op. cit., p. 14.

FIGURE B4–1 *Perspective of gallery interior, March 1967, by Louis I. Kahn. Courtesy of the Louis I. Kahn Collection, University of Pennsylvania and Pennsylvania Historical and Museum Commission. Copyright 1977.*

FIGURE B4–2 *Sketch, exterior view of the Kimbell Art Museum.*

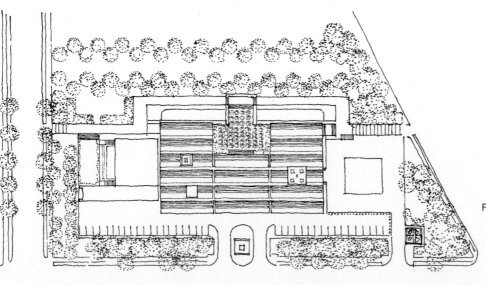

FIGURE B4–3 *Site plan. Redrawn from original drawings in the Louis I. Kahn Collection, University of Pennsylvania and Pennsylvania Historical and Museum Commission.*

0   40   80   120   N ▶

FIGURE B4–4 *Plan, gallery level.*
Redrawn from original drawings
in the Louis I. Kahn Collection,
University of Pennsylvania and
Pennsylvania Historical and
Museum Commission.

1. Entrance of the Trees
2. Portico
3. Lobby
4. Bookstore
5. Library
6. Gallery
7. North Court
8. Cafe
9. Auditorium
10. Fountain Court
11. Conservator's Court

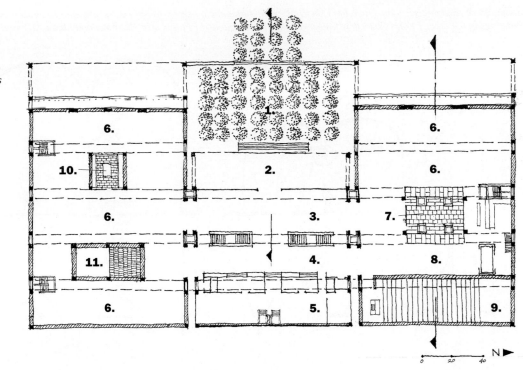

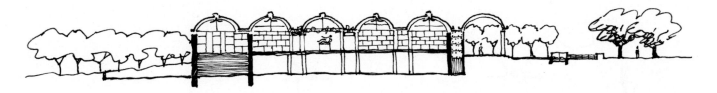

FIGURE B4–5 *Section. Redrawn from original drawings in*
the Louis I. Kahn Collection, University of Pennsylvania and
Pennsylvania Historical and Museum Commission.

FIGURE B4–6 *Cross-section showing entry progression*
through the "Entrance of the trees."

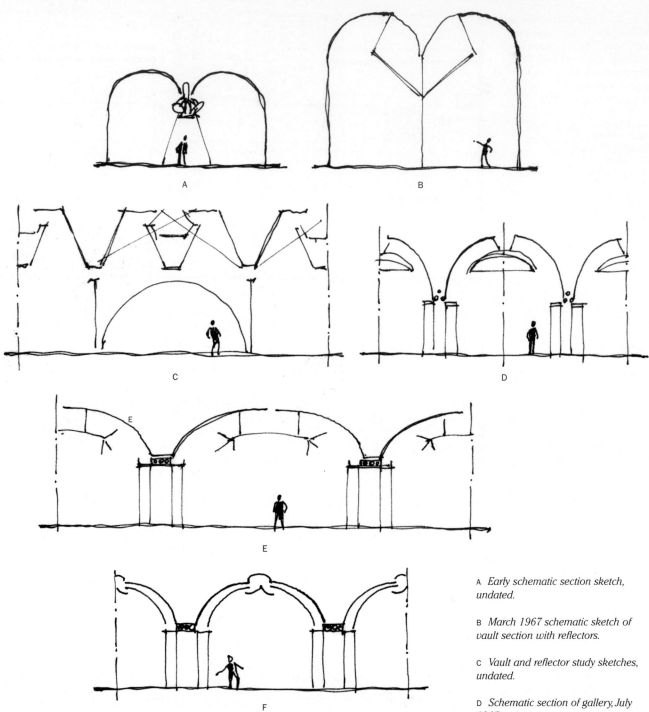

A *Early schematic section sketch, undated.*

B *March 1967 schematic sketch of vault section with reflectors.*

C *Vault and reflector study sketches, undated.*

D *Schematic section of gallery, July 1967.*

E *Schematic section of gallery, September 22, 1967.*

F *Final section, from March 4, 1969, study of reflector.*

FIGURE B4–8 *Exterior view from the southwest through the line of trees.*

FIGURE B4–9 *The grove of trees at the entry, as seen from the building. Photograph by M. Susan Ubbelohde.*

FIGURE B4–10 *Southwest corner of portico.*

FIGURE B4–11 *South end of entry portico with sun pattern. Photograph by Peter S. Stevens, author of* Patterns in Nature, Atlantic Monthly/Little Brown, 1974.

FIGURE B4–12 *Interior view of entry lobby.*

FIGURE B4–13 *View to the North Court as approached from the entry lobby.*

FIGURE B4–14 *The North Court with Pin Oak trees trained on a wire trellis to shade the court and block the view of the sky.*

FIGURE B4–15 *Lower level entry lobby from the parking lot on the east side, the "back door." The stairs ascend to the main entry lobby above.*

FIGURE B4–16 *View up the stairs to the main entry lobby.*

FIGURE B4–17 *View in the galleries past the Fountain Court.*

FIGURE B4–18 *The contrast between the light in the gallery room and the light in the Fountain Court.*

FIGURE B4–19 *View into the Fountain Court through its glazed wall on the west side.*

FigureB4–20 *View of the café. The North Court is to the left.*

Figure B4–21 *View into the Conservator's Court from the lower floor.*

Figure B4–22 *View of galleries across the axis of the cycloid shells.*

FIGURE B4–23 *View of a gallery with the daylight blocked from the slot in the shell. The* sacred light *is lost and the gallery becomes just a dark room.*

FIGURE B4–24 *View of gallery. Photograph by M. Susan Ubbelohde.*

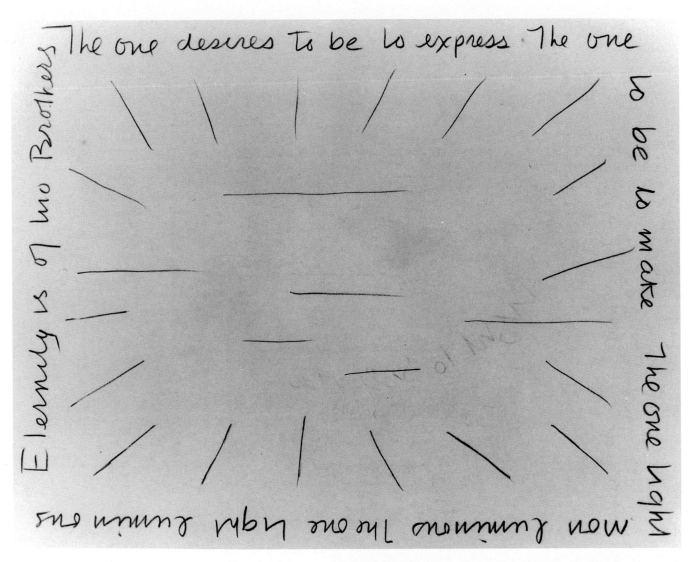

The one desires To be to express. The one

Eternity is of two Brothers

to be to make The one light

Eternity is of two Brothers

Non Luminous The one light Luminous

FIGURE B4–25 Eternity is of two Brothers, *sketch by Louis I. Kahn. Courtesy of the Louis I. Kahn Collection, University of Pennsylvania and Pennsylvania Historical and Museum Commission. Copyright 1977.*

INDEX